A Book Of

INTERNATIONAL BUSINESS ENVIRONMENT

For

MBA Semester - IV
As Per Revised Syllabus
Effective from June 2014

Mrs. Kiran Jotwani

M.A. (Economics), B. Ed

Mrs. Shraddha Omkar Chavan

MBA-IB & Marketing, PGDIB, BFT
Assistant Professor
Sankalp Business School

MBA - Sem. IV : International Business Environment ISBN 978-93-5164-264-0

Second Edition : January 2016
© : Authors

The text of this publication, or any part thereof, should not be reproduced or transmitted in any form or stored in any computer storage system or device for distribution including photocopy, recording, taping or information retrieval system or reproduced on any disc, tape, perforated media or other information storage device etc., without the written permission of Authors with whom the rights are reserved. Breach of this condition is liable for legal action.

Every effort has been made to avoid errors or omissions in this publication. In spite of this, errors may have crept in. Any mistake, error or discrepancy so noted and shall be brought to our notice shall be taken care of in the next edition. It is notified that neither the publisher nor the authors or seller shall be responsible for any damage or loss of action to any one, of any kind, in any manner, therefrom.

Published By :
NIRALI PRAKASHAN
Abhyudaya Pragati, 1312, Shivaji Nagar,
Off J.M. Road, PUNE – 411005
Tel - (020) 25512336/37/39, Fax - (020) 25511379
Email : niralipune@pragationline.com

Printed By :
REPRO INDIA LTD.
Mumbai.

☞ DISTRIBUTION CENTRES

PUNE
Nirali Prakashan : 119, Budhwar Peth, Jogeshwari Mandir Lane, Pune 411002, Maharashtra
Tel : (020) 2445 2044, 66022708, Fax : (020) 2445 1538
Email : bookorder@pragationline.com, niralilocal@pragationline.com

Nirali Prakashan : S. No. 28/27, Dhyari, Near Pari Company, Pune 411041
Tel : (020) 24690204 Fax : (020) 24690316
Email : dhyari@pragationline.com, bookorder@pragationline.com

MUMBAI
Nirali Prakashan : 385, S.V.P. Road, Rasdhara Co-op. Hsg. Society Ltd.,
Girgaum, Mumbai 400004, Maharashtra
Tel : (022) 2385 6339 / 2386 9976, Fax : (022) 2386 9976
Email : niralimumbai@pragationline.com

☞ DISTRIBUTION BRANCHES

JALGAON
Nirali Prakashan : 34, V. V. Golani Market, Navi Peth, Jalgaon 425001,
Maharashtra, Tel : (0257) 222 0395, Mob : 94234 91860

KOLHAPUR
Nirali Prakashan : New Mahadvar Road, Kedar Plaza, 1st Floor Opp. IDBI Bank
Kolhapur 416 012, Maharashtra. Mob : 9850046155

NAGPUR
Pratibha Book Distributors : Above Maratha Mandir, Shop No. 3, First Floor,
Rani Jhanshi Square, Sitabuldi, Nagpur 440012, Maharashtra
Tel : (0712) 254 7129

DELHI
Nirali Prakashan : 4593/21, Basement, Aggarwal Lane 15, Ansari Road, Daryaganj
Near Times of India Building, New Delhi 110002
Mob : 08505972553

BENGALURU
Pragati Book House : House No. 1, Sanjeevappa Lane, Avenue Road Cross,
Opp. Rice Church, Bengaluru – 560002.
Tel : (080) 64513344, 64513355,Mob : 9880582331, 9845021552
Email:bharatsavla@yahoo.com

CHENNAI
Pragati Books : 9/1, Montieth Road, Behind Taas Mahal, Egmore,
Chennai 600008 Tamil Nadu, Tel : (044) 6518 3535,
Mob : 94440 01782 / 98450 21552 / 98805 82331,
Email : bharatsavla@yahoo.com

niralipune@pragationline.com | www.pragationline.com
Also find us on www.facebook.com/niralibooks

Preface...

International Business conducts business transactions all over the world. These transactions include the transfer of goods, services, technology, managerial knowledge, and capital to other countries. The field of International Business is very dynamic, characterised by continuous changes in its variables which have a deep impact on the structure and nature of the global economy.

It thus gives us a feeling of immense pleasure and gratitude when placing before the students of MBA and other esteemed readers, the book of International Business Environment. The book is organised in a way that mirrors the revised syllabi of the MBA programme offered. However the book will also serve the needs of most students of International Business Environment. The subject matter is supported with suitable examples. The text has evolved out of the teaching experience, student interactions, various available text books, journals and magazines on the subject.

The topics in the book are arranged in a manner to facilitate easy reading and understanding by the student. Due care has been taken to simplify the language and illustrate the topics with diagrams, wherever necessary. The statistical data to support the various topics are up to date.

We would like to express our gratitude to our family members, Mr. Suresh Jotwani, Mr. Omkar Chavan, Mr. Chandrakant Chavan, Late Mrs. Uma Rajendra Salunke, Mr. Rajendra Salunke, and Mr. Rohan who continuously encouraged and motivated us to undertake and complete this task. We would also like to thank Mr. and Mrs. Pasalkar, Trustee of Sankalp Business School, and our colleagues.

We would also like to thank our publishers Mr. Dineshbhai Furia and Mr. Jignesh Furia of Nirali Prakashan for providing us the opportunity to meet the needs of thousands of students and their faculty. We are also thankful to the entire staff of Nirali Prakashan, Pune without whose unerring support and sustained effect, this book would not have seen the light of the day.

It is hoped that the book will be of great help to the students. Both our publisher and we will be thankful for any suggestions for the improvement of the book. We are confident that this text book will receive the patronage of all for whom it is intended.

Authors

Syllabus ...

1. **Environmental Context of International Business**

   Framework for analyzing international business environment - Domestic, foreign and global environments and their impact on international business decisions.

   Global Trading Environment: World trade in goods and services - Major trends and developments; World trade and protectionism - Tariff and Non-tariff barriers; Counter trade.

2. **International Financial Environment**

   Foreign investments - Pattern, Structure and effects; Movements in foreign exchange and interest rates and then impact on trade and investment flows.

3. **International Economic Institutions and Agreements**

   WTO, IMF, World Bank UNCTAD, Agreement on Textiles and Clothing (ATC), GSP, GSTP and other International agreements; International commodity trading and agreements.

4. **Multinational Corporations and their Involvement in International Business**

   Issues in Foreign investments, technology transfer, pricing and regulations; International collaborative arrangements and strategic alliances.

5. **Regional Economic Groupings in Practice**

   Regionalism vs. Multilateralism, Structure and functioning of EC and NAFTA; Regional economic cooperation. Emerging Developments and other Issues; Growing concern for ecology; Counter trade; IT and international business.

Contents ...

1. Environmental Context of International Business — 1.1 – 1.46

2. International Financial Environment — 2.1 – 2.24

3. International Economic Institutions and Agreements — 3.1 – 3.46

4. Multinational Corporations and their Involvement in International Business — 4.1 – 4.32

5. Regional Economic Groupings in Practice — 5.1 – 5.30

Case Studies — C.1 – C.30

University Question Paper - April 2015 — P.1 – P.1

Chapter 1...
Environmental Context of International Business

Contents ...

1.1 International Business
- 1.1.1 Introduction
- 1.1.2 Nature of International Business
- 1.1.3 Features of International Business
- 1.1.4 Modes of International Business
- 1.1.5 Importance of International Business
- 1.1.6 Essential Conditions for International Business

1.2 International Business Environment
- 1.2.1 Framework for Analysing International Environment: Domestic, Foreign and Global Environment and their Impact on International Business Decisions
- 1.2.2 Forces Influencing International Business Environment

1.3 Global Trading Environment: World Trade in Goods and Services
- 1.3.1 Changes in the Global Economy
- 1.3.2 Major Trends and Developments in Global Trading Environment
- 1.3.3 Trade Restrictions

1.4 World Trade and Protectionism
- 1.4.1 Meaning of Protectionism
- 1.4.2 Objectives of Protectionism
- 1.4.3 Forms of Protectionism
- 1.4.4 Arguments for Protectionism
- 1.4.5 Arguments Against Protectionism
- 1.4.6 Rising Trade Protectionism

1.5 Tariff and Non-Tariff Barriers
- 1.5.1 Introduction
- 1.5.2 Tariff Barriers
- 1.5.3 Non-tariff Barriers

1.6 Countertrade
    1.6.1 Types of Countertrade
    1.6.2 Advantages of Countertrade
    1.6.3 Disadvantages of Countertrade
- Points to Remember
- Questions for Discussion
- Multiple Choice Questions
- Project Questions

Learning Objectives ...
- To learn the reasons for firms entering into international business
- To be aware of the nature and importance of international business
- To understand the framework for analysing the international business environment
- To be able to explain the impact on domestic, foreign and global environments on international business decisions
- To study the major trends and developments in the global trading environment
- To learn the concepts such as protectionism, tariff and non-tariff barriers and counter trade

1.1 International Business

1.1.1 Introduction

International business consists of all commercial transactions - sales, investments, and transportation - that take place between two or more countries.

Private companies undertake such transactions for profit; governments may undertake them either for profit or for political reasons.

The basic tasks and functions of international business are almost the same as domestic business. But, for the sake of clarity, **international business may be understood as those business transactions that involve the crossing of national boundaries.**

Hence, International business transactions may include:
(i) Product presence in different markets of the world.
(ii) Production bases across the globe.
(iii) Human resource to contain a wide range of diversity.
(iv) Investment in international services like banking, tourism, advertising, construction.

(v) Transactions involving intellectual properties such as copyrights, patents, trademarks, process technology, etc.

1.1.2 Nature of International Business

What essentially happens in globalisation is the economic integration among the countries across the globe.

Internationalisation of business can be viewed as four – dimensional characteristics:

- Internationalisation of market presence
- Globalisation of supply chain
- Globalisation of capital base
- Globalisation of corporate mindset.

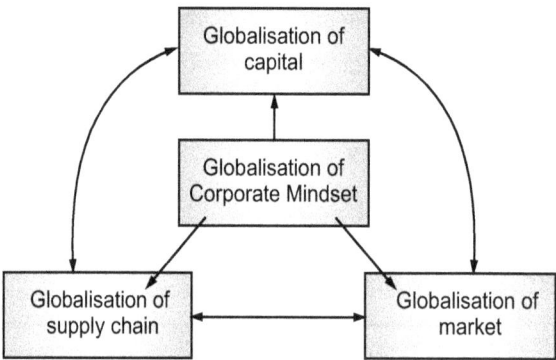

Fig. 1.1: Corporate Globalism

1.1.3 Features of International Business

The features of international business are:

1. Large Scale Operations: In international business, all the operations are conducted on a vast scale. For example, production and marketing activities are conducted on a large scale. At first, goods are sold in the local market and then the surplus goods are exported.

2. Integration of Economies: International business incorporates the economies of many countries. This is because it uses infrastructure from one country, labour from another country, and finance from another country. It designs the product in one country, produces its parts in many different countries and assembles the product in another country. It sells the product in many countries, i.e. in the international market.

3. Dominated by Developed Countries and MNCs: International business is dominated by developed countries and MNCs belonging to these countries. At present foreign trade is dominated by MNCs from USA, Europe and Japan. The reason behind this is that they have large financial and other resources. They have highly skilled employees and managers because they offer attractive salaries and other perks. They also have the best technology and R & D. Therefore, they produce quality goods and services at low prices, which helps them to capture and dominate the world market.

4. **Benefits to Participating Countries:** International business gives benefits to all participating countries. Though, major benefit is gained by the developed countries, the developing (poor) countries also get benefits. They get foreign capital and technology leading to more employment opportunities and rapid industrial development. This ultimately results in economic development of the developing countries. Therefore, developing countries open up their economies through liberal economic policies.

5. **Keen Competition:** International business has to face intense competition in the world market. The competition is between unequal partners i.e. developed and developing countries. In this keen competition, developed countries and their MNCs are in a favourable position because they produce superior quality goods and services at very low prices. Developed countries also have many contacts in the world market. So, developing countries find it very difficult to face competition from developed countries.

6. **Special Role of Science and Technology:** International business gives a lot of importance to science and technology. It helps the business to have large-scale production. Specialised technologies are used by developed countries, which help them to dominate the global business. International business helps them to transfer such top high-end technologies to the developing countries.

7. **International Restrictions:** Many restrictions are imposed on the inflow and outflow of capital, technology and goods. Various governments do not allow international businesses to enter their countries. They have implemented many trade blocks, tariff barriers, foreign exchange restrictions, and so on in order to restrict the entry of foreign firms. All this is harmful to international business.

8. **Sensitive Nature:** International business is very sensitive in nature. Any change in the political environment, economic policies, technology etc. has a huge impact on it. Therefore, marketing research should be conducted to find out and study these changes before entering into the international market. They must adjust their business activities and adapt accordingly to survive the changes.

1.1.4 Modes of International Business

A firm can engage in international business through various operating modes, including exporting and importing merchandise and services and licensing and foreign direct investment. The firm or individual exporting merchandise or a service will receive international earnings while the firm or individual importing merchandise or a service will make an international payment.

(A) Merchandise Exports and Imports

Merchandise exports consist of tangible (visible) products, i.e., goods that are sent to a foreign country for use or resale. **Merchandise imports** consist of tangible products, i.e., goods brought into a country for use or resale.

(B) Service Exports and Imports

Service exports and imports represent intangible (invisible), i.e., non-merchandise products.

1. **Tourism and Transportation:** When an American flies to Delhi on Air India and stays in an Indian-owned hotel, payments made to the airline and the hotel represent service export earnings (income) for India and service import payments (expenses) for the United States.

2. **Performance of Services:** Some services, such as banking, insurance, rentals, engineering, turnkey operations (construction, performed under contract, of facilities that are transferred to the owner when they are ready for operation), and management contracts (arrangements in which one firm provides personnel to perform management functions for another), net companies export earnings in the form of fees paid by a foreign client.

3. **Use of Assets:** Firms may receive export earnings, i.e., **royalties,** by allowing foreign clients to use their assets (trademarks, patents, copyrights, and other expertise). **Licensing agreements** are contracts that represent a transaction in which a licensor sells the rights to the use of its intellectual property to a licensee in exchange for a fee or royalty. **Franchising** is a special form of licensing in which the *franchisee* is granted additional control over the operation in exchange for the provision of additional support and services by the *franchisor*.

(C) Investments

Foreign investment consists of the ownership of foreign property for the purpose of realising a financial gain via profits, growth, dividends, and/or interest.

1. **Direct Investment: Foreign direct investment (FDI)** occurs when an investor gains a controlling interest in a foreign operation. *Sole ownership* represents 100% ownership of an operation; however, effective control can be realised with just a minority stake if the remaining ownership is widely dispersed. A **joint venture** represents a direct investment in which two or more parties share ownership.

2. **Portfolio Investment: Portfolio investment** is a non-controlling interest in a venture made in the form of either *debt or equity*. Often, firms use portfolio investment as part of their short-term financial strategy.

(D) International Companies and Terms to Describe them

There are numerous forms of **collaborative arrangements** through which companies work together internationally, such as joint minority ownership, licensing, management contracts, or other long-term contractual arrangements. A **strategic alliance** is more narrowly defined to indicate that the agreement is of critical importance to the competitive viability of one or more of the partners. The **multinational enterprise (MNE)** is a firm that takes a global approach to foreign markets and production, i.e., it is willing to consider markets and production sites anywhere in the world. The terms **multinational corporation (MNC)** and **transnational company (TNC)** may also be used in this context.

(E) Other Modes

Apart from the above modes of international business, some other commonly used modes of entry to International Market include:
- Contract manufacturing
- Management contracts
- Turn key projects
- Joint venture
- Mergers and acquisitions

1.1.5 Importance of International Business

The economic importance of international business is discussed below:

1. **Earn Foreign Exchange:** International business firms exports its goods and services all over the world. It helps to earn valuable foreign exchange. This foreign exchange is used to pay for imports. Foreign exchange helps to make the business more profitable and to strengthen the economy of its country.

2. **Optimum Utilisation of Resources:** International business firms make optimum utilisation of resources. This is because these firms produce goods on large scale for the international market. International business helps in utilising resources from all over the world. It uses the finance and technology of rich countries and the raw materials and labour of the poor countries.

3. **Achieve its Objectives:** International business achieves its objectives easily and quickly. The main objective of any international business is to earn high profits. This objective is achieved easily because it has high technology, best employees and managers. It produces high-quality goods. It sells these goods all over the world. All of this results in high profits for the international business.

4. **To Spread Business Risks:** International business spreads its business risk. This is because the business operations are not concentrated in one part but are spread all over the world. So, a loss in one country can be balanced by a profit in another country. The surplus goods in one country can be exported to another country. The surplus resources can also be transferred to other countries. All this helps to minimise the business risks.

5. **Improve Organisation's Efficiency:** Efficiency in an organisation is required in order to conduct international business operations. This is because without efficiency, firms will not be able to face the immense competition in the international market. So, all the modern management techniques are used to improve the efficiency. Most qualified and experienced employees and managers are hired. These people are trained regularly. They are highly motivated with very high salaries and other benefits such as international transfers, promotions, etc. All this results in high organisational efficiency, i.e. low costs and high returns.

6. **Get Benefits from Government:** International business gets many benefits, facilities and concessions from the government as it brings in a lot of foreign exchange for the country. It gets many financial and tax benefits from the government.
7. **Expand and Diversify:** International business can expand and diversify its activities. This is because it earns high profits. Government also provides financial help to these firms.
8. **Increase Competitive Capacity:** International business firms produce high-quality goods at lower cost. A lot of money is spent on advertising all over the world. It uses superior technology, management techniques, marketing techniques, etc. All this makes it more competitive. So, it can fight competition from foreign companies.
9. **Increased Domestic Business:** International business has certain spin-off. It may help to improve its domestic business. International business helps to improve the image of the company. There may be 'white skin' advantage associated with exporting when the domestic consumer gets to know that the company is selling a significant portion of the production abroad, they will be more inclined to buy from such a company,

1.1.6 Essential Conditions for International Business

Some essential conditions which need to be satisfied on part of the domestic economy as well as the firm for successful international business are:
1. **Orientation:** A global orientation on part of the business firms and suitable globalisation strategies are essential for international business.
2. **Business Freedom:** Unnecessary government restrictions which come in the way of globalisation, such as import restrictions, restrictions on sourcing finance, or foreign investments etc. should not be there. Thus, economic liberalisation is regarded as the first step towards facilitating globalisation.
3. **Support from the Government:** Unnecessary government restrictions should not be there, but at the same time government support can encourage globalisation. Government support may take form of policy and procedural reforms, development of common facilities such as infrastructural facilities, Research & Development support, and financial market reforms and in many other forms.
4. **Availability of Facilities:** The extent to which an enterprise can develop globally from home country base depends on the facilities available, for example the infrastructural facilities.
5. **Resources:** Resources are one of the important factors which often decide the ability of a firm to globalise. The companies that are resourceful find it easier to thrust ahead in the global market. Resources are finance, technology, R and D capabilities, managerial expertise, company and brand image, human resource etc.

However, it should be noted that many small firms have been successful in international business due to one or the other advantage that they possess.

6. **Competitive Advantage:** An important determinant of success in international business is the competitive advantage that the company enjoys. A firm may derive competitive advantage from one or more of the factors such as low costs and price, product quality, product differentiation, technological superiority, after sales service, marketing strength etc. At times small firms may have an edge over others in certain aspects of business.

1.2 International Business Environment

The environment of international business is regarded as the sum total of all external forces working upon the firm as it goes about its affairs in foreign and domestic markets.

The environment can be classified in terms of:
- domestic
- foreign
- international spheres of impact

The **domestic environment** is familiar to managers and consists of those uncontrollable external forces that affect its home market. **The foreign environment** can be those factors which operate in those countries within which the MNC operates. Generally, the factors are the same, but they can have differing impact from the home country situation. **International environment** is seen as the interaction between domestic and foreign factors and covers a wide spectrum of forces.

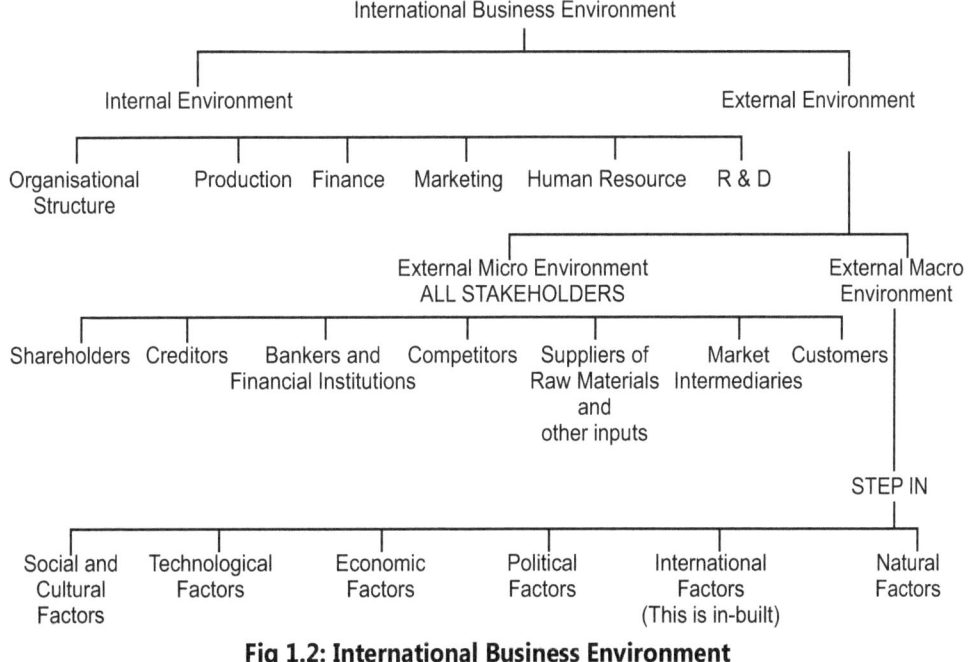

Fig 1.2: International Business Environment

1.2.1 Framework for Analysing International Environment: Domestic, Foreign and Global Environment and their Impact on International Business Decisions

The various factors can be divided broadly into three groups in order to understand the various factors constituting the international business environment. The classification is based on the location at which the environmental factors and forces operate and exist. The three groups are:

- domestic
- foreign
- global environments

Figure 1.3 shows the above three groups along with their components:

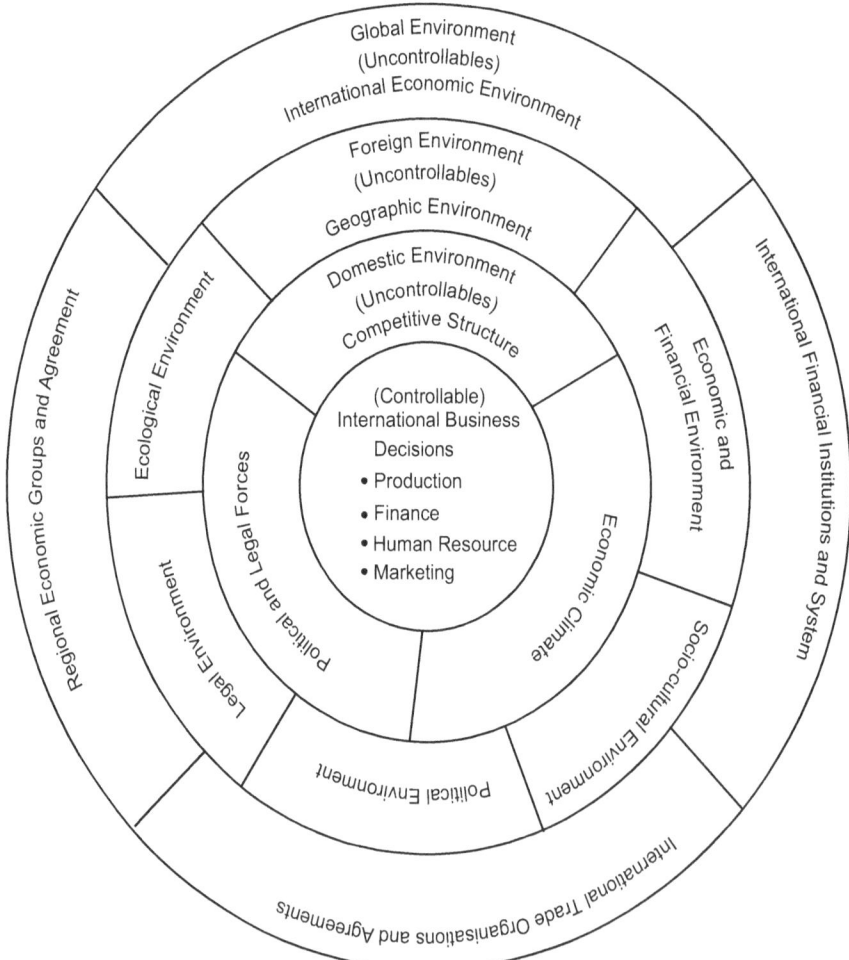

Fig. 1.3: Framework for International Business Environment

From the above figure the following conclusions can be drawn:
- The innermost circle represents the firm's business strategy and decisions with regard to production, finance, marketing, human resources and research activities. These strategies and decisions are called controllable as they are made by the firm and the firm can change them but within the constraints of the various environmental factors available.
- The **domestic environment** is represented in the next circle. Factors such as
    ✓ competitive structure,
    ✓ economic climate,
    ✓ political and legal forces which are essentially uncontrollable by a firm.

  These factors exert influence on the firm's foreign market operations. Lack of domestic demand or intense competition in the domestic market, for instance, have prompted many Indian firms to plunge into international business. Many firms internationalise their business operations as export promotion measures and incentives motivate them to do so. Firms are generally familiar with them and are able to readily react to them, since these factors operate on a national level.
- The foreign environment is represented in the third circle and consists of factors like:
    ✓ geographic and economic conditions,
    ✓ socio-cultural traits, political and legal forces,
    ✓ technological and ecological facets prevalent in a foreign country.

  Firms are generally not cognizant of these factors and their influence on business activities as they are being operative in the international market. The firm can neglect them only at the cost of losing business in the foreign markets. When the number of foreign markets in which a firm operates increases, the problem gets more complicated. Differences exist not only between domestic and foreign environments, but also among the environments prevailing in different foreign markets. Business strategies that are successful in one nation might fail miserably in other countries due to environmental differences. Hence an increased sensitivity towards the environmental differences and adaptation of business strategies to suit the differing market situation is required by the foreign market operations.
- The topmost circles or circle four represents the global environment. Global environment transcends national boundaries and is not confined in its impact to just one country. It influences the domestic as well as the foreign countries and it comprises of factors like:
    ✓ world economic conditions,
    ✓ international financial system,
    ✓ international agreements and treaties,
    ✓ regional economic groupings

  World-wide economic recession; international financial liquidity or stability; working of the international organisations such as World Trade Organisation (WTO),

International Monetary Fund (IMF), World Bank and the United Nations Conference on Trade and Development (UNCTAD); Agreement on Textiles and Clothing (ATC); Generalised System of Preferences (GSP); International Commodity Agreements; and initiatives taken at regional levels such as European Union (EU), North American Free Trade Association (NAFTA) and Association of South East Asian Nations (ASEAN) are some of the examples of global environmental forces having world-wide or regional influences on business operations.

1.2.2 Forces Influencing International Business Environment

The forces that influence international business are:
- Political Environment/forces
- Legal forces
- Cultural forces
- Technological forces
- Economic forces.

(1) Political Environment

It refers to the influence of the system of government and judiciary in a nation on international business. The system of government has a considerable impact on its business. The type and structure of government prevailing in a country decides, promotes, fosters, encourages, shelters, directs and controls the business of that country. A political system that is stable, honest, efficient, dynamic and which ensures political participation to the people, and assures personal security to its citizens, is a primary factor for economic development. Today's developed economies owe their success to a great extent to the political system. **John Kenneth Galbraith** comments, *"There is today no country with a stable and honest government that does not have or has not had a reasonably satisfactory state of economic progress."*

Political Risk: Corporate face political risk when they conduct business with the outside world. Political risk is politically motivated event that could adversely affect the long-term profitability or value of the firm. Political risks influence different firms in different ways. It can threaten the market of an exporter, the production facilities of a manufacturer, or the ability of a firm to repatriate its profits from a host country to its home country.

Political risk is common. It prevails in all countries and regions, regardless of political or economic system. It is very high in countries like Yugoslavia, Turkey, Iraq, Algeria, Sudan, Nigeria, Afghanistan, Somalia, Congo, Angola, Myanmar, and Indonesia. The political risk is almost non-existent in the US, Canada, Denmark, Australia, and Western European countries. Political risks arise when

(i) The host government make a decision adverse to the interests of the subsidiary.
(ii) When laws and government policies instituted by the firm's home country, adversely affect the firms that do business in a foreign country.
(iii) These risks can take the form of war and revolution, changes in law or policy. It can affect all aspects of international business, such as the right to ship goods to a country, or to own and operate a subsidiary there.

Type of Risks

Political risks can be

(A) Macro political risks

(B) Micro political risks

(A) Macro Risks

Below we give the macro risk and its impact on international business.

1. Expropriation of corporate assets without prompt and adequate compensation. **Impact -** Loss of future profits.
2. Barriers to repatriation of profits. **Impact -** No motivation to improve efficiency.
3. Confiscation of properties. **Impact -** Loss of assets and future profits.
4. Loss of technology or other intellectual property. **Impact -** Loss of future profits.
5. Campaigns against foreign goods: **Impact -** Loss of sales and increased costs of public relations campaign.
6. Mandatory labour legislations. **Impact -** Increased operating costs.
7. Civil Wars. **Impact -** Destruction of property, loss of sales, increased security costs, disrupted production runs.
8. Inflation. **Impact -** Increased operating costs.
9. Currency devaluations. **Impact -** Reduced values of repatriated earnings.

(B) Micro Political Risks

1. Kidnappings, terrorist, threats etc. **Impact -** Disrupted production, higher security costs, reduced productivity.
2. Increased taxation. **Impact -** Reduced after tax profits.
3. Official's dishonesty. **Impact -** Loss of business increased operating costs.

A macro political risk affects all international businesses in the same way. The taking of ownership of an entire industry that had been generated privately, as a plan to restructure an entire economy, is called nationalisation, which is a macro political risk. Communist governments in Eastern Europe and China expropriated private firms following World War. Recently, governments in Angola, Chile, Ethiopia, Peru, and Zambia have expropriated private firms. Field Marshall Ayub Khan nationalised four hotels of M. S. Oberoi without paying any compensation.

The level of macro political risk has been changing in recent years. China's entry into the WTO is a pointer to the changing environment in Asia. Vietnam's recent trade agreement with the US is another positive indicator. All these developments have certainly minimised the political risk, but it still continues to exist.

A micro political risk affects specific foreign business. Micro political risks include industry regulations, taxes, kidnapping and terrorist threats. India's decision in 1975 to reduce foreign equity to 40% and Peru's decision to nationalise its copper mines are examples of micro political risks. Another example is the bombing of the Chinese embassy in Belgrade by NATO forces in 1997. In retaliation, demonstrators in China thrashed KFC stores but did not touch Pizza Hut, though both are owned by US based company. The Chinese demonstrators thought Pizza Hut as Italian based company, therefore did not attack.

Managing Political Risk

International businesses employ different methods for managing political risks.

1. **Avoiding Investment:** The simplest way to manage is to avoid investing in a country ranked high on such risk. And where investments are done, plants may be wound up or transferred to some other country which may be considered safer.

2. **Adaptation:** It means incorporating risk into business strategies. MNCs incorporate risk by means of three strategies:
   a) **Local Equity and Debt:** This involves financing subsidiaries with the help of local firms, trade unions, financial institutions, and government. When McDonald's commenced franchise operations in India, it ensured that sandwiches did not contain any beef.
   b) **Developmental Assistance:** Offering development assistance allows an international business to assist the host country in improving its quality of life. For example, in Myanmar, the US oil company Unocal and France's Total (Energy Company) have invested billions of dollars to develop natural gas fields and also spent 56 million on local education, medical care, and other improvements.
   c) **Insurance:** This is the last means of adaptation. Companies buy insurance against the potential effects of political risk. Some policies protect companies when host government restrict the convertibility of their currency into parent country currency. Others insure against losses created by violent events, including war and terrorism.

   Most developed countries have created agencies to insure the firms against risks. For instance, The Overseas Private Investment Corporation (OPIC) insure US overseas investments against nationalisation, revolutions and foreign exchange inconvertibility. The Multilateral Investment Guarantee Agency (MIGA), a subsidiary of the World Bank provides insurance against political risks. Lloyd's of London also underwrites political risk insurance.

3. **Threat:** The firm may threaten the host country that the supply of materials, products or technology would be stopped if its functioning is disrupted. This is possible when the firm makes the host country to feel that the host country cannot do without the activities of the firm.

4. **Lobbying:** Influencing local politics through lobbying is another way of managing political risk. Lobbyists meet with local public officials and try to influence their position on issues relevant to the firm. Their ultimate objective is getting favourable legislation passed and unfavourable ones rejected.

5. **Terrorism Consultants:** To manage terrorism risk, MNCs hire consultants in counter terrorism to train employees to cope with the threat of terrorism.

(2) Legal Environment

Legal environment refers to the legal system existing in a country. The legal system refers to the rules and laws that regulate the behaviour of individuals and organisations. Failure to comply with the laws means that penalties will be inflicted by the courts depending on the seriousness of the offence.

The legal system of a country is very important to international business. A country's laws regulate business practice, define the manner in which business transactions are to be carried out and set down the rights and obligations of those involved in business deals.

The legal system in a country is also influenced by its political system. The government of a country defines the legal framework within which firms conduct business and often the laws that regulate business reflect the country's political ideology.

The legal system present in India should be emulated by all the countries. The legal resource is available to all – Indians or foreigners. Justice is meted to any petitioner. For example, GE got back the entire investment of $ 115 million from Dhabol once the latter went bust. The CEO, Scott Bayman, admitted that nowhere else this would have been possible.

Systems of Law: There are 4 basic legal systems prevailing around the world:

(i) Islamic Law, derived from the interpretation of the Quran and practised in countries where Muslims are in majority.
(ii) Common Law, derived from English law, is prevalent in countries which were under British influence.
(iii) Civil or Code Laws, derived from Roman law, practised in Germany, Japan, France, and non-Marxist and non-Islamic countries, and
(iv) Marxist legal system which has takers in Communist countries.

The main means of resolving international disputes are conciliation, arbitration, and litigation.

Conciliation, also known as mediation, is a nonbonding agreement between parties to resolve disputes by asking a third party to mediate. The function of the mediator is to carefully listen to each party and to explore, clarify and discuss the various practical options and possibilities for a solution with the intent that the parties will agree to it.

In arbitration the usual procedure is for the parties involved to select a disinterested and informed party or parties as referee to determine the merits of the case and make a judgement that both parties agree to honour. Although informal arbitration is workable, most arbitration is conducted under the auspices of one of the more formal domestic or international arbitration groups organised specifically to facilitate the resolution of commercial disputes. These groups have formal rules for the process and experienced arbitrators to assist. In most countries, decisions reached in formal arbitration are enforced under the law.

Litigation-seeking justice in a court is generally avoided by parties to an agreement. The costs incurred, the frustrating delays involved, fear of creating a poor image and damaging public relations, and extended aggravation make victories in law suits spurious.

To sum up, to settle any dispute – international or domestic – four steps are needed:

(i) Try to placate the affected party;
(ii) If this does not work conciliate;
(iii) If this also fails, seek arbitration; and
(iv) If arbitration fails; resolve through litigation.

Areas of concern for MNCs: The immediate legal issues that bother MNCs most are the following: protection of IPRS, product liability and safety, competition laws, bribery and corruption, advertising and sales promotion, contracts, shipping of goods, labour laws, and environmental laws.

(a) IPRS: Property that results from people's intellectual talent and abilities is called intellectual property and includes designs, novels, patents, trademarks, copyrights, computer software, and secret formulae such as one used for making Coca Cola. Such laws are a very important stimulus to innovation and creative work.

(b) Product Liability and Safety: Most countries have laid down product safety laws which bind manufacturers to produce safe products. Product liability holds manufacturers and sellers responsible for damage, injury, or death caused by defective products. Affected parties can sue both for monetary compensation through civil law suits, or imprisonment through criminal lawsuits.

(c) Competition among Businesses: Competition laws are enforced to break monopolies and protect consumer interests. In India there is the Competition Law.

(d) Bribes and Corrupt Practices: Bribery is a deliberate attempt to persuade someone (usually someone in position or power) to act improperly in favour of the party offering bribes in the form of money or gifts. Bribery is the root cause for corruption. International businesses are known to bribe officials to get favour. Investigations of the US based MNCs in the 1970s and of Italian firms in the 1990s, along with much anecdotal information from several years, indicate that the practice has been widespread.

(d) Advertising and Sales Promotion: Multinational businesses spend huge sums across the globe for advertising their products. Like advertising in domestic markets, there are temptations to make exaggerated claims and tell untruths while conveying messages about the products to be sold in international markets. Almost all nations have laws to prevent such false claims. Advertising aimed at children is closely regulated. More than 40 countries prohibit or limit such advertising, reasoning that children cannot intelligently assess the contents of commercial ads. It is essential that the international manager must learn that he or she should seek legal advice from local practiners and strategise local advertising appropriately.

(e) Contracts: A contract is an agreement by the parties concerned to establish a set of rules to govern a business transaction. Contract law plays a major role in international business transactions, because of the complexities arising from the differences in the legal systems of participating countries and because the host government in many developing and communist countries is often a third party in the contract.

(f) Carriage of Goods: Another area of concern to international business relates to the carriage of goods across countries. It includes the liability of international carriers (the liability of an air carrier for death or personal injury or a passenger or damage to property is determined by the Warsaw Convention of 1929); Ocean shipping (the liability of the carrier – chartered or common carrier – for damage or loss to ocean going goods, in most nations of the world is governed by the Hague Rules); issues in maritime and marine cargo insurance law (loss is minimised through insurance, insuring cargo is an essential element in international business). Cargo insurance is usually handled through a broker. Rates vary depending on the risk involved in the shipment. The well-known name in cargo insurance is Lloyd's of London.

(g) Labour Laws Across the World: Yet another area of concern for an MNC relates to labour legislation prevailing in different countries. Four main issues relating to labour are:

- employee dismissals;
- working conditions;
- discrimination
- child labour.

(h) Environmental Laws: International environmental law has lately become a topic of considerable interest. There have been large-scale international environmental disasters such as the Chernobyl nuclear plant disaster, the Sandoz Chemical spill into the Rhine River, and various oil tanker spills. At the same time, concern over the possible thinning of the ozone layer and global warming has intensified. As a result, nations have been enacting legislations and entering into treaties concerning the environment.

A way of fighting pollution by any nation is to enact legislation outlawing import of the offending products. The Regional approaches are- banning export of hazardous materials; North American Environmental Treaties and NAFTA; the Single European Act 1985 for the EU; Regional marine treaties among nations sharing bodies of water; and the ASEAN Agreement on the Conservation of Nature and Natural Resources for Asian countries.

The Global approach is – the WTO; global ban on toxic substances such as DDT, dioxins; Hazardous Wastes and their disposals; the Climate Control Convention.

(3) Cultural Environment

For an international manager, business culture – the way Indians, Germans, Japanese and others do business – is more important. More than just cultural differences in business etiquette, business culture represents norms, values, and beliefs that pertain to all aspects of doing business in a particular environment. Business cultures tell people the correct, acceptable ways to conduct business in a society. Business culture also provides the guides for everyday business interactions. For example, what to wear to a meeting, when and how to use the business cards and so on, are types of business etiquettes taught by the business culture.

It has been observed that organisation-specific and occupation-specific cultures tend to develop within national and business cultures. Organisational culture refers to the philosophies, ideologies, values, assumptions, beliefs, expectations, attitudes, and norms that knit an organisation together and are shared by its employees.

Different occupational groups such as physicians, professors, lawyers, accountants, and crafts people have distinct cultures, called occupational cultures. Occupational cultures are the norms, beliefs, and expected ways of behaving of people in the same occupational groups, regardless of which organisations they work for. The occupational cultures cannot be ignored by the international manager, notwithstanding the dominance of national and business cultures.

Implications for International Business

Global businesses are the repositories of multiculture. Multiculturalism means that people from different cultures interact regularly. An MNC is just another world. It has a home country and has several host countries where the head office and subsidiaries interact regularly. Managing multiculturalism is essential for every international firm. Four tasks are essential: **spreading cross-country literacy** (doing business in different cultures requires adaptation to conform to the nuances of that culture. No firm is expected to change the local culture to suit its needs and expectations.); removing **cross-cultural illiteracy** (firms should ensure that home-country executives are cosmopolitan enough to understand how differences in culture affect the practice of international business.

In 1991 Hitachi set up a department to educate executives about other cultures); **culture and competitive advantage** (culture may sound abstract but the norms and values prevalent in a society do influence the costs of doing business in the country. These costs decide the ability of enterprises to establish a competitive advantage in the global marketplace); **managing diversity** (it means establishing a heterogeneous workforce to perform to its potential in an equitable work environment where no member has an advantage or a disadvantage. Managing diversity is a challenge for an international manager. The challenge is to create a work environment in which each person can perform to his or her potential and therefore compete for promotions on merit basis alone).

Tackling the Culture Factor: There are 3 general categories of national responsiveness:
(i) Product adaptation;
(ii) Individual adjustment;
(iii) Institutional adaptation.

(4) Technological Environment

Technological environment wields considerable influence on international business.

The most fundamental effect of technology is greater productivity in terms of both quality and quantity. This is the main reason why technology at all levels is adopted. Research & Development assumes considerable relevance in organisations as technology advances.

With the advent of technology, jobs tend to become more intellectual or upgraded. Introduction of new technology dislocates some workers unless they are well-equipped to work on new machines.

Not only jobs become more intellectual and knowledge-oriented but they also have the incumbents tended to become highly professional and knowledgeable. An organisation that has adopted the latest technology is flush with scientists, engineers, MBA's college graduates, and knowledge workers as teammates.

A by-product of technological advancement is the ever-increasing regulation imposed on business by the government of the land and stiff opposition from the public. The host government has the powers to investigate and ban products that are directly harmful or hurt the sentiments of a section of society.

The phenomenal growth of the Internet and the associated World Wide Web has made e-commerce possible. E-Commerce is contributing to a growing percentage of cross-border transactions. While e-commerce focuses on marketing and sales processes, E-business emphasises integration of systems, processes, organisations, value chains, and markets.

Technological breakthroughs have facilitated globalisation of production. Along with the globalisation of production, technological innovations have facilitated the internationalisation of markets.

Three features of technology are conspicuous- change, widespread effects and self-reinforcement.

Technology management involves its awareness, acquisition, adaption, advancement and abandonment phases.

(5) Economic Environment

Economic environment of international business is examined from 6 dimensions: classification of countries on income basis, classification on economic orientation, region wise categorisation, trade policies, economic institutions and transition economies

On income basis, there are developed and developing countries. Economic system seeks to group nations into those following capitalism, socialism or mixed economy. Based on region the classification gives us a big list of country classification, East Asia and Pacific,

Europe and Central Asia, Latin America and the Caribbean, Middle East and North Asia, etc. Transition economies are those that are transforming themselves from command economies to market economies. Several institutions, treaties and conventions have their impact on international business.

All these classifications of economic nature have impact on international business.

To conclude, business environment is influenced by host of internal and external forces. Internal forces can be easily managed. It is the external forces that have a deep impact on global business.

1.3 Global Trading Environment: World Trade in Goods and Services

Since World War II, the global environment has shown tremendous growth. Global growth has been accompanied by a change in the pattern of trade, which reflects on-going changes in structure of the global economy. Some of the major changes that can be noticed are:

- the rise of regional trading blocks,
- deindustrialisation in many advanced economies,
- the increased participation of former Communist countries,
- emergence of China and India in the world market.

Characterised by a movement of goods, services, labour and capital across borders, countries are becoming economically co-dependent. There exist better support linkages among the smaller and larger enterprises as well among the marginalised producers.

In the past two decades, global trade patterns have changed tremendously. Emerging markets (EMs) now account for 42% of world exports, up from 19% in 1990, or 52% excluding intra-EU trade. With China emerging as a mega trader, it has put Asia in the center of the global supply chain.

With countries no longer trading in goods so much as in 'tasks', such as design or assembly, trade is increasingly unbundled. Before the final product reaches consumers, the components and partial assemblies are traded several times.

As compared to goods trade, the service trade is expanding faster since it involves better communications. Services cannot always easily be measured at the border and some estimates put them at 40% of total trade now.

Trade growth has averaged about 1.4 times GDP growth. There has been only a marginal increase of world exports as it has risen only 5%, while the nominal GDP is up by 10%. Growth in developed countries is accelerating, while manufacturing, still the driver of goods trade, is still not doing well. Numerous bilateral trade pacts have been agreed in recent years and new multilateral trade pacts are in the works. Constraints such as lower trade finance availability and rising protectionism are fading.

1.3.1 Changes in the Global Economy

The important changes in the global economy are:

1. With the emergence of regional trading blocks, which sees members trading with each other, erect barriers to trade with non member, it has shown a significant impact on the pattern of global trade. Some important blocs are the NAFTA and European Union, which have led to trade creation between members, even though countries that are outside the block have suffered from trade diversion.

2. Many of these advanced economies have experienced deindustrialisation, with less national output generated by their manufacturing sectors.

3. The collapse of communism led to the opening up of many former communist countries. These countries have increased their share of world trade by taking advantage of their low production costs, especially their low wage levels.

4. India and China, some of the newly industrialised countries, have increased their share of world trade including manufacturing exports. China has surely shown a sharp increase in the share of world trade and has emerged as an economic super power. Its share of world trade has increased in all areas and has not limited to clothing and toys. For example, in 1995, the US had captured nearly 25% of global trade in hi-tech goods, while China had only 3%. By 2005, the US share had fallen to 15%, while China's share had risen to 15%. *(Source: European Central Bank - ECB, Occasional Paper - China and India's Role in Global Trade and Finance, 2008)*

1.3.2 Major Trends and Developments in Global Trading Environment

Intense competition among countries, industries, and firms on a global level is a recent development owed to the coming together of several major trends. Among these trends are:

1. Forced Dynamism: Since the environment in international trade is always changing, it is a complex topic. International trade is forced to give way to trends that shape the cultural, economic environment and political. Businesses are pushing the limit of economic technology, culture, politics and growth which also changes the global society and global economic context. Another point to be kept in mind is that factors that are external to international trade are forcing international trade to change in the way they operate.

2. Cooperation among Countries: Countries cooperate with each other in thousands of ways through international organisations, treaties, and consultations. When such cooperation takes place, it encourages the globalisation of business by removing any restrictions placed on it and by designing a framework that reduces uncertainties about what the company can and cannot do. Some of the reasons that companies cooperate are:

(i) To gain reciprocal advantages,

(ii) To attack problems they cannot solve alone, and

(iii) To deal with concerns that lie outside anyone's territory.

Agreements on a variety of commercially related activities, such as transportation and trade, allow nations to gain reciprocal advantages. Groups of countries have also agreed to protect the property of foreign-owned companies and to permit foreign-made goods and services to enter their territories with fewer restrictions.

Countries cooperate on problems they cannot solve alone, such as by coordinating national economic programmes (including interest rates) so that global economic conditions are minimally disrupted, and by restricting imports of certain products to protect endangered species.

Countries also agree on how to exploit areas that are outside their territories which include outer space, seas, oceans etc.

2. Liberalisation of Cross-border Movements: Every country restricts the movement across its borders of goods and services as well as of the resources, such as workers and capital. Due to these restrictions, international trade hits a road block as the restrictions can be changed at any time and hence the ability to sustain international trade is uncertain. There has been a change in the recent decade where government imposes fewer restrictions on cross border movement which allows the organisation to take advantage of international opportunities. The Government has decreased the number of restrictions due to the following factors:

(i) Having very few international restrictions will give consumers better access to a greater variety of goods and services at lower prices,

(ii) Producers will become more efficient by competing against foreign companies, and

(iii) If they reduce their own restrictions, other countries will do the same.

4. Transfer of Technology: Technology transfer is the process by which commercial technology is circulated. This may not be a legal contract but involves communication by the transferor to the recipient. Non commercial technology transfer is also included which are found in international agreements between the developed and developing nations. Such agreements may relate to infrastructure or agricultural development, or to international cooperation in the fields of research, education, employment or transport.

5. Growth in Emerging Markets: The growth of emerging markets has impacted international trade in every way (e.g., India, China, Brazil, and other parts of Asia and South America especially). The emerging markets have simultaneously increased the potential size and worth of current major international trade while also facilitating the emergence of a whole new generation of innovative companies.

1.3.3 Trade Restrictions

Though there are a number of advocates of free trade, international trade is generally characterised by the existence of various trade barriers or trade restrictions. International trade is restricted by tariffs and non-tariff measures.

Meaning

"Trade barriers refer to the government policies and measures which obstruct the free flow of goods and services across the national borders".

A trade restriction is an artificial restriction on the trade of goods and/or services between two countries. It is the by-product of protectionism.

However, the term can be viewed differently because what one part may see as a trade restriction another may see as a way to protect consumers from inferior, harmful or dangerous products.

Trade restrictions aims at:

- Protecting domestic industries or certain other sectors of the economy from foreign competition;
- Making the Balance of Payments position more favourable;
- Conserving the foreign exchange resources of the country;
- Promoting indigenous R & D;
- Guarding the country against dumping of goods;
- Curbing conspicuous consumption and mobilise revenue for the government.

Trade barriers/restrictions may be broadly divided into two groups- (i) tariff barriers and (ii) non-tariff barriers.

Trade restrictions are government-induced restrictions on international trade. The restrictions can take many forms, including the following:

- Tariffs;
- Non-tariff barriers to trade;
- Import licenses;
- Export licenses;
- Import Quotas;
- Subsidies;
- Voluntary Export Restraints;
- Embargo;
- Currency devaluation;
- Trade restriction.

Most trade barriers work on the same principle, i.e., imposition of some sort of cost on trade that raises the price of the traded products. If two or more nations repeatedly use trade barriers against each other, it results in trade war.

There is a general agreement among the economists that trade barriers are detrimental and decrease overall economic efficiency. Free trade involves the removal of all such barriers, except perhaps those considered necessary for health or national security.

Impact of Trade Restrictions

- Trade restrictions are often criticised for the impact that they have on the developing economy.
- Trade restrictions such as taxes on food imports or subsidies for farmers in developed economies lead to overproduction and dumping on world markets, thus lowering prices and affecting poor-country farmers.
- Tariffs tend to be anti-poor, with low rates for raw commodities and high rates for labour-intensive processed goods.
- Another negative aspect of trade restrictions is that it would cause a limited choice of products and would thus force customers to pay higher prices and accept inferior quality.
- Trade restrictions are barriers to free trade. Before exporting or importing to other nations:
  (a) they must be aware of restrictions that the government imposes on the trade;
  (b) they need to make sure that they are not violating the restrictions by checking those related regulation on tax or duty;
  (c) they probably need a licence in order to ensure a smooth export or import business and reduce the risk of penalty of violation;
  (d) sometimes the situation becomes even more complicated with the changing of policy and restrictions of a country.

1.4 World Trade and Protectionism

1.4.1 Meaning of Protectionism

Trade disputes *between countries happen because one or more parties either believes that trade is being conducted unfairly, on an uneven playing field, or because they believe that there is one or more economic or strategic justifications for import controls.*

Protectionism *represents any attempt to impose* **restrictions on trade** *in goods and services.* Trade protection is the deliberate attempt to limit imports or promote exports by putting up barriers to trade. Protectionism is still widely practiced, even though the arguments are in favour of free trade and increasing trade openness. The aim is to cushion domestic businesses and industries from overseas competition and prevent the outcome resulting from the inter-play of free market forces of supply and demand.

1.4.2 Objectives of Protectionism

1. To protect domestic industry from foreign competition.
2. To direct the foreign trade in accordance with national priorities.

3. To promote indigenous research and development.
4. To conserve foreign exchange resources of the country.
5. To make the balance of payments position favourable.
6. To curb conspicuous consumption.
7. To mobilise revenue for government.
8. To discriminate against certain countries.

1.4.3 Forms of Protectionism

Some of the important forms of Protectionism are:

1. **Tariffs**: A tax that raises the price of imported products and causes a contraction in domestic demand and an expansion in domestic supply – for example, the average import tariff on goods entering the Russian economy is 10%, although there will be higher rates for a number of products.
2. **Intellectual property laws** (patents and copyrights).
3. **Quotas – quantitative (volume) limits** are the amount of imports allowed or a limit to the amount of imports permitted into a country at a given time and period.
4. **Domestic Subsidies**: Government financial help (state aid) for domestic businesses facing financial problems e.g. subsidies for car manufacturers or loss-making airlines.
5. **Voluntary Export Restraint Arrangements:** The two countries sign a deal where they limit the amount of their exports to one another over a said period of time.
6. **Preferential State Procurement Policies:** Where a government favours local/domestic producers when finalising contracts for state spending e.g. infrastructure projects
7. **Technical barriers to trade** including **product labelling rules and stringent sanitary rules**, food safety and environmental standards. Due to these barriers, they increase the product compliance cost and also impose monitoring costs on export agencies in many countries. Huge scale vertically integrated transnational businesses can cope with these non-tariff barriers but many of the least developed countries do not have the some technical sophistication to overcome these barriers.
8. **Financial Protectionism:** For example when a national government instructs its banks to give priority when making loans to domestic businesses.
9. **Exchange Controls:** Limiting the foreign exchange that can move between countries.
10. **Import Licensing:** Governments grants importers the license to import goods.

11. **Export Subsidies:** is a type of payment which encourages domestic production by lowering costs. Soft loans can be used to fund the 'dumping' of products in overseas markets.
12. **Murky or Hidden Protectionism:** A government subsidy that is paid only when consumers buy locally produced goods and services. Deliberate intervention in currency markets might also come under this category.

1.4.4 Arguments For Protectionism

1. **Fledging Industry Argument:** Certain industries possess a possible comparative advantage but have not yet exploited economies of scale. Short-term protection allows the 'infant industry' to develop its comparative advantage at which point the protection could be relaxed, leaving the industry to trade freely on the international market.
2. **Protection of Strategic Industries:** The government may also wish to protect employment in strategic industries, although value judgements are involved in determining what constitutes a strategic sector. This might involve attempting to reduce long-term dependence on certain imports.
3. **Protection of jobs** and improvement in the balance of payments.
4. **Externalities and Market Failure:** Protectionism can also be used to internalise the social costs of de-merit goods, or to correct for environmental market failure in the supply of certain imports.
5. **Anti-dumping Duties:** Goods are dumped when they are sold for export at less than their normal value. Dumping is a type of predatory pricing behaviour and a form of price discrimination. Some examples of disputes about alleged dumping have included
   (a) India complaining about the dumping of bus and truck tires from China and Thailand.
   (b) EU shoemakers alleging that Chinese and Vietnamese shoe manufacturers have illegally dumped leather, sports and safety shoes in the EU market.
   (c) In 2009 EU imposed temporary "anti-dumping" taxes on Chinese wire, candles, iron and steel pipes, and aluminium foil from Armenia, Brazil and China.
6. **Diversification:** It is necessary to have a diversified industrial structure for an economy to be strong and reasonably self-sufficient. A country relying too much on foreign countries undertakes a number of risks. Changes in political relations and international economic conditions may put the country into difficulties. Hence, a diversified industrial structure is necessary to maintain stability and acquire strength.

7. **Employment:** Protection has been advocated also as a measure to stimulate domestic economy and expand employment opportunities.
8. **Key Industries:** It is also argued that a country develop its own key industries because the development of other industries and the economy depends a lot on the output of key industries.

1.4.5 Arguments Against Protectionism

1. **Market Distortion:** Protection can be an ineffective and costly means of sustaining jobs.
2. **Higher Prices for Consumers:** Tariffs increase the prices faced by the consumers and lag in the inefficient sectors of competition. Foreign producers are punished and they encourage the allocation of resources both globally and domestically.
3. **Loss of Economic Welfare:** Tariffs create a deadweight loss of consumer and producer surplus. Welfare is reduced through higher prices and restricted consumer choice.
4. **Regressive Effect on the Distribution of Income:** Higher prices that result from tariffs hit those on lower incomes hardest, because the tariffs (e.g. on foodstuffs, tobacco, and clothing) fall on those products that lower income families spend a higher share of their income.
5. **Production Inefficiencies:** Some organisations are protected from competition and hence they have little motivation to reduce the production costs.
6. **Reduction in Market Access for Producers:** Export subsidies depress world prices and damage output, profits, investment and jobs in many developing countries that rely on exporting primary and manufactured goods for their growth.
7. **Trade Wars:** Retaliatory actions increase the costs of importing new technologies affecting LRAS. There is the danger that one country imposing import controls will lead to "retaliatory action" by another leading to a decrease in the volume of world trade.
8. **Second best Approach:** Protectionism is a 'second best' approach to correcting for a country's balance of payments problem or the fear of structural unemployment. Import controls go against the principles of free trade. In this sense, import controls can be seen as examples of government failure arising from intervention in markets.
9. **Negative Multiplier Effects:** If one country imposes trade restrictions on another, the resultant decrease in trade will have a negative multiplier effect affecting many more countries because exports are an injection of demand into the global circular flow of income.

1.4.6 Rising Trade Protectionism

The rise in trade over the last few decades is attributable to a concerted effort to bolster international economic co-operation. The creation of the General Agreement on Tariffs and Trade (GATT) and other multilateral agencies like the IMF and World Bank that advocate trade liberalisation lowered barriers to trade, especially in terms of tariffs.

According to the 14th Global Trade Alert (GTA) report published in September 2013, countries have taken 2134 new measures since 2008 that almost certainly discriminate against foreign commercial interests (CEPR 2013a). Out of these, 1,814 measures are still in place. In addition, there are another 235 measures still in force that could hamper foreign commercial interests. While some of these measures are now being slowly unwound, the concern is that protectionism could remain a drag on global trade growth (Figures 1.4).

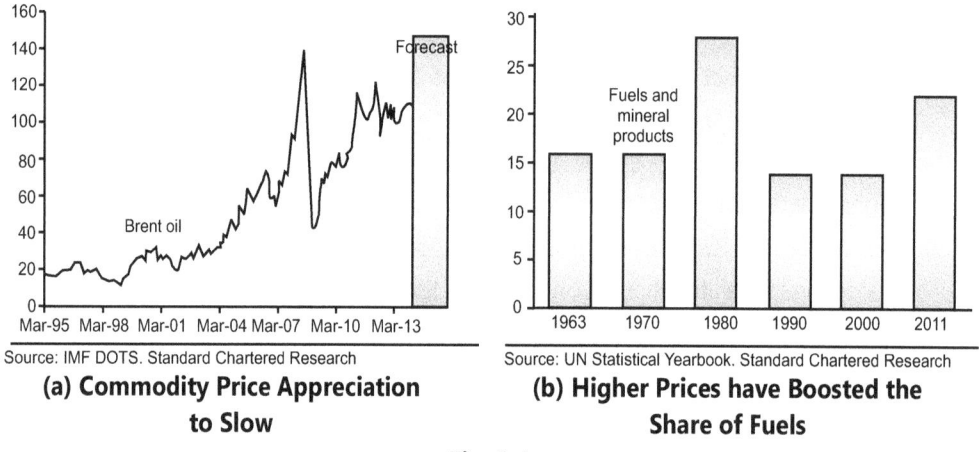

Source: IMF DOTS. Standard Chartered Research
(a) **Commodity Price Appreciation to Slow**

Source: UN Statistical Yearbook. Standard Chartered Research
(b) **Higher Prices have Boosted the Share of Fuels**

Fig. 1.4

The lack of progress on the Doha round of talks, launched in 2001, has also been a point of concern. Some economists have blamed the creation of bilateral and free-trade agreements for the lack of progress on global trade agreements. They also argue that these bilateral agreements reduce international trade efficiency by 'diverting' trade to preferred but less efficient destinations.

According to the World Trade Organisation (WTO), the number of Preferential Trade Agreements (PTA) and Bilateral Investment Treaties (BIT) more than tripled between 1990 and 2010. Approximately 300 PTAs are currently in operation and many more under negotiation. Around half of these PTAs are bilateral and almost two-thirds are between developed and developing countries (World Trade Report 2013).

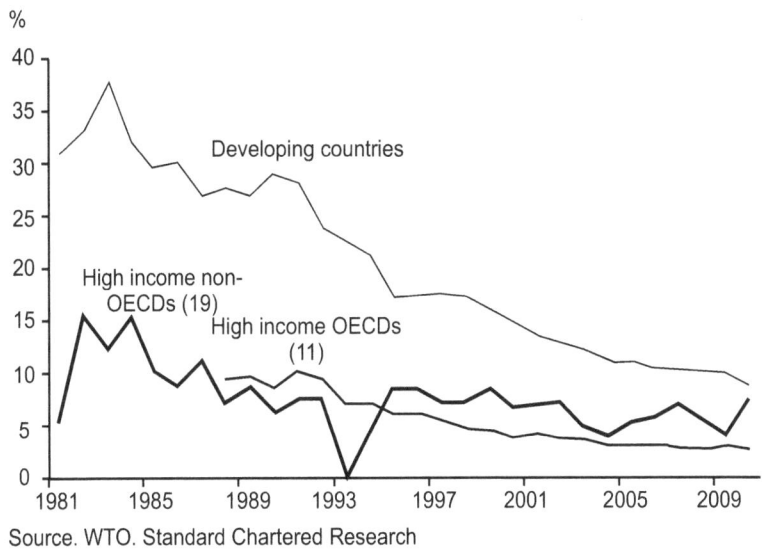

Fig. 1.5: Trends in Average Most Favoured Nations Applied Rates

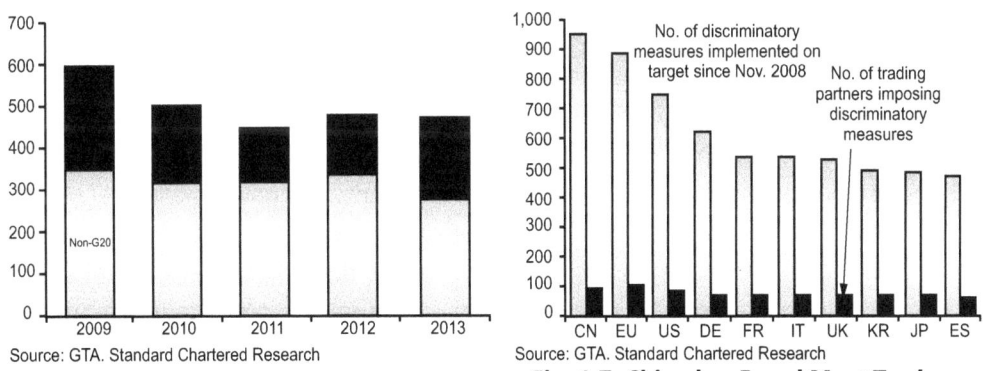

Fig. 1.6: Trade Protectionism has Fallen Back

Fig. 1.7: China has Faced Most Trade Discrimination

The conclusion of the WTO 'Bali package' in December 2013 under the Doha round of talks could yet prove to be a shot in the arm for global trade talks. The Bali package assists trade facilitation by simplifying customs procedures and reducing the red tape around trade. The WTO calculates the benefit of reducing trade costs by between 10-15% under the Bali package to be between USD 400bn and USD 1tn. There has recently been progress on trade agreements that cover large parts of the global economy. Recent academic work suggests that PTAs are not necessarily inefficient, as they can facilitate wider trade agreements by establishing standards and procedures and lowering domestic political opposition to wider global deals.

The Trans-Pacific Partnership (TPP) and the Transatlantic Trade and Investment Partnership (TTIP) together would cover 60% of the global economy once in force. According to Petri and Plummer (2012), the TPP could result in a boost to Asia-Pacific trade, with potential trade gains of nearly USD 2tn per year once full integration is achieved. In addition, agreements like the Regional Comprehensive Economic Partnership (RCEP) in Asia may provide a further fillip to South-South trade.

The concern is that these trade agreements may be difficult to complete, as they are no longer about simply reducing tariffs on certain products or commodities. With tariffs already very low, these agreements are focused on harmonising the regulatory environment around trade across regions and tackling twenty-first century concerns such as intellectual property rights and financial services oversight. This would require individual economies to be willing to give up sovereignty over how these markets are regulated domestically, which might be hard to get approved in national parliaments.

1.5 Tariff and Non-Tariff Barriers

1.5.1 Introduction

Though there are a number of advocates of free trade, international trade is generally characterised by the existence of various trade barriers.

Trade barriers refer to the government policies and measures which obstruct the free flow of goods and services across national borders.

Governments use many rationales and seek a range of outcomes when they try to influence exports or imports. We now review the instruments that governments use to try to do so. Because a country's trade policy has repercussions abroad, retaliation from foreign governments looms as a potential obstacle to achieve the desired objectives. Therefore, the choice of the instrument of trade control is crucial because each type may incite different responses from domestic and foreign groups.

Main Goals of Imposing Trade Barriers

The main goals of imposing trade barriers are:

(a) To protect domestic industries or certain other sectors of the economy from foreign competition;
(b) To promote indigenous research and development;
(c) To guard against dumping;
(d) To conserve the foreign exchange resources of the country;
(e) To make the Balance of Payments position more favourable;
(f) To control conspicuous consumption; and
(g) Mobilise revenue for the government.

One way to understand trade control instruments is by distinguishing two types that differ in their effects:
- Those that indirectly affect the amount traded by directly influencing the *prices* of exports or imports;
- Those that directly limit the *amount* of goods that can be traded.

Thus, trade barriers can be broadly divided into two groups:

(I) Tariff Barriers

(II) Non-Tariff Barriers (NBTs).

1.5.2 Tariff Barriers

When it comes to explaining tariffs, we need to start by distinguishing tariff barriers (which directly affect either prices) and non-tariff barriers (which may directly affect either price or quantity).

Tariffs in international trade refer to the duties or taxes imposed on internationally traded products when they cross the national borders.

- A tariff, also called a **duty,** is the common type of trade control and a tax that government levy on a good shipped internationally.
- Governments charge a tariff on a good when it crosses an official boundary-whether it be that of a nation, say Mexico, or a group of nations like the EU, that have agreed to impose a common tariff on goods entering their block.
- Tariff is a very important instrument of trade protection. However, mostly because of the efforts of the WTO aimed at trade liberalisation, in the industrial countries, there has been a substantial reduction in the tariffs on manufactured goods over the last fifty years.
- Although the tariff rates are still fairly high in the developing countries, many of them have also been progressively reducing the tariff levels.
- It is also true that WTO prefers tariff barriers to non-tariff barriers as tariffs are generally regarded as less restrictive than other methods of protection like quantitative restrictions.

Classification of Tariffs

On different criteria, we can classify tariffs as discussed below:

(A) On the basis of the origin and destination of the goods crossing the national boundary, tariffs may be classified into three categories:

- **Export Tariffs:** An export duty is a tax imposed on a commodity originating from the duty-levying country destined for some other country. That is, tariffs collected by the exporting country are called export tariffs.

- **Transit Tariffs:** A transit duty is a tax imposed on a commodity crossing the national frontier originating from and destined from other countries. That is, if tariffs are collected by a country through which the goods have passed, they are transit tariffs.

- **Import tariffs:** An import duty is a tax imposed on a commodity originating abroad and destined for the duty-levying country. That is, tariffs collected by importing countries are called import tariffs. Import tariffs are by far the most common tariffs.

Import tariffs raise the price of the imported goods by placing a tax on them that is not placed on domestic goods, thereby giving domestically produced goods a relative price advantage.

A tariff may be protective even though there is no domestic production in direct competition. For example, a country that wants its residents to spend less on foreign goods and services may raise the price of some foreign products, even though there are no close domestic substitutes, to curtail demand for imports.

(B) On the basis for quantification of the tariff, tariffs may be classified into the following three categories:

- **Specific Duties:** A government may assess a tariff on a per unit basis, in which case it is applying a specific duty. Thus, a specific duty is a flat sum per physical unit of the commodity imported or exported. Thus, a specific import duty is a fixed amount of duty levied upon each unit of the commodity imported.

- **Ad-Valorem Duties:** A government may assess a tariff as a percentage of the value of the item, in which case it is an ad valorem duty. Thus, these duties are levied as a fixed percentage of the value of commodity imported or exported. Thus, while the specific duty is based on the quantum of the commodity imported/exported, the ad-valorem duty is based on the value of the commodity imported/exported.

- **Compound Duties:** When a commodity is subject to both specific and ad-valorem duties, the tariff is generally referred to as compound duty. Thus, if it assesses both a specific duty and ad valorem duty on the same product, the combination is a compound duty.

A specific duty is straightforward for customs officials to assess because they do not need to determine a good's value on which to calculate a percentage tax.

The raw materials frequently enter developed countries free of duty; however, if processed e.g. coffee beans to instant coffee powder, developed countries then assign an import tariff. Because an ad valorem tariff is based on the total value of the product, meaning the raw materials and the processing combined.

Developing countries argue that the **effective tariff** on the manufactured portion turns out to be higher than the published tariff rate. For example, a country may charge no duty on coffee beans but may assess a 10% ad valorem tariff on instant coffee. Thus, if $5 for a jar of instant coffee covers $2.50 in coffee beans and $2.50 in processing costs, the $0.50 duty is effectively 20% on the manufactured part as the coffee beans could have entered free of duty. This challenges the developing countries to find markets for their manufactured products.

- **Sliding Scale Import Duty**: Sliding scale import duty is imposed on ad valorem basis or on specific basis. Often, sliding scale import duty is levied on a specific basis. For example, no import duty is imposed on 1 watch brought into the country by an Indian tourist returning from a trip abroad. Then, ₹ 50 is charged per watch imported between 50 and 100 watches and may be ₹ 100 per watch on imported watches for the quantity of 101 and 200 and so on.

(C) On the basis of its application between different countries, the tariff system may be classified into three categories:

- **Single-Column Tariff:** This tariff is also known as uni-linear tariff system, which provides a uniform rate of duty for all like commodities without making any discrimination between countries.

- **Double-Column Tariff:** Under this system there are two rates of duty on some or on all commodities. Thus, the double-column tariff discriminates between countries.

The double-column tariff system may be further sub-divided into:

(i) **General and Conventional Tariff:** It consists of two schedules of tariffs i.e. the general and the conventional. The general schedule is fixed by the legislature at the start. On the other hand, the conventional schedule results from the conclusion of commercial treatise with other countries.

(ii) **The Maximum and Minimum System:** It consists of two autonomously determined schedules of tariff - the maximum and the minimum. The minimum schedule applies to those nations who have obtained the concession as a result of the treaty or through 'Most Favoured Nation' (MFN) pledge, while the maximum schedule applies to all other countries.

- **Triple-Column Tariff:** This system consists of three autonomously determined tariff schedules: the general, the intermediate and the preferential. The first two i.e. the general and the intermediate tariff schedule are similar to the maximum and minimum rates (under double-column tariff system). The preferential rate was generally applied in the case of trade between the mother country and its colonies.

(D) On basis of the purpose that the tariff serves, it may classified into the following three categories:

- **Revenue Tariff:** Tariffs also serve as a source of governmental revenue. Import tariffs are of little importance to developed countries, usually costing more to collect than they yield. However, tariffs are a major source of revenue in many developing countries. This is because government authorities in these countries may have more control over determining the amounts and types of goods crossing their borders and collecting a tax on them than they do over determining and collecting individual and corporate income taxes. Although revenue tariffs are most commonly collected on imports, some countries charge export tariffs on raw materials. Transit tariffs were once a major source of revenue for countries, but governmental treatise has nearly abolished them.

Thus, sometimes the main intention of the government in imposing tariff may be to obtain revenue. When raising revenue is the primary motive, the rates of duty are generally low lest imports be highly discouraged, thus defeating the aim of mobilising revenue for the government. Revenue tariffs tend to fall on articles of mass consumption.

- **Protective Tariff:** This tariff is intended mainly to accord protection to domestic industries from foreign competition. In general, the rates of duty tend to be very high, as only high rates of duty curtail imports to a significant extent.

- **Countervailing and Anti- dumping Duties:** Countervailing duties may be imposed on certain imports when they have been subsidised by foreign governments. And, anti-dumping duties are applied to imports which are being dumped on the domestic market at a price either below their cost of production or substantially lower than their domestic prices. These two types of tariffs are generally penalty duties as an addition to the regular rates.

(E) On the basis of the production, distribution, consumption, it may classified into following four categories:

- **Single Stage:** It means the Department will collect tax at the first stage which means from the distributor or manufacturer only. There is not going to be tax collection from subsequent stages like dealers and retailers as they will be out of the tax chain. Single stage tax structure will encourage proliferation of illegal trading activities.

- **Cascade:** This tax is also called as tax on tax. A tax that is levied on a goods at each stage of the production process up to the point of being sold to the final consumer. Cascade tax can create higher tax revenues compared to a single stage tax, because tax is imposed on top of the tax.

- **Value Added Tax:** A Value-Added Tax (VAT) or also Goods and Services Tax (GST) is a form of consumption tax. From the perspective of the buyer, it is a tax on the purchase price. From that of the seller, it is a tax only on the value added to a product, material, or service, from an accounting point of view, by this stage of its manufacture or distribution.

- **Excise:** An excise is an inland tax on the sale, or production for sale, of specific goods or a tax on a good produced for sale, or sold, within a country or licenses for specific activities. Excises are distinguished from custom duties, which are taxes on importation. Excises are inland taxes, whereas customs duties are border taxes.

On the basis of the origin and destination of the goods crossing the national boundary.	On the basis for quantification of the tariff.	On the basis of its application between different countries.	On basis of the purpose that the tariff serves.	On the basis of the production, distribution, consumption.
Export Tariffs	Specific Duties. Ad-Valorem Duties.	Single-Column tariff.	Revenue tariff.	Single stage
Transit Tariffs.	Compound Duties.	Double-Column tariff.	Protective tariff.	Value added
Import Tariffs.	Sliding Scale Import Duty.	Triple-Column tariff.	Countervailing and anti-dumping duties.	Cascade
				Excise

Effects of Tariffs on an Economy

Tariff affects an economy in different ways, as pointed below:

(1) Protective Effect: An import duty is likely to increase the price of the imported goods. This increase in the price of imports is likely to reduce imports and increase the demand for domestic goods. Import duties may also enable the domestic industries to absorb higher production costs. As a result of the protection given by the application of tariffs, the domestic industries are able to expand their output.

(2) Revenue Effect: A tariff means increased revenue for the government, unless of course, the rate of tariff is so prohibitive that it completely stops the import of the commodity subject to the tariff.

(3) Consumption Effect: The rise in prices resulting from the import duty usually reduces the consumption capacity of the people.

(4) Redistribution Effect: If the import duty causes an increase in the price of domestically produced goods; it amounts to redistribution of income between the consumers and producers in favour of the producers. Further, a part of the consumer income is transferred to the exchequer by means of the tariff.

(5) Employment Effect: The tariff may cause a switch over from spending on foreign goods to spending on domestic goods. This higher spending within the country may cause an expansion of domestic income and employment.

(6) Terms of Trade Effect: In an attempt to maintain the previous level of imports to tariff imposing country, if the exporter reduces the prices, the tariff imposing country is able to get their imports at a cheaper price. Other things being equal, this will improve the terms of trade of the country imposing the tariff.

(7) Competitive Effect: The competitive effect of the tariff is, in fact, an anti-competitive effect in the sense that protection of domestic industries from foreign competition may enable the domestic industries to obtain monopoly power with all its associated evils.

(8) Balance of Payment Effect: Tariffs, by reducing the volume of imports, may help the country to improve its balance of payments position.

Tariff Structure - Developing Countries

The prevailing tariff structures in industrial countries are highly harmful to developing countries.

1. Although most tariffs in industrial nations are low, but on certain commodities it remains prohibitively high.
2. Tariffs on many consumers', agricultural and labour-intensive goods are 10-20 times higher than the overall average tariff. For example, US import tariffs on clothes and shoes average 11% and go as high as 48%. Other industrial economies are no different. For example, the EU applies tariffs of up to 236% on meat, 180% on cereals, and 17% on chocolates. In contrast, its tariffs on raw materials and electronics rarely exceed 5%.
3. Developing countries that export primarily agricultural and labour-intensive goods, such as textiles, and clothing, are hard hit by industrial countries' tariff policies. For example, on imports of $2.4 billion from Bangladesh (a major clothing exporter), the U.S. collected duties of $ 331 million in 2001- slightly more than the $ 330 million it collected on $ 30 billion of imports from France.
4. Thus, poor countries like Bangladesh, that are beginning to move from subsistence agriculture and dependency on exports of primary commodities into light manufacturing, face the highest effective tariffs, on average, 4 or 5 times, those faced by the richer economies.
5. To worsen the matters further, tariffs applied to similar categories of consumer goods are often higher on the cheaper goods than on luxury versions. For example, the U.S. tariff on imported silk shirts is only 1.9% while it is 20% on cotton shirts, and 32.5% on synthetic fibre shirts.
6. In other words, the tariff structure on these products is regressive taxes on the poor, who can least afford to pay.
7. Unfair tariff structures are not limited to textiles alone. Another type of discriminatory tariff is tariff-escalation- when tariffs increase with the degree of processing involved in the product. Cocoa beans are taxed at lower rate than cocoa butter, which is taxed at a lower rate than chocolate and tariff escalation is also seen in many major developing countries.

1.5.3 Non-tariff Barriers

Non-tariff Barriers (NTBs), some of which are described as *new protectionism* measures (tariffs are regarded at traditional barriers), have grown considerably, particularly since the beginning of 1980s. The export growth of many developing countries has been seriously affected by NTBs.

According to a World Bank study, NTBs in major industrial countries affect more than one-third of imports from developing countries as compared to more than one-fourth from all countries.

The NTBs are categorised into two groups:

(i) **The first group** includes those tariffs which are generally used by developing countries to prevent foreign exchange outflows, or those which are due to the chosen strategy of economic development. These traditional NTBs include import licensing, import quotas, foreign exchange regulations and canalisation of imports.

(ii) **The second group** of NTBs are those which are mostly used by developed countries to protect domestic industries which have lost international competitiveness and/or which are politically sensitive for governments of these countries. One of the most important new protectionism measures under this group is Voluntary Export Restraint (VER).

Extent and Effect of NTBs

- Over the years, the NTBs have been becoming more extensive and intensive. Today, they are not confined to the labour intensive products where the developing countries like India have a cost advantage, but also cover sophisticated products; Japan and newly industrialising countries (NICs) like South Korea are also among the most affected countries by NTBs.
- The NTBs tend to offset favourable effects of the GATT negotiations, particularly of the Tokyo Round, on trade liberalisations like the reductions in the average levels of tariffs.
- In fact, several advanced countries like the US, which were the high advocates of free trade, increasingly resort to several NTBs, particularly against the developing countries and also certain economically powerful countries like Japan.

Forms of NTBs (NTBs for Quantity Controls)

There are different forms of NTBs. The NTBs which have significant restrictive effects are described as *hard-core* NTBs. Governments use non-tariff regulations and practices to affect directly the quantity of imports and exports. A brief account of the NTBs is given below:

1. **Voluntary Export Restraint (VER):** VER is a bilateral arrangement instituted to restrain the rapid growth of exports of specific manufactured goods from Japan and the newly industrialising countries. The U.S. and the EC have, thus, regulated several imports.

   A variation of an import quota is the so-called **Voluntary Export Restraint (VER).** Essentially, the government of Country A asks the government of Country B to reduce its companies' exports to Country A voluntarily. Here, the term 'voluntarily' is misleading; typically either Country B volunteers to reduce its exports or else Country A may impose tougher trade regulations.

   Procedurally, VER has unique merits. A VER is much easier to switch off than an import quota. In addition, the appearance of a "voluntary" choice by a particular country to constrain its shipments to another country tends not to damage political relations between those countries as much as an import quota does.

   A country may establish *export quotas* to assure domestic consumers of a sufficient supply of goods at a low price, to prevent depletion of natural resources, or to attempt to raise export prices by restricting supply in foreign markets. To restrict supply, some countries band together in various commodity agreements, such as those for coffee and petroleum, which then restrict and regulate exports from the member countries.

2. **Embargoes:** A specific type of quota that prohibits all forms of trade is an **embargo.** Regarding quotas, countries/group of countries may place embargoes on either imports or exports, on whole categories of products regardless of origin or destination, on specific products with specific countries or on all products with given countries. Governments impose embargoes in the effort to use the economic means to achieve political goals. For example, when U.S. imposed embargo on Cuba it was conceived to weaken the Cuban economy and thus induce a demoralised populace to overthrow the Communist regime.

3. **"Buy Local" Legislation:** Another form of quantitative trade control is so-called 'buy local legislation'. Government purchases form a large part of the total expenditures in many of the countries; and generally governments favour domestic producers. At times, governments specify a domestic content restriction i.e. a certain percentage of the product must of local origin. Sometimes they favour domestic producers through price mechanism. For example, a government agency may buy a foreign-made product only if the price is at some predetermined margin below that of a domestic competitor.

4. **Standards and Labels:** Countries can devise classification, labelling, and testing standards to allow the sale of domestic products but obstruct that of foreign-made ones. For example, the requirement that companies indicate on a product where it is made provides information to consumers who may prefer to buy products from certain nations. In addition, countries may dictate their terms on content information to be displayed on the packaging. These technicalities add to a firm's production costs, particularly if the labels have to be translated for each export market.

Further raw materials, design, and labour increasingly come from many countries, so most of the products today are of such mixed origin that they are difficult to be sorted out. For instance, the U.S. stipulated that any cloth "substantially altered" in another country must identify that country on its label. As a result, designers like Gucci and Versace must declare "Made in China" on the label of garments that contain silk from China.

The objective of *standards* is to protect the safety or health of the domestic population. However, some foreign companies argue that standards are just another method of providing protection to domestic producers. Further, it is argued that there's no way of knowing to what extent products are kept out of countries for legitimate safety and health reasons or are arbitrarily kept to safeguard domestic production.

5. **Specific Permission Requirements:** Some countries require that potential importers or exporters secure permission from government authorities before conducting trade transactions. This requirement is called as an **import or export license**. A company may have to submit samples to government authorities to obtain an import licence. Thus, this procedure can restrict imports or exports directly by denying permission or indirectly because of the cost, time, and uncertainty involved in the process.

6. **Foreign-exchange Control:** It is a similar type of control. It requires an importer of a given product to apply to a government agency to secure the foreign currency to pay for the product. Thus, failure to grant the exchange obstructs foreign trade.

7. **Administrative Delays:** Intentional administrative delays create uncertainty and raise the cost of carrying inventory. However, competitive pressure moves countries to improve their administrative systems.

8. **Reciprocal Requirements:** Governments sometimes require exporters to take merchandise in lieu of money or to promise to buy merchandise or services, in place of cash payment, in the country to which they export. This requirement is common in the defence or aerospace industries where the importer does not have enough foreign currency. For example, Indonesia bought Russian jets in exchange for merchandise like rubber.

9. **Countertrade:** For instance, McDonnell Douglas sold helicopters to the UK government but had to equip them with Rolls-Royce engines (made in the UK) as well as transfer much of the technology and production work to the UK. Such transactions are called *countertrade or offsets*. In other words, more frequently reciprocal requirements are made between countries with ample access to foreign currency that want to secure jobs or technology as part of the transaction. All things being equal, companies avoid countertrade. However, some companies have developed competencies in these types of arrangements.

10. **Restrictions on Services:** Services are the fastest-growing sector in international trade. When taking decision about restrictions about trade in services, countries typically consider four factors:

- **Essentiality:** Certain industries are termed as industries that serve strategic purposes or because they provide social assistance to their citizens. As such, countries sometimes prohibit private companies, foreign or domestic, in some sectors because they feel the services should not be sold for profit. In other cases, they set price controls for private competitors or subsidise government-owned service organisations, creating disincentives for foreign private participation.

- **Not-for-profit Services:** Certain sectors like mail, education, and hospital health services are often not-for-profit sectors in which few foreign firms compete. When a government privatises these industries, its customary preference for local ownership and control of essential services may preclude foreign firms from competing. Certain essential services in which foreign firms are sometimes excluded are media, communications, banking and utilities.

- **Standards:** Governments limit foreign entry into many service professions to ensure practice by qualified personnel. The licensing standards of these personnel vary by country and include such professionals as accountants, electricians, gemologists, hairstylists, lawyers, and teachers.

  There is little reciprocal recognition in licensing from one country to another because occupational standards differ substantially. Thus, for example, that an accounting or legal firm from one country faces obstacles in another country. The company must hire professionals within each foreign country or else try to earn certification abroad. But, obtaining the certificate can be difficult because examinations will be in a foreign language and generally emphasise materials different from those in the home country.

- **Immigration:** Satisfying the standards of a particular country are no guarantee that foreigners can then work there. Further, governmental regulations often require that an organisation, domestic or foreign, search extensively for qualified personnel locally before it can even apply for work permits for personnel it would like to bring in from abroad. Even if no one is available, hiring a foreigner is still difficult.

11. Quantitative Restrictions (Quotas): The quota is the most common type of quantitative import or export restriction, limiting the quantity of a product that can be imported or exported in a given time frame, typically per year. **Import quotas** normally raise prices for two reasons: (i) they limit the supply, and (ii) they provide little incentive to use price competition to increase sales.

12. Administered Protection:

- **Safeguard Action:** Safeguard action, under WTO article XIX which enables countries to undertake temporary restrictions against import surges threatening the viability of domestic industries.

- **Health Standard:** Several health and product standards imposed by developed countries hinder the export developing countries because of added cost of technical requirement.
- **Customs Procedures:** Certain customs procedures of many countries become trade barriers. For example, studies point out that frequent changes of Japan's customs regulations are themselves a significant barrier to exporters, especially those not affiliated with Japanese overseas joint-venture.
- **Consular Formalities:** A number of countries insist on certain consular formalities like certifications of export documents by the respective consulate, of the importing country. This becomes a trade barrier when fees charged for this is very high or the procedure is very cumbersome.

Non-Trade Barriers and India's Exports

The problem of NTBs on India's exports has been growing. The impact of conventional NTBs on exports of marine products and leather and leather goods to developed countries is only marginal. However, exports of metal goods and readymade garments from India have suffered due to NTBs in developed economies. Extension and intensification of NTBs is bound to severely restrict India's export expansion in these two relatively important export sectors of the economy.

Apart from the actual imposition of these NTBs, the 'noise' created is often enough to drive out the exporters and bring a fall in exports. NTBs and their administration bring about undesirable change in the structure of domestic industry and in the distribution of rewards between rent, profit and wage incomes.

The uncertainty they create has an adverse effect on capacity creation and investment in the industry. NTBs prevent the industry from making full use of technological potential and economies of scale. These facts were well seen in the survey of garment firms in India.

The study of the Asian Development Bank (ADB) points out that in case of NTBs, Indian exporters have not taken full advantage of the scope which exists. Thus, improvements in domestic capability will surely yield export expansion, at least in the short-run.

The problem of NTBs has increased for Indian exports. The indications are that India may have to face more problems in future. NTBs are often employed when a country's exports to a country increases considerably, causing problems to the importing country, or when the exporting country does not tow the economic or political lines of the powerful importing country. According to an estimate of the Government of India (2002), about 44% of the total exports of India to the US faced some or the other form of NTBs.

In short, a large part of Indian exports to industrial countries encounter NTBs. Developing country exports are hit hard by industrial country's NTBs.

Disadvantages of NTBs

(i) The non-tariff barriers are less transparent, difficult to identify, and their impact on exporting countries is almost impossible to quantify.

(ii) They are against the widely accepted principles of non-discrimination and transparency in measures to restrict trade.

(iii) The costs to the country imposing the NTB, and to the world as a whole, are higher than under an equivalent tariff.

(iv) NTB is unfair, because they do not treat exporters equally. Often it is the exporters with the least bargaining power whose exports are most reduced.

(v) Though the NTBs are adopted to protect certain interests of the importing countries, but the fact remains that both the exporting and importing countries are adversely affected by the protection.

(vi) NTBs cause higher prices for consumers, loss in tariff revenue for governments, inefficient resource allocation, and diminished competition.

(vii) NTBs seriously affect many exporting countries. A developing country that exports to developed countries faces considerable NTBs. In some cases it has seen that the impact is very severe. For example, the VER (Voluntary Export Restraint) covering the tapioca exports of Thailand to the EC, established in 1982, caused its tapioca exports to fall by 40% and its export earnings fell by about $ 300 million, which was 10% of Thailand's total export earnings from the EC.

(viii) An Asian Development Bank study has observed that through the exercise of various forms of administrative protection, non-tariff barriers have increased in importance in absolute terms and have been applied with increasing discrimination, causing bilateral trade arrangements in many cases to reign over more globally efficient multilateral trade arrangements and thus threatening the gains to the less developed countries of negotiated tariff reductions.

(ix) Apparel exports of the developing countries were the most affected because of such NTBs, via the Multi-Fibre Arrangement (MFA). Several country studies give examples of lost apparel exports, declining production and employment due to reporting, certification and other problems involved in administering bilateral MFA agreements.

NTBs also cause diversion of production and exports. For example, some Indian textile and apparel firms decided to set up manufacturing facilities in Nepal to circumvent MFA quota controls of their exports from India, and to avoid local costs of purchasing added quota rights. Likewise, exporters have attempted to diversify their exports to non-quota countries.

1.6 Countertrade

Countertrade is a term that covers a huge range of commercial mechanisms for reciprocal trade. Though it exists in many forms, it mainly always involves the payment which is being made in goods or services instead of money. Countertrade occurs when MNCs sell to customers abroad and they in turn pay the MNCs in terms of goods. In some countries, countertrade is a condition of the buying organisation importing goods from elsewhere.

Countertrade is an important means of trade used by developing countries. It is a system of international trading which helps the government reduce inequity in trade between them and other countries. It basically is the direct or indirect exchange of goods for other goods instead of money. Countertrade is often used when a foreign currency is in short supply, or when a country applies foreign exchange controls, which are limits imposed on the availability of foreign currencies to importers for the purchase of foreign products. Countertrade is used as a development technique which is used by developing countries to control trade.

1.6.1 Types of Countertrade

Countertrade can take several different forms which can be used separately or in conjunction. The important forms are:

1. Direct Offset

A direct offset occurs once a seller of a product to be imported into a foreign country agrees to purchase parts or materials used to produce the product. Due to the profit earned by the local foreign company selling components to the seller, the direct offset reduces the price of the imported good, keeping in mind that the main goal is to improve the trade imbalances between the two countries. Consequently, the purchaser of the foreign good doesn't necessarily benefit from the direct offset, but the economy of the foreign country does.

2. Indirect Offset

The idea behind an indirect offset is the same as a direct offset, but the offset doesn't involve the same trade transaction. When a international government requires an importer to make long term investment in the country's economy, it is known as an indirect offset. A typical example could be construction of a factory which will create jobs and help build the country's economy.

3. Switch Trading

This type of countertrade occurs when a third country has a trading relationship with two other countries that have a significant imbalance in trade. The third country will purchase what the second country needs from the first country, and then trade it to the first country in exchange for a product that the third country needs.

Take an example of three countries: A, B, C. The country C has a huge trade difference with A, which means it imports more from A than it exports to. C has a trade surplus with B. C needs to import tin from A, but it doesn't have enough hard currency or credit acceptable to A. A easily sells to B. Hence B agrees to buy the tin that C needs from A and then swaps it with C for goods that B needs from C.

4. Counterpurchase

A counter purchase occurs when a foreign exporter agrees to purchase goods or services from the importing country as a requirement of the sale. The goods that the exporter agrees to purchase are not used as components in the product being exported to the foreign country. For example, a large multinational conglomerate may have an aerospace division and a grocery store chain. The company may agree to buy its tropical fruits from the foreign country in exchange for the foreign country permitting the sale of the company's airplanes.

5. Barter

The easiest form of countertrade to understand is the Barter. *It's simply trading one good for another.* For example, a country rich in oil but poor in steel may trade oil for steel with a country that has plenty of steel but not much oil.

1.6.2 Advantages of Countertrade

1. It gives access to markets for companies that may otherwise be closed to them.
2. Increases sales
3. Overcomes currency controls and exchange problems
4. It helps conserve foreign currency reserves of the importing country
5. Overcomes credit difficulties
6. Gains foreign contracts for future sales
7. Allows disposal of declining products
8. Clean up bad debt situations
9. Gain competitive edge over competition
10. Find lower cost purchasing sources
11. Expand or maintain foreign markets

1.6.3 Disadvantages of Countertrade

1. No "in house" use of goods offered by customers
2. Time consuming and complex negotiations
3. Ambiguity
4. Costs are at a high
5. Difficult to resell goods by offsets
6. The brokerage cost is also included which is an added expenditure
7. Getting businesses in which firm may have no knowledge
8. Since commodities are involved, it is risky

Points to Remember

- **International business** may be understood as those business transactions that involve the crossing of national boundaries.
- **Domestic environment** consists of factors such as competitive structure, economic climate, and political and legal forces which are essentially uncontrollable by a firm.
- **Foreign environment** consists of factors like geographic and economic conditions, socio-cultural traits, political and legal forces, and technological and ecological facets prevalent in a foreign country.
- **The Forces that influence the international business are:**
  1. Political Environment/forces
  2. Legal forces
  3. Cultural forces
  4. Technological forces
  5. Economic forces.
- **A trade restriction** is an artificial restriction on the trade of goods and/or services between two countries. It is the by-product of protectionism.
- **Protectionism** represents any attempt to impose restrictions on trade in goods and services. The aim is to cushion domestic businesses and industries from overseas competition and prevent the outcome resulting from the inter-play of free market forces of supply and demand.
- **Protectionism can come in many forms including the following:**
  1. Tariffs
  2. Quotas
  3. Voluntary Export Restraint Arrangements
  4. Intellectual property laws
  5. Technical barriers to trade
  6. Preferential State Procurement Policies
  7. Export Subsidies
  8. Domestic Subsidies
  9. Import Licensing
  10. Exchange controls
  11. Financial Protectionism
  12. Murky or Hidden Protectionism
- **Trade barriers** refer to the government policies and measures which obstruct the free flow of goods and services across national borders.
- **Countertrade** is a system of international trading that helps governments reduces imbalances in trade between them and other countries. It involves the direct or indirect exchange of goods for other goods instead of currency.

Questions for Discussion

1. Explain the nature of International Business. Illustrate with a diagram.
2. Discuss the different characteristics of International Business.
3. Explain the importance of the study of International Business.
4. Elaborate the framework for analysing the international business environment.
5. Explain the impact on domestic, foreign and global environments on international business decisions.
6. Discuss the trends and developments in the global trading environment.
7. What do you understand by the term protectionism?
8. Elaborate various tariff and non-tariff barriers.
9. What are the various types of counter trade?

Multiple Choice Questions

1. Which of the following is a driver of globalisation?
   (a) Weak competition
   (b) Technological advance
   (c) Economies of scale are being exploited to the maximum
   (d) Trade barriers and controls on inflows of foreign direct investment
2. Why should managers have an understanding of trade protectionism?
   (a) Trade protectionism target factor endowments, thus affecting the best country to locate the Production Facility.
   (b) Trade protectionism affects a company's ability to sell abroad and ability to compete at home.
   (c) Trade protectionism affects the number of people permitted to practice a specific profession.
   (d) Trade protectionism prevents companies' enactment of merger and acquisition agreements.
3. Which of the following is NOT an example of a "non-tariff barrier" to the free flow of goods and services in accordance with comparative advantage?
   (a) Import quotas
   (b) Government procurement provisions that favour home products
   (c) Specific duty of ₹ 1.00 per unit on each imported item
   (d) Voluntary export quotas
4. An import quota specifies the ____ amount of a good that can be imported into a country; a step to becoming more protectionist would involve ____ in the quota.
   (a) Maximum; an enlargement   (b) Maximum; a reduction
   (c) Minimum; an enlargement   (d) Minimum; a reduction

5. A country gains from international trade if its post trade _____ point lies outside its production possibility frontier.
   (a) autarky
   (b) production
   (c) consumption
   (d) all of the above

6. Which of the following are used as non-tariff barriers?
   (a) Government procurement policies
   (b) Health and safety standards
   (c) Domestic content laws
   (d) All of the above

7. Protectionism can come in many forms including the following:
   (a) Tariffs
   (b) Quotas
   (c) Voluntary Export Restraint Arrangements
   (d) All the above

8. The Forces that influence the international business are:
   (a) Political Environment/forces
   (b) Legal forces
   (c) Cultural forces
   (d) All of the above

9. A trade restriction is an artificial restriction on the trade of goods and/or services between no countries.
   (a) True
   (b) False

10. Domestic environment consists of factors such as competitive structure, economic climate, and political and legal forces which are essentially uncontrollable by a firm.
    (a) True
    (b) False

ANSWERS

| 1. (b) | 2. (b) | 3. (c) | 4. (b) | 5. (c) |
| 6. (d) | 7. (d) | 8. (d) | 9. (b) | 10. (a) |

Project Questions

1. Do you think Indian firms should go global? Why don't they remain content with domestic market, which is vast?
2. What do you believe makes foreign business activities more complex than purely domestic ones?

Chapter 2...

International Financial Environment

Contents ...

- 2.1 Foreign Investment
    - 2.1.1 Meaning
    - 2.1.2 Types of Foreign Investment
    - 2.1.3 Motivations/Objectives of FDI
    - 2.1.4 Significance of FDI
    - 2.1.5 Advantages and Disadvantages of FDI
    - 2.1.6 Impact of FDI
    - 2.1.7 Patterns of Foreign Investment
    - 2.1.8 Structure of Foreign Investment
    - 2.1.9 Effects of Foreign Investment
    - 2.1.10 Factors Affecting Foreign Investment
- 2.2 Exchange Rates
    - 2.2.1 Types of Exchange Rate
    - 2.2.2 Exchange Rate Regimes
    - 2.2.3 Factors which Influence Exchange Rate
    - 2.2.4 Foreign Exchange Fluctuations
    - 2.2.5 Foreign Exchange Effects are Far-Reaching
    - 2.2.6 Impact of Movements in Foreign Exchange on Trade and Investment Flows
- 2.3 Interest Rate
    - 2.3.1 Factors which Influence Interest Rate
    - 2.3.2 Impact of Movements in Interest Rates on Trade and Investment Flows
- Points to Remember
- Questions for Discussion
- Multiple Choice Questions
- Project Questions

Learning Objectives...

- To understand the pattern and structure of foreign investment
- To study the positive as well as negative effects of foreign investment
- To learn the impact of foreign exchange movements on trade and investment
- To be able to explain the impact of interest rate movements on trade and investment

2.1 Foreign Investment

2.1.1 Meaning

Foreign investment is the flow of capital from one nation to another in exchange for significant ownership stakes in domestic companies or other domestic assets. As part of their investments, foreigners take an active role in the management. Between countries of equal economic stature, foreign investment works both ways.

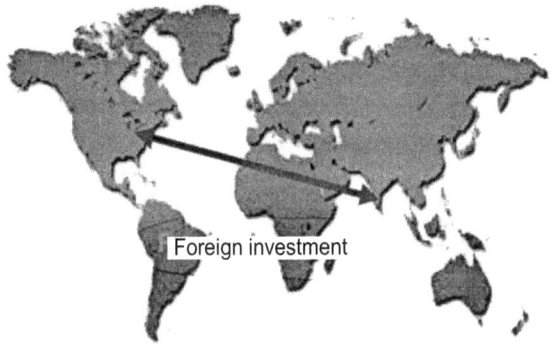

Due to globalisation, many MNCs have investments in quite a few countries. They see foreign investment as a positive sign and as a source for future economic growth.

2.1.2 Types of Foreign Investment

There are four types of foreign investment:

1. Foreign Direct Investment (FDI),
2. Foreign Portfolio Investment (FPI),
3. Official flows,
4. Commercial loans.

The way in which the loan is given and how engaged the investor is with the receiver of the loan, is the main difference between these types of foreign investment.

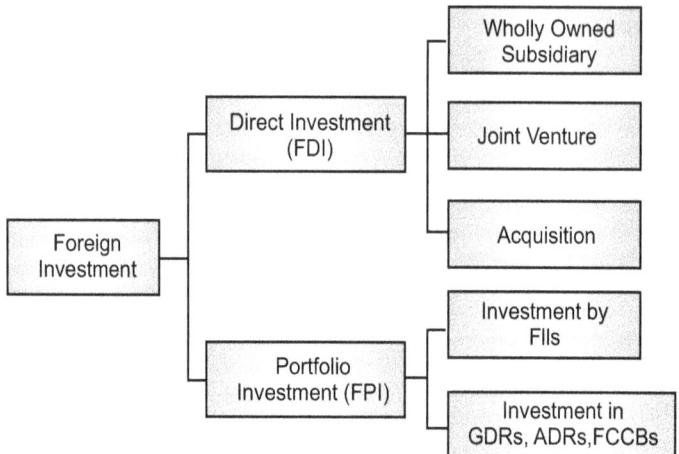

Fig 2.1 Types of Foreign Investment

1. **Foreign direct investment** (FDI) is a component of a country's national financial accounts. FDIs occur when a company invests in a business that is located in another country. It is the investment of foreign assets into domestic structures, equipment and organisation, but it does not include the foreign investment made in the stock markets. In order for a private foreign investment to be considered an FDI, the company that is investing, must have not less than 10% of the shares belonging to the foreign company. The firm that is investing is known as the **parent company**, and the foreign country is known as the **subsidiary of the parent company.**

   The types of FDI are:
   - Wholly Owned Subsidiary
   - Joint Venture
   - Acquisitions

2. **Foreign Portfolio Investment:** When foreign investments are made by a company, FPIs can also occur. Any individual, who has mutual funds, can also make FPI. FDI allows the investing company to own shares of the subsidiary company, while FPI may be just temporary. The investment instruments usually traded in FPI are stocks and bonds. A company that has stocks and bonds from a foreign company does not necessarily have a share in that company in which it is investing.

3. **Official Flow:** Instead of the foreign investment occurring between companies, official flow occurs between **nations**. A country that is more developed or prosperous will invest money in a less developed country. The less developed nation will receive financial support as well as technology and aid in economic and government management.

4. **Commercial loan:** occurs in the form of a bank loan and is another type of foreign investment. This investment occurs between businesses or nations that are in different countries. It usually occurs between larger organisations though it can also be made by an individual.

Until the 1980s, Commercial loans were the most common kind of foreign investment. This was especially true in cases where investments were going to the governments and companies of developing countries. After the 1980s, FDIs and FPIs are more common. The term globalisation is normally used to describe the phenomenon of an increased use of FPIs and FDIs. FPIs and FDIs are private investments, while commercial loans are issued by banks and which are backed by the government.

2.1.3 Motivations/Objectives for FDI

- Sales Expansion
- Resource acquisition
- Diversification
- Minimise the competitive risk

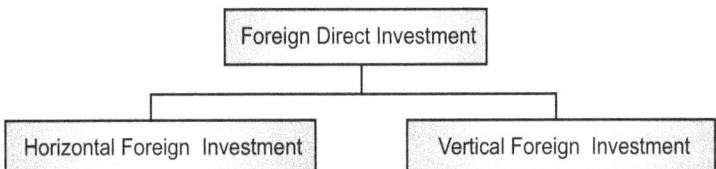

1. **Horizontal Foreign Investment (HFI):** It refers to the investment of the firm in a foreign country to produce the same products which it produces in its home country. HFI implies that FDI is undertaken in the same industry by the firm as it operates in the home country.

   For Example: Electrolux is a Swedish firm which is manufacturing household appliances like washing machine, refrigerators, etc invested in Asia and Europe for producing similar household appliances.

2. **Vertical Foreign Investment (VFI):** It is integration process in the production. Vertical FDI occurs **when** a multinational decides to acquire or build an operation that either fulfills the role of a supplier (backward vertical FDI) or the role of a distributor (forward vertical FDI).

   For Example: an American retailer that builds a store in China is trying to earn more money by exploring the Chinese market.

   - **Backward Vertical Integration** (BVI) implies that the firm directly invests in a foreign country to produce intermediate goods that are meant to be used as inputs in its domestic production process.

- **Forward Vertical Investment (FVI)** implies that the firm invests in foreign country in producing the final stage goods or assembly of product to market it directly to foreign buyers.

2.1.4 Significance of FDI

1. Through foreign direct investment (FDI) corporations extend their business activity into foreign countries.
2. The main object of FDI is to acquire or retain control over markets and/or productive resources.
3. Major areas of FDI are: oil, coal and ores, as well as service sector including banking/finance, legal services, marketing and distribution.

Thus, capital movement in the form of foreign investment is advantageous to the economies of both the lending and borrowing nations.

2.1.5 Advantages and Disadvantages of FDI

Advantages	Disadvantages
Inflow of equipment and technology: Foreign expertise is important factor in improving the existing technical process in country.	Crowding of local industry.
Competitive advantage and Innovation: Advances in technology and process improves competitiveness of countries in the domestic economy.	Conflict of laws.
Financial resources for expansion: FDI provide financial investment which is the back-bone of the expansion.	Loss of control.
Employment generation: FDI can create jobs. In an effort to increase productivity, skilled and semiskilled workers are needed.	Effect on natural environment.
Contributing to export growth.	Effect on local culture.
Improve consumer welfare through reduced cost, wider choice and **improved quality**.	

2.1.6 Impact of FDI

FDI constitutes both positive and negative impacts. FDI has certain **positive impact on the host country's economy through capital and technology transfer. These include;**

➢ Management know-how and expertise
➢ New products

- Production Technology
- Machinery
- Skilled labour force
- Propelling industrial advancement
- Diversification
- Improve substitutions
- Employment Creation
- Stimulation to domestic economy (through new ideas, products, technology, skills and Capital)
- Intensification of competition

Negative impact of FDI includes:
- Over dependence of the host country on foreign technology
- Threats to domestic industries
- Distortions in wages/salaries structure
- Deterimental effects on culture, values and lifestyles
- Political purpose and distortions

2.1.7 Patterns of Foreign Investment

Foreign Direct investments are made in the form of:
- fixtures,
- machinery,
- equipment
- buildings.

Mostly via mergers and acquisitions, this type of investment is achieved. This has been the primary mechanism for investment for traditional manufacturing and it has been proven to be very efficient. Increasing changes in foreign investment can be noticed due to the fact that in the last decade or so, there has been a rise in the number of technology startups along with a rise in internet usage. Many of these high tech start-ups are very small companies that have grown out of research and development projects often affiliated with major universities and with some government sponsorship.

These companies, unlike the traditional manufacturers, do not require huge warehouses and manufacturing plants in order to store their inventory. Software based companies can be housed almost anywhere and hence making a huge investment in them does not require big layouts for machinery, fixtures etc.

Large companies still play a major role in investment activities in small, high tech companies. However these large companies are not acquiring the smaller companies entirely. The most important reason is the risk which is associated with such high tech ventures. The major risk here is that you do not sell enough of the product that you manufactured. However, you have added additional capacity and in the case of multinational corporations this capacity can be used in a variety of ways.

In high tech ventures the product tends to require significant development time. While when one looks at the software type products, the product is constantly changing even before it hits the marketplace. Hence the decision on making the investments gets more complicated. When you invest in fixtures and machinery, you know what the real and book value of your investment will be. When you invest in a high tech venture, there is always an element of uncertainty. Unfortunately, the recent spate of dot.com failures is quite illustrative of this point.

The lingering role of technology and intellectual property has changed the foreign direct investment playing field. Companies still make foreign investments but are now finding new ways to accomplish their goals due to the unexpected situations of technology investments. Consider the following:

1. **Licensing and Technology Transfer:** In promoting collaboration between the academic and business communities, tech transfers and licensing have been essential. With some help from a variety of government agencies in the form of grants for RandD as well as other financial assistance for such things as incubator programs, once timid college researchers are now stepping out and becoming cutting edge entrepreneurs.

    These strategic alliances have had a serious impact in several high tech industries, including but not limited to:
    - medical and agricultural biotechnology,
    - computer software engineering,
    - telecommunications,
    - advanced materials processing,
    - ceramics,
    - thin materials processing,
    - photonics,
    - digital multimedia production
    - publishing,
    - optics and imaging
    - robotics and automation.

Licensing agreements allow companies to take full advantage of new and exciting technologies while limiting their overall risk to royalty payments until a particular technology is fully developed and thus ready to put new products into the manufacturing pipeline. Industry clusters are now growing up around the university labs where their derivative technologies were first discovered and nurtured.

2. **Portfolio Investment:** For most of the latter part of the 20th century when FDI became an issue, a company's portfolio investments were not considered a direct investment if the amount of stock and/or capital was not enough to garner a significant voting interest amongst shareholders or owners. However, two or three companies with "soft" investments in another company could find some mutual interests and use their shareholder power effectively for management control. This is another form of strategic alliance, sometimes called "shadow alliances". So, while most company portfolio investments do not strictly qualify as a direct foreign investment, there are instances within a certain context that they are in fact a real direct investment.

3. **Joint Venture and other Hybrid Strategic Alliances:** Joint venture is bi-lateral, i.e., it involves two parties who are within the same industry who are partnering for some strategic advantage. One very good reason why many joint ventures only involve two parties is the difficulty in integrating different corporate cultures. With two domestic companies from the same country, it would still be very difficult. However, with two companies from different cultures, it is almost impossible at times. This is probably why pure joint ventures have a fairly high failure rate only five years after inception. Joint ventures involving three or more parties are usually called syndicates and are most often formed for specific projects such as large construction or public work projects that might involve a wide variety of expertise and resources for successful completion. In some cases, syndicates are actually easier to manage because the project itself sets certain limits on each party and close cooperation is not always a prerequisite for ultimate success of the endeavour.

4. **Reciprocal Distribution Agreements:** Actually, this type of strategic alliance is more trade-based, but in a very real sense it does in fact represent a type of direct investment. Basically, two companies, usually within the same or affiliated industries, agree to act as a national distributor for each other's products. The classical example is to be found in the furniture industry. A U.S.-based manufacturer of tables signs a reciprocal distribution agreement with a Spanish-based manufacturer of chairs. Both companies gain direct access to the other's distribution network without having to pay distributor support payments and other related expenses found within the distribution channel and neither company can hurt the other's market for its

products. Without such an agreement in place, the Spanish manufacturer might very well have to invest in a national sales office to coordinate its distributor network, manage warehousing, inventory and shipping as well as to handle administrative tasks such as accounting, public relations and advertising.

2.1.8 Structure of Foreign Investment

1. **Cautious Optimism Returns to Global Foreign Direct Investment (FDI):** After the 2012 slump, global FDI returned to growth, with inflows rising 9 per cent in 2013, to $1.45 trillion. UNCTAD projects that FDI flows could rise to $1.7 trillion in 2015 and $1.8 trillion in 2016, with relatively larger increase in developed countries. Vulnerability in some markets including regional instability and risks related to policy uncertainty, could negatively affect the expected upturn in FDI.

2. **Developing Economies Maintain their Lead in 2013:** The Foreign Investment flow increased by 9% - $566 billion to developed countries (which account for 39% of the global flows). Developing economies increased 54% - $778 billion! Transition economies took the remaining $108 billion. Developing and transition economies now constitute half of the top 20 ranked by FDI inflows.

3. **FDI Outflows from Developing Countries also Reached a Record Level:** Transition economies along with Developing economies invested $553 billion, or 39 percent of global FDI outflows, compared with only 12 percent at the beginning of the 2000. Developing economies' Transnational corporations (TNCs) are acquiring foreign associates from developed countries that are located in their areas.

4. **Mega-regional Groupings Shape Global FDI:** There are three regional groups namely TPP,TTIP, RCEP, that are under negotiation and each one of them account for a quarter or more of the global FDI flows. TTIP is declining while the others are in ascendance. Asia-Pacific Economic Cooperation (APEC) remains the largest regional economic cooperation grouping, with 54 % of global inflows.

5. **The Poorest Countries are Less and Less Dependent on Extractive Industry Investment:** The share of the extractive industry in the value of Greenfield projects was 26 percent in Africa and 36 percent in LDCs, in the past decade. However these shares are on the decline. 90% of the value of announced projects in Africa and in LDCs is made up of manufacturing and services. Private equity FDI is keeping its powder dry. Outstanding funds of private equity firms increased to a record level of more than $1 trillion. At a decline of 11%, the cross border investment was $171 billion and they accounted for 21% of the value of cross-border mergers and acquisitions. Relatively subdued activity in recent years and funds available for investment, the potential for increased private equity FDI is significant .

6. **State-owned TNCs are FDI Heavyweights:** At least 550 State-owned TNCs are present as estimated by UNCTAD, from both developing as well as developed countries. There are more than 15,000 foreign affiliates and foreign assets of over $ 2 trillion.

2.1.9 Effects of Foreign Investment

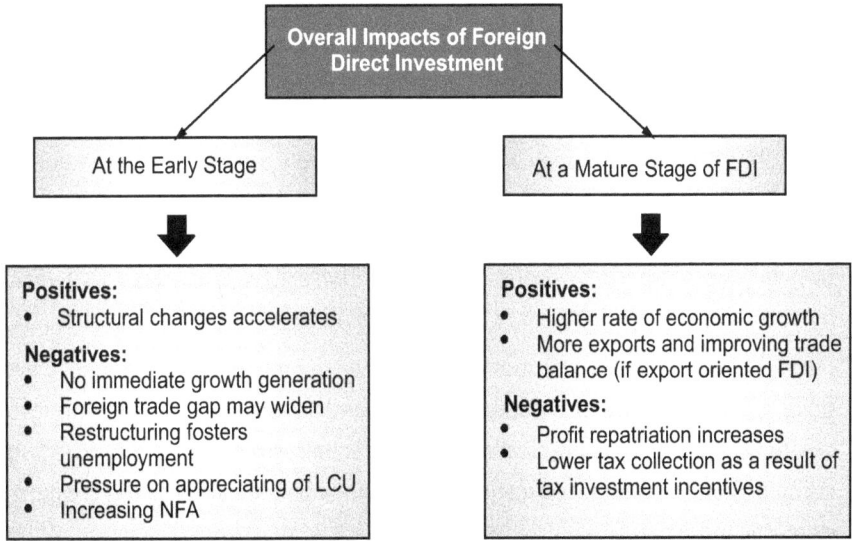

Based on :

HUNYA, G. (2001) : Impact of FDI on Economic Growth and Restructuring in CEECs. WIIW Working Paper, WIIW Spring Seminar 2001. The Vienna Institute for International Economic Studies (WIIW), Vienna, 2001.

POESCHL, J. (2001) : "The Central and Eastern European Countries on the Road to the EU". Lecture at the University of Economics in Prague, April, 2001.

Fig. 2.2: Effects of Foreign Investment

(A) Positive Effects of Foreign Investment for MNEs

1. **Access to Markets:** An effective way to enter the market is through the FDI. There are some countries that can limit foreign access into their domestic markets. Starting a business in the foreign markets is a good way to gain access.

2. **Access to Resources:** Natural resources, such as precious metals, can be acquired by the FDI. To develop oil fields, for example, tremendous FDIs are made by the Oil companies.

3. **Reduces Cost of Production:** If the labour market is cheaper and the regulations are less restrictive in the target foreign market, a good means to reduce the cost of

production is the FDI. For example, by moving the operations to developing countries, the shoe and clothing industries have greatly reduced their costs of production.

(B) Positive Effects of Foreign Investment to Foreign Countries

1. **Source of External Capital and Increased Revenue:** FDI can be a tremendous source of external capital for a developing country, which can lead to economic development. Take for example, a company that starts a factory in a developing country – local labour, equipment and materials will be needed to start the factory which is an advantage to the developing country. With the startup of the factory, new jobs and foreign money will help improve the economy. It doesn't end there, as once the factory has been constructed, local employees need to be hired and some local material and service may also be used and hence further jobs are created and this may open up some more businesses. These new jobs mean that locals have more money to spend, thereby creating even more jobs.

   From the products and activities in the factory, tax revenue is generated. Developing governments can use this capital infusion and revenue from economic growth to create and improve its physical and economic infrastructure such as building roads, communication systems, educational institutions and subsidising the creation of new domestic industries.

2. **Development of New Industries:** Not always, does a MNE own all the foreign entities. Sometimes, it is the local company that develops an alliance with the foreign investor and thereby helps to develop a new industry. The developing country gets to establish a new industry and market, and the MNE gets access to a new market through its partnership with the local firm.

3. **Learning:** By exposing local businesses and citizens, national and local governments to new business practice, economic concepts, technology, management techniques, the FDI helps them in this indirect manner, as this will help them develop local business and industries.

(C) Negative Effects of Foreign Investment to MNEs

1. **Unstable Economic Conditions:** The market conditions in the developing world can be quite unstable and unpredictable. Much of FDI takes place in the developing world, which is just developing its economic systems.

2. **Unstable Political and Legal System:** Political and legal systems may be unstable or underdeveloped. Corruption and unstable political system often pose a threat. The legal system may be underdeveloped.

(D) Negative Effects of Foreign Investment to the Foreign Countries

1. **Race to the Bottom:** Developing nations are forced into a race to the bottom regarding labour and regulations in order to attract foreign investors who seek cheap labour and non-existent or relaxed regulation to maximise its profit potential. The stripping of natural resources, abusive labour practices and severe environmental damage to the foreign country, are not acceptable in the developed world.

2. **Crowd out Local Development:** Foreign investment may also crush the local competition, resulting in problems in long-term economic development.

3. **Undue Political Influence:** MNEs exercise a lot of power in a developing country due to the capital it brings in to the country. Deals that may not be in the best interests of the citizens can bring down a country if a corrupt government is willing to accept these deals.

2.1.10 Factors Affecting Foreign Investment

1. **Stable, Predictable Macroeconomic Policy:** Companies must have the confidence that the economy in which they make an investment will be managed in a competent and predictable way. Simply stated, investors must believe that the rules of the game will not change in the middle of a contest.

2. **An Effective and Honest Government:** An investor must be able to rely upon the integrity of the host government and its ability to maintain law and order.

3. **A Large and Growing Market:** The size and potential for growth of country's domestic market, especially the purchasing power of its customers, are key. Companies do not seek to invest in a market where there is little potential to make profit.

4. **Freedom of Activity in Market**: The strength of the competition, as well as the degree of government (theirs and ours) interference to entering a country's market, the more attractive it becomes as an investment site for international investors.

5. **Minimal Government Regulation**: The cost of government regulation and intervention in the affairs and profits of private companies must be kept to minimum.

6. **Property Rights and Protection:** Private property must be protected. The likelihood that a company's real or intangible (patents, copy rights, etc.) property will be stolen must be avoided.

7. **Reliable Infrastructure:** The ability to consummate transactions and get products and services to market is also critical. Whether it is reliable transportation, power generation, insurance and accounting services, a competent financial system or other basic factors, investments cannot yield a sufficient or reliable financial return without them.

8. **Availability of High-quality Factors of Production:** While the investors brings capital, technology and management to the table, the quality of the indigenous work force and the availability of local raw materials are also key ingredients in the recipe for success.

9. **A Strong Local Currency:** The local currency must retain its value. If you make an investment in dollars and then the local assets (valued in the local currency) are devalued, you have lost part or possibly all of your original dollar-based investment.

10. **The Ability to Remit Profits, Dividends and Invests:** If you cannot get your money out of the country, why invest.

11. **A Favorable Tax Climate:** Although tax incentives geared to attract initial investments are important, a company's final investment decision is usually based on how a country's taxation will affect the normal operating environment once the venture is off the ground.

12. **Freedom to Operate Between Markets:** A company must be able to source goods and services from its operating unit in one market in order to serve other markets or to maximise its global efficiency by trading among its operating entities in different countries to 'round out' its product line.

Courtesy: John D. Sullivan, 'Prospering in the global economy', Economic reforms today, no. 1, 2000

2.2 Exchange Rates

The national currency's quotation in respect to foreign ones is known as exchange rate. For example,

If, $1 = ₹ 60 then

The exchange rate of a dollar is 60 Rupees

So if a product cost ₹ 120, in dollars it would cost $2.

Exchange rate is a conversion factor, a ratio or multiplier depending on the direction of conversion.

If the exchange rate can freely move, the exchange rate may turn out to be the fastest moving price in the economy, bringing together all the foreign goods with it.

2.2.1 Types of Exchange Rate

Some types of exchange rates are:

1. **Nominal Exchange Rate and Real Exchange Rate:** Nominal exchange rates *are established on currency financial markets called "forex markets", which are similar to stock exchange markets*. The newspaper usually report the daily quotation and the rates are usually established in continuous quotations. Central bank may also fix the nominal exchange rate.

Real exchange rates *are nominal rate corrected somehow by inflation measures.*

For example:

Country X has an inflation rate of 20%

Country Y has an inflation rate of 10%

No changes in the nominal exchange rate took place

Then, Country A has a currency whose real value is: 20% - 10% = 10% higher than before

Higher prices mean an appreciation of the real exchange rate, other things equal.

2. **Bilateral Exchange Rate:** Number of currencies taken into account. Bilateral exchange rates clearly relate to two countries' currencies. They are usually the results of matching of demand and supply on financial markets or in banking transaction.

   Bilateral exchange rates may also be calculated from triangular relationships:

   Example:

   Exchange rate dollar / rupee is 60 and

   Dollar / Tanzanian shilling is 60000 then,

   ₹1 = 1000 Tanzanian shillings

   No direct rupee/shilling transaction needs to take place.

3. **Multilateral Exchange Rate:** Multilateral exchange rates are computed in order to judge the general dynamics of a country's currency toward the rest of the world. Different currencies are chosen, and a set of relative weights are chosen, after which the "effective" exchange rate of the country's currency is computed.

   For example,

   A basket of 40% US dollars and 60% Indian Rupees

   10% suffered from a value loss in respect to the dollar and 40% to mark will be said having faced an "effective" loss of

   $10\% \times 0.6 + 40\% \times 0.4 = 22\%$.

   Some countries impose the existence of more than one exchange rate, depending on the type and the subjects of the transaction. Multiple exchange rates then exist, usually referring to commercial vs. public transactions or consumption and investment imports. This situation requires always some degree of capital controls.

   In many countries, beside the official exchange rate, the black market offers foreign currency at another, usually much higher, rate.

2.2.2 Exchange Rate Regimes

An **exchange-rate regime** is the way an authority manages its currency in relation to other currencies and the foreign exchange market. It is closely related to monetary policy and the two are generally dependent on many of the same factors.

"**Freely floating exchange rate**" will be the name of currency institutional regime when the exchange rate can freely move. It is also known as "flexible" exchange rate as well.

Floating rates are the most common exchange rate regime today. For example, the dollar, euro, yen, and British pound all are floating currencies. However, since central banks frequently intervene to avoid excessive appreciation or depreciation, these regimes are often called managed float or a dirty float.

A "*managed floating exchange rate regime*" takes place, when the central bank timely and significantly intervenes on the currency market. The central bank may have an explicit target.

A loss in currency value in "freely" and "managed" floating regimes is called as "*depreciation*", whereas an increase of currency's international value will be called "appreciation". If the dollar rise from 10,000 yen to 12,000 yen, then it has shown an appreciation of 20%. At the same time, the yen has undergone a 8.3% depreciation.

Fixed Exchange rates are those that have direct convertibility towards another currency. In case of a separate currency, also known as a currency board arrangement, the domestic currency is backed one to one by foreign reserves.

By offering to supply or buy any quantity of domestic or foreign currencies at that rate, the central banks can also declare a fixed exchange rate. This is known as "*fixed exchange rate*".

When a loss of value occurs, usually due to market or purposeful policy action, it is known as "*devaluation*"; similarly an increase of international value is a "*revaluation*".

When a split of fixed exchange rates with an adverse devaluation or even the end of that regime in favour of a floating exchange rate occurs, it is known as a "currency crisis". It can dominate the attention of the public, policymakers and entrepreneurs, both in advance and after. An extreme national engagement to fixed exchange rates is the transformation of the central bank in a mere "currency board" with no autonomous influence on monetary stock. The bank will automatically print or lend money depending on corresponding foreign currency reserves. Thus, exports, imports and capital inflows (e.g. FDI) will largely determine the monetary policy.

Monetary unions phase out the national currencies in favour of one currency. There are some countries that may join the union and set up the economic and financial policies, especially if there are clear conditions for entering into the monetary area. If a country exists a monetary union, it will rouse a large depreciation of the national currency. Depending on trade elasticity, on foreign debt of the country, on how the exit is managed and on the overall institutional conditions, this can lead to massive internal poverty or a large export led growth.

2.2.3 Factors which Influence Exchange Rate

Supply and demand determine the exchange rates. If there is a demand for Indian goods then the rupee would appreciate. The factors that affect the exchange rate are:

1. **Inflation:** Let's say the inflation in USA is less as compared to other countries, then exports from USA will be more competitive and there will be a demand for the dollar. Foreign goods will be less competitive and hence US citizens will buy the local goods and less of the imported stuff.

   Countries that have a lower inflation rate will see an increase in the value of their currency.

2. **Interest Rates:** If the interest rates in Japan rise as compared to the other developing countries then it will be more attractive to deposit money in the Japanese banks. A better rate of return will be obtained from saving in the Japanese banks and thereby increasing the demand for Yen. This is known as "hot money flows" and is important in the short run factor of determining the value of a currency. Higher interest rates cause an appreciation.

3. **Speculation:** If investors believe that the Yen will increase in the future, they will demand more now to be able to make a profit. Therefore movements in the exchange rate do not always reflect economic fundamentals, but are often driven by the sentiments of the financial markets.

4. **Change in Competitiveness:** The value of the exchange rate can also increase if the Japanese goods are more competitive and attractive and this is important for determining the long run value of the Yen.

5. **Relative Strength of other Currencies:** In 2010 and 2011, the value of the Japanese Yen and Swiss Franc rose because markets were worried about all the other major economies – US and EU. Therefore, despite of low interest rates and low growth in Japan, the Yen kept appreciating.

6. **Balance of Payments:** When the values of imports (of goods and services) are greater than the value of exports, a deficit on the current account occurs. If there is a surplus of financial and capital gains then all is smooth flowing, but if a country struggles to attract enough capital inflows to finance a current account deficit, it will cause the currency to depreciate.

7. **Government Debt:** If the government is in debt, the value of the debt can influence the exchange rate. If markets fear a government may default on its debt, then investors will sell their bonds causing a fall in the value of the exchange rate. Take for example, if markets feared the US would default on its debt, foreign investors would sell their holdings of US bonds. This would cause a fall in the value of the dollar.

8. **Government Intervention**: In some countries, their government often attempts to influence the value of their currency. For example, China has sought to keep its currency undervalued to make Chinese exports more competitive. They can do this by buying US dollar assets which increases the value of the US dollar to the Chinese Yuan.

9. **Economic Growth / Recession:** During a recession, interest rates usually fall, and hence a recession may cause depreciation in the exchange rate.

2.2.4 Foreign Exchange Fluctuations

Foreign Exchange or Currency fluctuations are a natural outcome of the floating exchange rate system that is the norm for most major economies. When exchange rate of one country is compared with another, it is influenced by numerous fundamental and technical factors. The factors are

- relative supply and demand of the two currencies,
- economic performance,
- outlook for inflation,
- interest rate differentials,
- capital flows,
- technical support
- resistance levels etc.

Since these factors keep on fluctuating, the currency values also fluctuate according to the fluctuation of the factors. Although a currency's level is largely supposed to be determined by the underlying economy, the tables are often turned, as huge movements in a currency can dictate the economy's fortunes.

2.2.5 Foreign Exchange Effects are Far-Reaching

Most people do not pay particularly close attention to exchange rates because most of their business and transactions are conducted in their domestic currency. Exchange rates for a normal person, comes only during foreign travel, import payments or overseas remittances.

A misleading notion that many people make is that having a stable domestic currency is beneficial as it becomes cheaper to travel abroad, however an overly strong currency can exert a significant drag on the underlying economy over the long term, as entire industries are rendered uncompetitive and thousands of jobs are lost. Some consumers disregard a weak domestic currency as the cross border shopping and travelling abroad becomes expensive and hence a weak currency can actually benefit in more economic benefits.

Directly or indirectly, therefore, currency levels affect a number of key economic variables. They may play a role in the interest rate you pay on your mortgage, the returns on your investment portfolio, and the price of groceries in your local supermarket, and even your job prospects.

2.2.6 Impact of Movements in Foreign Exchange on Trade and Investment Flows

Fluctuations in the Exchange rate have an impact on the following factors of the economy:

1. **Merchandise Trade:** Merchandise trade refers to the country's internal trade / exports and imports. When the currency is weak, it will encourage exports thereby making imports expensive and decreasing a nation's trade deficit.

   Let us look at an example to understand this concept. Let's say there is an exporter from Australia who sold a million radios at $10 each to a buyer in Paris at an exchange rate of EUR 1 = Aus $1.25. The Cost of the radio to the Parisian was Euro 8 per radio. The buyer is now asking for a discount as he wants to place a larger order and since the dollar has declined to 1.35 per euro, the exporter can give the buyer a price break while still maintaining the $10 mark. Imagine the new price is Euro 7.5 that amounts to a 6.25% discount and in Aus $ ut would be $10.13 at the current exchange rate. The depreciation in your domestic currency is the primary reason why your export business has remained competitive in international markets. A significantly stronger currency can reduce export competitiveness and make imports cheaper, which can cause the trade deficit to widen further, eventually weakening the currency in a self-adjusting mechanism. But before this happens, industry sectors that are highly export-oriented can be decimated by an unduly strong currency.

   Economic growth: The basic formula for an economy's GDP is $C + I + G + (X - M)$

   where,

   C = Consumption or consumer spending, the biggest component of an economy

   I = Capital investment by businesses and households

G = Government spending

(X – M) = Exports minus imports, or net exports.

From this equation, it is clear that the higher the value of net exports, the higher a nation's GDP. Net exports have an inverse correlation with the strength of the domestic currency.

2. **Capital Flows:** When a government is strong, the economy is dynamic and the currency is stable, the foreign capital will tend to flow into the country. If a country wants to attract investment capital from foreign investors, then it must have a stable currency, else the prospect of exchange losses imposed by currency depreciation will deter overseas investors.

There are two main types of Capital Flows:

✓ *foreign direct investment* (FDI), in which foreign investors take stakes in existing companies or build new facilities overseas;

✓ *foreign portfolio investment*, where foreign investors invest in overseas securities.

In growing economies like India and China, whose growth would be constrained if capital was unavailable, FDI is a critical source of funding.

FDI is often preferred as compared to FPI since FPI is similar to "hot money" which can leave the country when the going gets tough. This is known as "capital flight".

3. **Inflation:** For countries that are substantial importers, a currency that is devalued can result in "imported inflation". A sudden decline of 20% in the domestic currency may result in imported products costing 25% more since a 20% decline means a 25% increase to get back to the original starting point.

4. **Interest Rates:** A key consideration for most central banks when setting monetary policy is the exchange rate level. For example, former Bank of Canada Governor Mark Carney said in September 2012 speech that the bank takes the exchange rate of the Canadian dollar into account in setting monetary policy. Carney said that the persistent strength of the Canadian dollar was one of the reasons why Canada's monetary policy had been "exceptionally accommodative" for so long.

A strong domestic currency exerts a pull on the economy, achieving the same end result as tighter monetary policy.

2.3 Interest Rate

Home loan interest rates have come a full cycle, in the past 7 years. The interest rates started hardening from the year 2006. The interest rates have started going down, from this year.

Due to global recession, exports started to decrease, which had an adverse impact on the sentiments of the consumer who in turn started cutting down their expenses. This led to a lower GDP. The Reserve Bank of India (RBI) announced cuts in its key policy rates and ratios, and it further cut its key policy rates and ratios many times to provide a stimulus to the economy and industry.

2.3.1 Factors which Influence Interest Rate

Potential borrowers need to track some points to get an idea on the possible movement of interest rates. There are some important factors that govern the movement of interest rates.

1. **Economy:** The general economic conditions are among the prime factors that influence the movement of interest rates. When the economy is growing, secure sources of earnings are present with the people who in turn have a better confidence to borrow and spend such as buying a house or car. Hence there is a demand for funds and it also influences the rate of interest to go on a rise. In a recessionary economic condition or slowdown, the interest rates tend to go down due to the opposite happening.

2. **Inflation:** Another important feature that governs interest rates on loans is the rate of inflation. When it comes to lending, the lender prefers to lend where the interest rates are higher than the rate of inflation else they will have a negative growth. Hence if there is a rise in the rate of inflation, then a higher interest rate is expected, whereas a drop in the rate of inflation points towards a softer interest rate.

3. **RBI Moves:** In a recessionary economic condition or slowdown, the interest rates tend to go down due to the opposite happening. Based on the economic conditions from time to time, the RBI keeps tuning these parameters.

4. **Stock Market Conditions:** Through equity expansions in the stock markets or borrowings from financial institutions, corporates meet their needs of funds. Companies to go in for the equity expansion route when optimistic there are trends in the stock markets. This reduces the demand for funds through borrowing. When the market condition is slow, it will make the corporate move towards the borrowing path which increases the demand for funds.

5. **International Borrowings:** The economic conditions of international markets have also started playing an important role in deciding the interest rate direction. The global economic conditions influence the lending pattern of foreign investors to domestic companies, and thus compete with domestic sources of funds in the market.

6. **Fiscal Deficit and Government Borrowings:** The government borrows money from the market to fund its fiscal deficit. A rising fiscal deficit (as percentage of the GDP) indicates that the government will have to borrow more from the market. This puts an indirect upward pressure on the borrowing rates in the market.

2.3.2 Impact of Movements in Interest Rates on Trade and Investment Flows

Exchange rates, inflation and interest rates are all correlated. If the interest rate is influenced, the central banks can apply control over both inflation and exchange rates, and changing interest rates impact inflation and currency values. When the interest rates are high in an economy, lenders are offered a higher return as compared to other countries and hence higher interest rates attract foreign capital and will cause the exchange rate to go up. The opposite relationship exists for decreasing interest rates - that is, lower interest rates tend to decrease exchange rates. Rather than just the interest rate paid on risk free securities, the price of the currency depends more on the economy. While higher interest rates would most certainly result in a short-term inflow of investment, it would also reduce aggregate demand, thus making other areas of the economy less likely to be invested in.

The interest rate is the rate which is charged or paid for the use of money or more precisely the cost of borrowing. According to **Gross and Trevino** *a relatively high interest rate in a host country has a positive impact on inward foreign investment.*

Points to Remember

- **Foreign investment** is the flow of capital from one nation to another in exchange for significant ownership stakes in domestic companies or other domestic assets.
- **Four types of foreign investment:**
    - ✓ FDI
    - ✓ FPI
    - ✓ official flows
    - ✓ Commercial loans
- **Foreign Direct investments** are made in the form of the overwhelming majority of foreign direct investment is made in the form of
    - ✓ fixtures,
    - ✓ machinery,

- ✓ equipment
- ✓ buildings.
- Due to foreign investments advantages for the MNEs, there is easy access to markets and resources. It reduces cost of production.
- **Due to foreign investments advantages for the foreign countries are:**
  - ✓ Source of external capital and increased revenue,
  - ✓ Development of new industries,
  - ✓ learning.
- The national currency's quotation in respect to foreign ones is known as exchange rate. Exchange rate is a conversion factor, a ratio or multiplier depending on the direction of conversion.
- **Nominal exchange rates** are established on currency financial markets called "forex markets", which are similar to stock exchange markets
- Real exchange rates are nominal rate corrected somehow by inflation measures.
- **Some of the factors influencing exchange rate are:**
  - ✓ Inflation
  - ✓ Interest rate
  - ✓ Speculation
  - ✓ Change in competitiveness
  - ✓ Relative strength of other currencies
  - ✓ balance of payment
  - ✓ government debt
  - ✓ government intervention
  - ✓ economic growth
- When exchange rate of one country is compared with another, it is influenced by numerous fundamental and technical factors
- The exchange rate of one currency versus the other is influenced by numerous fundamental and technical factors. The factors are:
  - ✓ relative supply and demand of the two currencies,
  - ✓ economic performance,
  - ✓ outlook for inflation,
  - ✓ interest rate differentials,

- ✓ capital flows,
- ✓ technical support and
- ✓ resistance levels
- Economic growth: The basic formula for an economy's GDP is C + I + G + (X – M)

Questions for Discussion

1. Discuss the pattern and structure of foreign investment.
2. Elaborate positive and negative effects of foreign investment.
3. Describe the factors influencing foreign exchange movements and the impact of foreign exchange movements on trade and investment.
4. Explain the factors influencing interest rate movements and the impact of interest rate movements on trade and investment.

Multiple Choice Questions

1. FDI stands for
   - (a) Foreign Direct Income
   - (b) Foreign Direct Investment
   - (c) Foreign Director Investment
   - (d) Foreign Dictatorship Income

2. FPI stands for
   - (a) Foreign Portfolio Investment
   - (b) Foreign Portfolio Income
   - (c) Foreign Perfect Investment
   - (d) Foreign Perfect Income

3. Which is a type of foreign investment?
   - (a) FDI
   - (b) FPI
   - (c) Commercial loan
   - (d) All the above

4. The market conditions in the developing world can be quite unstable and unpredictable.
   - (a) True
   - (b) False

5. The national currency's quotation in respect to foreign ones
   - (a) Foreign Direct Investment
   - (b) Exchange Rate
   - (c) Foreign Portfolio Investment
   - (d) Foreign Income

6. If the exchange rate is: $1 = ₹ 60 what will a ₹ 30000 car cost in dollars?
   - (a) $1000
   - (b) $300

(c) $500 (d) $30000

7. What is / are the factors that influence the Exchange Rate?
   (a) Inflation
   (b) Interest rates
   (c) Government Debt
   (d) All the above

8. The basic formula for an economy's GDP is C + I + G + (X – M). What does G stand for?
   (a) Consumption or consumer spending, the biggest component of an economy
   (b) Capital investment by businesses and households
   (c) Government spending
   (d) All the above

9. Joint Venture is a type of:
   (a) FPI
   (b) FDI
   (c) Commercial Loan
   (d) Official Flow

10. Which factor affects the interest rate?
    (a) Inflation
    (b) Commercial Loan
    (c) Official flow
    (d) Exchange rate

ANSWERS

| 1. (c) | 2. (a) | 3. (d) | 4. (a) | 5. (b) |
| 6. (c) | 7. (d) | 8. (c) | 9. (b) | 10. (a) |

Project Questions

1. Examine the FDI policies of the Government of India and discuss how foreign investment can be attracted more effectively towards the public sector industries.

2. If the dollar appreciates relative to the euro, will the German camera you have wanted become more or less expensive? What effect do you imagine this change will have on American demand for German cameras?

Chapter 3...

International Economic Institutions and Agreements

Contents ...

- 3.1 World Trade Organisation
    - 3.1.1 Introduction
    - 3.1.2 Evolution
    - 3.1.3 Difference between GATT and WTO
    - 3.1.4 Objectives of WTO
    - 3.1.5 Structure of WTO
    - 3.1.6 Principles of WTO
    - 3.1.7 Functions of WTO
    - 3.1.8 Impact of WTO
- 3.2 International Monetary Fund (IMF)
    - 3.2.1 Introduction
    - 3.2.2 Origin of IMF
    - 3.2.3 Objectives of IMF
    - 3.2.4 Functions of IMF
    - 3.2.5 Future Vision
    - 3.2.6 Organisation and Management of IMF
    - 3.2.7 India and the IMF
    - 3.2.8 Critical Evaluation of the IMF
- 3.3 World Bank
    - 3.3.1 Introduction
    - 3.3.2 Establishment
    - 3.3.3 Principles of the World Bank
    - 3.3.4 Objectives of the World Bank
    - 3.3.5 Functions of the World Bank
    - 3.3.6 Policies of the World Bank in their Lending Operations
    - 3.3.7 Different Lending Operations

- 3.3.8 Other Activities
- 3.3.9 Critical Evaluation
- 3.3.10 The World Bank and India
- 3.4 UNCTAD
  - 3.4.1 Introduction
  - 3.4.2 Objectives of UNCTAD
  - 3.4.3 Functions
  - 3.4.4 Activities
- 3.5 Agreement on Textiles and Clothing (ATC)
  - 3.5.1 Introduction
  - 3.5.2 Purpose of ATC
  - 3.5.3 Main Provisions of ATC
- 3.6 Generalised System of Preferences (GSP)
- 3.7 Global System of Trade Preferences (GSTP)
- 3.8 International Commodity Trading and Agreements
  - 3.8.1 Introduction
  - 3.8.2 Prerequisites for Negotiation
  - 3.8.3 Obsolete Principles Versus Realities
  - 3.8.4 Economic Effects
  - 3.8.5 Current Pressures Favouring Agreements
  - 3.8.6 Alternatives
  - • Points to Remember
  - • Questions for Discussion
  - • Multiple Choice Questions
  - • Project Questions

Learning Objectives ...

- To understand the objectives and functions of IMF
- To study the objectives and functions of World Bank
- To learn the role and functions of WTO
- To know about the evolution of WTO
- To be able to explain various International Economic Agreements including UNCTAD, ATC, GSP and GSTP
- To study the International commodity trading and agreement

3.1 World Trade Organisation

3.1.1 Introduction

The World Trade Organisation (WTO) is an organisation that proposes to supervise and liberalise international trade. The organisation deals with regulations and guidelines of trade between participating countries by providing a framework for negotiating and formalising trade agreements and a dispute resolution process aimed at enforcing participant's loyalty to WTO agreements, which are signed by representatives of member governments and approved by their parliaments.

3.1.2 Evolution

From early times, the need for a world trade body was felt. On the recommendations of the Bretton Woods Conference in 1994, the International Trade Organisation (ITO) was proposed to be set up along with the World Bank and IMF.

The ITO was not set up, but in its place GATT was established by the U.S, U.K., and some other countries in 1947.

It was soon realised that GATT was based in favour of the developed countries and was called as the 'rich men's club'. Due to this, the developing nations insisted on setting up of ITO, but U.S.A opposed to this proposal. To solve the issue, the UN appointed a committee in 1963. The committee recommended the United Nation Conference on Trade and Development (UNCTAD). As such UNCTAD came into being in 1964 and could manage to secure some concessions for the developing nations.

Table 3.1: Illustrates the Negotiations in GATT's Different Rounds

Period	Round	Negotiations Outcome
1947	Geneva Round	Birth of GATT. 45,000 tariff concessions representing half of world trade.
1949	Annecy Round	Modest tariff reductions.
1950-51	Torquay Round	In relation to 1948 level, 25% tariff reductions.
1955-56	Geneva Round	Moderate Tariff reductions.
1961-62	Dillon Round	Tariff reductions.
1963-67	Kennedy Round	Modest reduction for agricultural goods, anti-dumping code, average tariff reduction of 35% on industrial goods.
1973-79	Tokyo Round	34% for industrial goods (tariff reduction). Non-tariff trade barrier code.
1986-94	Uruguay Round	Tariffs, non tariff measures, rules, services, intellectual property rights, dispute settlement, creation of WTO.

WTO was established on 1st January 1995. The Uruguay round of GATT negotiations concluded on 15th December 1993 and ministers had given their political backing to the results by signing the Final Act at a meeting in Marrakesh, Morocco in April 1994.

India, along with 123 ministers besides the EC countries signed the Final Act incorporating the 8th Round of multilateral trade negotiations. The 'Marrakesh Declaration' of 15th April 1994 affirmed that the results of the Uruguay Round would 'strengthen the world economy and lead to more trade, investment, employment and income growth throughout the world'.

The Final Act consists of:

(i) WTO Agreement covers the formation of the organisation and the rules governing its working;
(ii) The Ministerial decisions and declarations which contain important agreements covering subjects like trade in goods, services, intellectual property rights, plurilateral trade, dispute settlement rules, etc.

WTO is the embodiment of the Uruguay Round results and the successor to the General Agreement on Tariffs and Trade (GATT). WTO has a larger membership than GATT, the present number stands at 151 and India is one of the founder members of WTO.

WTO is GATT plus a lot more. It is a more powerful body with enlarged functions than the GATT and is envisaged to play a major role in the world economic affairs. *To become a member of the WTO, a country must completely accept the provisions of the Uruguay Round.*

3.1.3 Difference between GATT and WTO

WTO is not a simple extension of GATT; it completely replaces its predecessor and has a very different character. The major differences between GATT and WTO are as follows:

GATT	WTO
1. GATT had a small Secretariat managed by a Director General.	1. WTO has a large Secretariat and a huge organisational set up.
2. GATT was Adhoc and provisional.	2. WTO and its agreements are permanent.
3. GATT had contracting parties.	3. WTO has members.
4. GATT was set of rules, a multilateral agreement, with no institutional foundation. There were separate agreements on separate issues which were not binding on members. Any member could stay out of an agreement. Only those who signed the agreement could be penalised for default.	4. The agreements which form part of WTO are permanent and binding on all members. Action can be taken against any defaulting members by all the member states.
5. GATT had no legal status.	5. WTO has a legal status similar to that of the World Bank and the IMF.

... (Contd.)

GATT	WTO
6. GATT rules applied to trade in merchandise goods. Trade in services was included in Uruguay Round but no agreement was arrived at.	6. In addition to goods, WTO covers trade in services and trade-related aspects of intellectual property rights.
7. GATT system allowed existing domestic legislation to continue even if it violated a GATT agreement.	7. WTO does not permit this.
8. GATT was less powerful, dispute settlement system was slow and less efficient, and its ruling could be easily blocked.	8. WTO is more powerful than GATT; dispute settlement mechanism is faster and more efficient, very difficult to block the rulings.
9. GATT was a forum where the member countries met once in a decade to discuss and solve world trade problems. There used to be long negotiating rounds that took decades to complete.	9. WTO is a properly established rule-based world trade organisation where decisions on agreements are time-bound and any extension in dateline is only by consensus.

3.1.4 Objectives of WTO

WTO's main objective is to help trade flow smoothly, freely, fairly and predictably.

WTO reiterates the objectives of GATT, which are as follows:

(i) In the area of trade and economic, its efforts shall be conducted with a view to raise standard of living and incomes, promote full employment, expand production and trade in goods and services.

(ii) To allow for optimum utilisation of world's resources and fulfil the objective of sustainable development, seeking both:
   (a) Protect and preserve the environment;
   (b) To enhance the means that are consistent with respective needs and concerns at different levels of economic development.

(iii) To take positive steps to ensure that developing countries, especially 'the least developed ones', secure a better share of growth in world trade commensurate with the needs of their economic development.

(iv) To ensure linkages between trade policies, environmental policies and sustainable development. Thus, *monitoring national trade policies.*

(v) To establish procedures for resolving trade disputes among members.

(vi) WTO aims at promoting trade flows by encouraging nations to adopt non-discriminatory and predictable trade policies. Thus, *administering the WTO trade agreements.*

(vii) To develop an integrated, more viable and durable multilateral trading system including:
  (a) the GATT;
  (b) the results of past liberalisation efforts;
  (c) the results of the 9th Round, i.e., Uruguay round of multilateral trade negotiations.
(viii) Cooperating with other international organisations like the IMF and IBRD and its affiliated agencies with a view to achieving greater coherence in global economic policy making.
(ix) Administering the mechanism for settling trade disputes between the member countries.
(x) Providing technical assistance and training for developing countries.

3.1.5 Structure of WTO

(i) Fig. 3.1 shows the structure of the WTO is dominated by its highest authority - *The Ministerial Conference*. This body is composed of representatives of all WTO members. The members meet every two years and the body is empowered to make decisions on all matters under any of the multilateral trade agreements.

(ii) The day-to-day work of the WTO is entrusted to a member of subsidiary bodies mainly, the **General Council** also compared to all WTO members, which is required to report to the Ministerial Conference.

(iii) The General Council convenes in two particular forms:
  (a) The Dispute Settlement Body and
  (b) The Trade Policy Review Body.

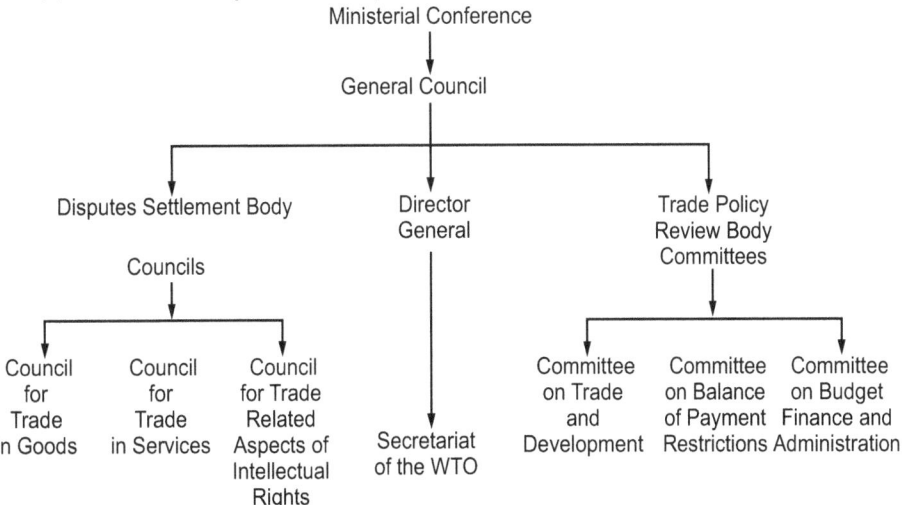

Fig. 3.1: Structure of WTO

(iv) The General Council delegates responsibility to three bodies viz.

   (a) The Council of Trade in Goods,

   (b) Trade in Services,

   (c) Trade-Related aspects of Intellectual Property Rights.

(v) The Council for Goods supervises the implementation and functioning of all the agreements covering trade in goods. The latter two Councils have responsibility for their respective WTO agreements.

(vi) Three others bodies are set up by the Ministerial Conference who report to the General Council.

   (a) **The Committee on Trade and Development** is concerned with issues relating to the developing nations and particularly to the 'least-developed' among them.

   (b) **The Committee on Balance of Payments** concerned with consultations among WTO members and nations that resort to trade restrictive measures to cope with their BOPs difficulties.

   (c) **Committee on Budget, Finance and Administration** relates to WTO's financing and budget.

Each of the plurilateral agreements of the WT such as civil aircraft, government procurement, dairy products and bovine meat establish their own management bodies, which are required to report the General Council.

3.1.6 Principles of WTO

The following are the principles of WTO:

1. **Non-Discrimination:** WTO is built on a foundation of non-discrimination which has two major components:

   (a) **Most Favoured Nation Rule:** The Most Favoured Nation rule (MFN) has been an important feature of international trade policy for a long time. The Most Favoured Nation rule forbids discrimination between like products originating in, or intended, for different countries.

   (b) **National Treatment:** National Treatment means that foreign imported goods, after they cross the border, should be treated no less favourably than domestically-produced goods. The fundamental principle behind the national treatment is to make sure that tax and domestic regulation are not used to restrain trade.

2. **Binding and Enforceable Commitments:** Tariff commitments are made by WTO members during trade negotiations. These negotiations are bilateral (one country to one country) during the agreement process, and then become multilateral (all countries together) after a country has joined WTO.

When a country agrees to the WTO, these commitments are listed in a schedule with ceiling bindings or maximum tariff rate. A country cannot exceed these bound rates without negotiating with its trading partners. It could mean compensating them for loss of trade. If satisfaction is not attained, the complaining country may refer the matter to the WTO dispute settlement body.

3. **Transparency:** WTO members are required to publish their trade regulations and to make sure any decisions affecting trade are reported to other WTO members and to the WTO Secretariat itself. The WTO also has a Trade Policy Review Mechanism (TPRM) which periodically reviews the laws and regulations of a WTO-member country.

4. **Single Undertaking:** All WTO agreements are held together as a single undertaking. This means that member countries cannot choose which agreement they will join. The WTO, and all of its agreements, is a single package that member states must join on an 'all or nothing' basis.

5. **Safety Valves:** In certain conditions, governments are allowed to restrict trade. For example, under the Agreement on Safeguards, a country is authorised to restrict temporarily products from which a surge in imports caused or is threatening to cause serious injury to a specific domestic industry.

3.1.7 Functions of WTO

The functions of WTO are:
(i) WTO provides a forum for multilateral trade negotiations. That is, WTO acts as a forum for negotiations among its members concerning their multilateral trade.
(ii) It administers the understanding on rules and procedures governing the Settlement of Disputes of the Agreement.
(iii) It co-operates with other international institutions- IMF and the World Bank and its affiliated agencies – involved in global economic policy-making.
(iv) Provision of technical assistance and training for developing countries.
(v) WTO acts as a management consultant for world trade. Experts on the panel of WTO scan the world economic environment and make observations on contemporary issues.
(vi) WTO maintains trade-related database. Members are required to notify in detail various trade measures and statistics.
(vii) It provides the framework for the implementation, administration and operation of the Plurilateral Trade Agreements relating to trade in civil aircraft, government procurement, trade in dairy products and bovine meat.
(viii) It oversees national trade policies.
(ix) WTO acts as a watchdog of international trade, constantly examining the trade regimes of individual members.

From the above mentioned functions it clarifies that WTO does not aim at economic or political integration, but it seeks to promote free trade among member countries.

3.1.8 Impact of WTO

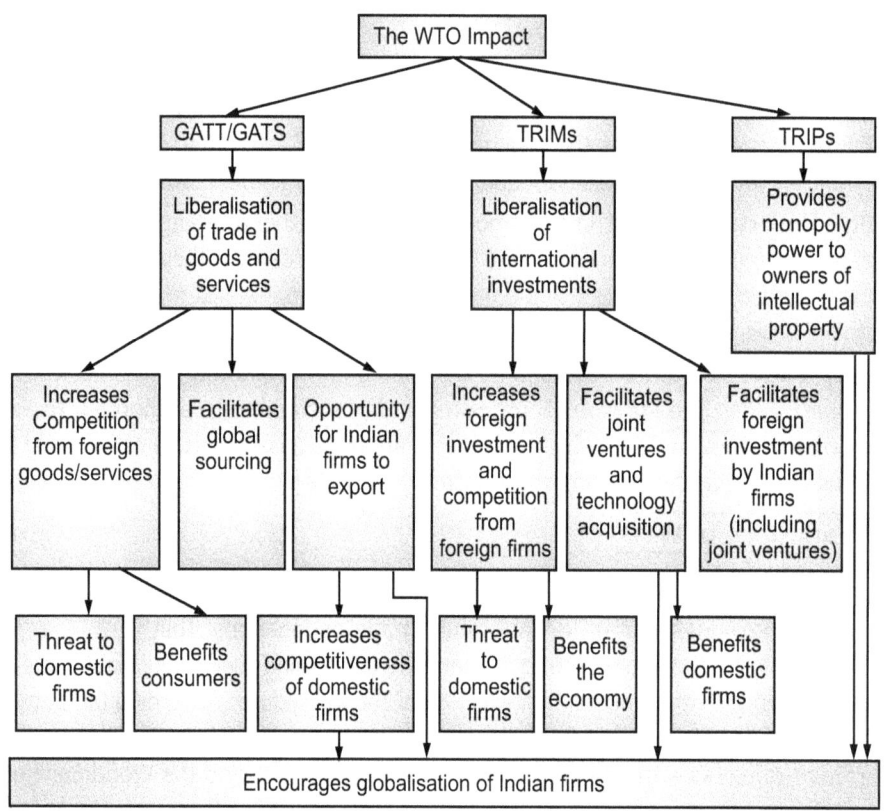

Fig. 3.2: The WTO Impact

Table 3.2: Groups and Issues in the URUGUAY ROUND

Negotiating Groups	Main Issues
Track I : Group of Negotiations on Goods	
1. Tariffs	• Reduction and elimination of existing tariff. • Tariff escalation. • Formula approach or product by product Approach.
2. Non – tariff Measures	• Reduction /elimination of any non-tariff measures including quantitative restrictions • How to establish equivalence for bilateral negotiation.

		• Whether to treat unjustified quantitative restriction (QRs) as negotiable or whether to insist on rolling back these QRs.
3.	Natural Resource-based Products	• Tariff escalation. • Use of quantitative restrictions. • Access to supplies. • Products coverage in the group's work.
4.	Textile and Clothing	• What procedure could be used to integrate trade in textiles and clothing into the working of GATT; in effect, how to dismantle the MFA.
5.	Agriculture	• Improved market access through reduction of impact barriers. • Increased discipline over measures not conforming with the GATT, including direct and indirect subsidies, quotas, also reduction of subsidies which do not conform with GATT.
6.	Tropical Products	• Increased liberalisation of processed and semi-processed tropical products. • Tariff and non-tariff liberalisation. • How much reciprocity should be required of developing countries. • Coverage by products.
7.	GATT Articles	• Articles on tariff bindings, customs union, balance of payments, state trading, waivers etc. are to be reviewed.
8.	MTN Agreements and Arrangement	• Improvement, classification on expansion of code.
9.	Safeguards	• Selectivity, transparency, digressively, structural adjustment, etc.
10.	Subsidies and Countervailing Measures	• Review of the MTN agreement on subsidies and countervailing measures. • Definition of subsidy. • Discipline on export subsidies.

11. Trade Related Aspects of Intellectual Property Rights (TRIPs), Including Trade in Counterfeit Goods	• Clarify GATT provisions. • Ensure measures and procedures to enforce IPR.
12. Trade Related Investment Measures	• To elaborate on further provision.
13. Dispute Settlement	• Effective enforcement of panels conclusion. • Improvement of the efficiency and transparency.
14. Functioning of the GATT System	• Enhanced surveillance in the GATT to enable monitoring of trade policies and practices of contracting parties. • Improved functioning of the GATT as decision-making institution.
Track II : Groups of Negotiations on Services	
15. Services	• Definition and statistical issue. • Broad concepts on principles and rules for trade in services. • Coverage of multilateral discipline. • Foreign investment. • International labour mobility. • Right of establishment, etc.

Source: D.M. Mithani "International Economics", Himalaya Publication House, 1999, PP 336-337

3.2 International Monetary Fund (IMF)

3.2.1 Introduction

There are several international organisations, funding and assisting the development, particularly, of developing economies. Indeed, great is the impact of these institutions like IMF, World Bank, Regional Development Banks like the Asian Development Bank (ADB). The economic policies and programmes of member countries which take financial assistance from these organisations may be influenced by the policies and conditions of assistance of these organisations. Several schemes of IMF extend financial assistance to countries having balance of payment problems. Besides, financial assistance, IMF provides different types of technical assistance too.

3.2.2 Origin of IMF

The IMF was established on 27th December, 1945 with 29 countries as members and it began its financial operations on 1st March, 1947. It is the result of the Bretton Woods Conference of Nations held in 1944. The objective was to discuss the major international economic problems, including reconstruction of the economies ravaged by the world war. The principal aim was to avoid economic mistakes of the 1920s and 1930s.

The attempts made by many countries to return to the old Gold Standard System after the First World War failed miserably. The Great Depression of the 1930s forced every country to abandon the gold standard. As a result, every country adopted purely nationalistic policies whereby almost every nation imposed trade restrictions, exchange controls and resorted to exchange depreciation to encourage exports. This led to severe decline in world trade and the depression deepened further.

It was against this background that 44 nations assembled at the United Nations Monetary and Financial conference at Bretton Woods, New Hampshire (USA) from 1st July to 22nd July, 1944.

IMF endeavours to maintain international monetary and national macro-economic stability and to promote orderly development of global trade.

IMF started functioning from 1st March, 1947 and at the beginning of May 2008, IMF had 185 members.

IMF is the central institution of the international monetary system – the system of international payments and exchange rates among national currencies. Its objective is to prevent crises in the system by encouraging countries to adopt sound economic policies. It is a fund that can be utilised by members for temporary financing to iron out and correct balance of payments problems.

Membership to IMF is open to every country that controls its foreign relations and is able and prepared to fulfil the obligations of membership. Membership in the World Bank (IBRD) is by virtue of being a member of the Fund. A close working relationship exists between the Fund and the WTO and the Bank for International Settlements (BIS).

3.2.3 Objectives of IMF

IMF's *Statutory Purposes* has been laid down in Article I of the Original Articles of Agreement and they have been upheld in the two amendments that were made in 1969 and 1978 to its basic Charter.

According to the Articles of Agreement, the purposes/objectives of the IMF are:

1. To promote international monetary co-operation through a permanent institution. This institution would provide as machinery for consultation and collaboration on international monetary problems.
2. To facilitate the expansion and balanced growth of international trade and to contribute thereby to the promotion and maintenance of high levels of employment

and real income and to the development of productive resources of all members, as primary objectives of economic policy.
3. To promote exchange stability, to maintain orderly exchange arrangements among members and to avoid competitive exchange depreciation.
4. To assist in the establishment of a multilateral system of payments in respect of current transactions between members and in the elimination of foreign exchange restrictions which hamper the growth of world trade.
5. To give confidence to members by making the general (pool of resources) resources of the Fund temporarily available to them under adequate safeguards. This provides them with opportunity to correct maladjustments in their balance of payments without resorting to measures that would damage national or international prosperity.
6. To shorten the duration and lessen the degree of disequilibrium in the international balance of payments of members.
7. The Fund shall be guided in all its policies and decisions by the purposes set forth in this Article.

To fulfil the above objectives, the IMF:

(a) Monitors economic and financial developments and policies of the member countries and at the global level and gives policy advice to its members based on its nearly six decades of experience.
(b) Lending to member countries with balance of payments problems, not just to provide temporary financing but to support adjustments and reform policies aimed at correcting the underlying problems.
(c) Provides the governments and central banks of its member countries with technical assistance and training in its areas of expertise.

3.2.4 Functions of IMF

IMF is the only international agency whose activities involve active dialogue with virtually every country on economic policies. IMF is the principal forum for discussing not only national economic policies in a global context, but also endeavours its efforts towards the stability of international monetary and financial system.

IMF performs the following functions:

1. **Determination of Par Values:** One of the objectives of IMF is to assure exchange rate stability. Usually countries express the value of their funds fixes minimum and maximum limit in which once determined exchange rate can make changes in the external value of its currency within this limit. Changes in exchange rate is possible only after prior permission of IMF. If member nation ask for such permission in that case they have to take action within 72 hours. It gives permission only if 2/3 members are in favour of it.

2. **Financial Assistance:** The fund has a variety of facilities for leading its resources to member countries. Leading by the fund is linked to temporary assistance to members in financing disequilibrium in their BOP on current account.
3. **Reserve Tranche:** If a member has less currency with fund than its quota, the difference is called "Reserve Tranche". It can draw up to 25% of their Reserve Tranche. No interest has been charged on such drawings but need to repay within period of 3 to 5 years.
4. **Credit Tranche:** A member can draw further annually from balance quota in 4 installments up to 100% from quota it is "called Credit Tranche". Such borrowings are conditional and members have to satisfy fund of adopting a viable programme. The limit is increased to 300% of their quota due to rising problems of countries. Other credit facilities are:
    - **Buffer Stock Financing Facility:** It was credited in 1969 for financing commodity buffer stock by member countries. The facility is equivalent to 30% of borrowing member's quota. Repurchase are made in 3 to 5 years but the member is expected to cooperate with the fund by establishing commodity prices within the country.
    - **Extended Fund Facility (EFF):** It was created in 1974, under EEF, the fund provides credit to member countries to meet their balance of payments deficits for longer period and in amounts larger than their quotas under normal credit facilities. EFF provides credit up to a period of 10 years and loans up to 300% of a member quota are allowed. It depends upon the performance criteria and drawing installments.
    - **Supplementary Financing Facility (SFF):** It was established in 1977 under which stand by agreements to member countries to meet serious BOP deficits that are large in relation to their economies and their quotas. The facility has been extended to low income developing member countries to reduce the cost of borrowing under SFF to such countries.
    - **Structural Adjustment Facility (SAF):** It is started in 1986 to provide concessional adjustment to poorer developing countries. Under this facility loans are granted to them to solve BOP Problems and to carryout medium term micro-economic and structural adjustment programme. The rate of interest charged is only 5% to 11% with the principle repayable over 5 to 10 years with a five year grace period.
    - **Enhanced Structural Adjustment Facility:** It was started in 1987 to provide medium term finance. The objective eligibility and basic features of this programme is same like Structural adjustment facility but eligible members can receive a great deal and more assistance. 100% of the quota over 3 years programme period, with provision for up to 250% in exceptional circumstances.
    - **Compensatory and Contingency Finance Facility:** This finance facility started in 1998 to provide timely compensation for temporary shortfalls or excess in import costs due to factors beyond the control of the members. Contingency finance is

within 95% of quota. Besides workers remittance and travel receipts, shortfall in other services such as receipts from pipelines, canals, shipping, transportation, construction and insurance have been included.

- **Systematic Transformation Facility:** In 1993 the IMF established to help Russia and other Asian republics to face BOP crises.
- **Emergency Structural Adjustment Loans**: It was established in early 1999 to help the Asian and Latin American countries inflicted with the financial crisis. Under it, such countries are given short term loans - 3% to 9% above the funds normal interest rate which are to be repaid in a short period.
- **Contingency Credit Line (CCL):** It was created in April 1999 to protect fundamentally sound countries from the contagion of financial crisis occurring in other countries, rather than from domestic policy weakness. Only countries that over the medium term can finance BOP comfortably and enjoy healthy financial sectors, 7 strong debtor creditor relations are considered in CCL.

5. **Other Facilities:** IMF sends specialist and experts to help the countries and they solve BOP and exchange rate problems of member countries. They confer with local officials and suggest monetary, fiscal and other measures in their reports. The fund has set up three departments to solve banking and fiscal problems of countries.
    - **Central banking service department** which helps member countries with the services of its experts to run and mange their central banks and reform their banking fund system.
    - The IMF Institutes conduct **short term training programme** for the officers of member countries relating to monetary, fiscal, banking and BOP policies.
    - Fiscal affairs department **renders advice** to member countries concerning their fiscal matters.

3.2.5 Future Vision

(a) To promote sustained non-inflationary economic growth that benefits all people of the world.
(b) Work as the centre of competence for the stability of the international financial system.
(c) Focus on its core macroeconomic and financial areas of responsibility, working in a complementary fashion with other institutions, set up to safeguard global public goods.
(d) Adapting continuously to changing circumstances.

The Bretton Woods Conference which led to the foundation of IMF and the environment in which IMF functions are now different. The number of successful mature economies has grown from a handful at the end of World War II to a significant now. The number of 'emerging markets' (with substantial international trade) has grown. Some countries will no longer need to borrow from IMF; others to borrow occasionally a large amount and still others might borrow on concessional terms than to borrowing from the Fund's ordinary resources on market terms. Both the private markets and official agencies such as IMF will have to be prepared for these and other developments.

3.2.6 Organisation and Management of IMF

1. The Board of Governors is the highest authority governing the IMF. In this, all member countries are represented. Each member country appoints a Governor (usually the country's minister of finance or the Governor of its Central Bank) and an alternate Governor. The Board decides on major policy issues.

2. The Executive Board consists of 24 Executive Directors, with the Managing Director as a chairman. The executive board usually meets 3 times a week, at the organisation's headquarters in Washington D.C. The IMF's 5 largest shareholders are United States, Japan, Germany, France, and United Kingdom – while China, Russia, and Saudi Arabia have their own seats on the Board.

3. Interim committee was established in October 1974 to advise the board of Governors on supervising the management and adaptation of the international monetary system in order to avoid disturbances that might threaten.

3. The Development Committee, is a joint committee of the Board of Governors of the IMF and the World Bank, advises and reports to the governors on development policy and other matters of concern to developing nations.

4. International Monetary and Financial Committee is a committee of Governors that deals with the issues relating to the international monetary system.

The IMF has a weighted voting system: the larger a country's quota in the IMF (determined by its economic size), the more votes it has.

3.2.7 India and the IMF

- India is one of the 44 countries which participated in the Bretton Woods conference held in 1944; as such India is one of the founder members of the fund.
- Till 1970 India's quota in the Fund was the 5th and it had the power to appoint a permanent executive director. With the increase in the fund quota after May 1970, the quotas of Japan, Canada and Italy increased more than that of India. As such India ceased to hold a permanent position as Executive Director of the Fund. India's position in the fund quota came to 13th as its quota declined from 2.09% to 1.96%.

India and the IMF have had a friendly relationship, which has been beneficial for both. The IMF has provided India with loans over the years and this has helped the country to grow. The IMF has also praised India for it has been able to maintain average growth of its economy.

India's Relations with the IMF

India and the IMF have a positive relationship. The IMF has provided financial assistance to India, which has helped in boosting the country's economy. The IMF praised the country for it was able to avoid the Asian Financial crisis in 1999 and was able to maintain the average rate of growth of its economy. The Managing Director of the IMF Rodrigo De Rato visited India in May 2005. In 2005, the IMF said that the budget of India is very positive for it points that the economy of the country will grow at the rate of 6.7%.

IMF said that the reasons behind the economy's growth of India are that the RBI has been able to control inflation and has also handled its monetary policies very skilfully. The IMF has suggested that India can become a financial super power by bringing in more reforms in its economic policies that will increase its growth rate to 8%.

3.2.8 Critical Evaluation of the IMF

The main **advantages** that have accrued to the world from the functions of the IMF:

- Under this system, the Fund is able to accumulate a sizeable stock of the national currencies of different countries, which it uses to meet the foreign exchange requirements of the member countries.
- The establishment of the fund has given boost to the setting up of a multilateral trade and payments system.
- By lending foreign currencies to member countries against their national currency, the fund has helped them to eliminate short-term disequilibrium in their balance of payments.
- The rates of exchange under the IMF had not fluctuated much as they used to do before its establishment.
- Before the establishment of the Fund, different countries of the world often resorted to competitive currency devaluation to boost their exports. No member country can now devalue its currency without the prior consent of the fund.
- The fund does not interfere in the internal economic affairs of member countries nor tries to influence their economic and monetary policies.
- Prof. Halm has referred the Fund as an "International Reserve Bank". The IMF has been able to secure for its members all the advantages of Gold Standard without its disadvantages – by introduction of SDR system. The new system is less expensive and more flexible than the old Gold Standard.

The functioning of the IMF is often subjected to **criticism (and suggestions)** on the following grounds:

At first we evaluate the IMF policies:

By 2005, the IMF was committing loans to some 49 countries that were struggling with economic and currency crises. All IMF loan packages come with conditions attached. In general, the IMF insists on a combination of tight macroeconomic policies, including cuts in public spending, higher interest rates and tight monetary policy. It often pushes for the reregulation of sectors formerly protected from domestic and foreign competition, privatisation of state-owned assets, and better reporting from banking sector. These policies are designed to cool overheated economies by controlling inflation and curtailing government spending and debt.

Recently, this set of policy prescription has come in for tough criticisms from many observers.

1. Inappropriate Policies: The IMF's "one-size-fits-all" approach to macroeconomic policy is inappropriate for many countries. Critics argue that in the case of the Asian crisis, the tight macroeconomic policies imposed by the IMF are ill-suited to countries that are suffering not from excessive government spending and inflation, but from a private-sector debt crisis with deflationary undertones. For example, in South Korea, the government had been running a budget surplus for years and inflation was low at about 5%. South Korea had the second strongest financial position of any country. Despite this, critics say, the IMF insisted on applying the same policies that it applies to countries suffering from high inflation.

The IMF required South Korea to maintain an inflating rate of 5%. And, with given fall in the value of its currency and subsequent rise in the price of imports such as oil, critics claimed that inflationary pressures would increase in South Korea. The reason is that to hit a 5% inflation rate, the country would be forced to apply an unnecessary tight monetary policy. Further short-term interest rates in South Korea did jump from 12.5% to 21% immediately after the country signed its deal with the IMF. Increasing interest rates made it difficult for companies to service their already excessive short-term debt obligations, and critics used this as evidence to argue that the cure prescribed by the IMF may actually increase the probability of widespread corporate defaults, not reduce them.

2. Moral Hazard: Another criticism against the IMF is that its rescue efforts are creating a problem known to economists as moral hazard. Moral hazard arises when people behave recklessly because they know that they will be saved if situations go adverse. Critics point out that many Japanese and western banks were far too willing to lend large amounts of capital to overleveraged Asian companies during the boom years of the 1990s. These critics argue that the banks were forced to pay the price of their rash lending policies, even if that means some banks must close. Only by taking such drastic action, the argument goes, will banks learn the error of their ways and not engage in rash lending in the future. By providing support to these countries, the IMF is reducing the probability of debt default and in effect bailing out the banks whose loans gave rise to this situation.

3. Lack of Accountability: Critics point out that the IMF has become too powerful for an institution that lacks any real mechanism for accountability. The IMF has determined macroeconomic policies in those countries, yet according to critics such as noted economist Jeffrey Sachs, the IMF, with a staff of less than 1,000, lacks the expertise required to do a good job. According to Sachs, evidence of this lack in expertise, can be found in the fact that when the IMF claimed the success with the Thai and South Korean governments only months before both countries lurched into crisis.

Certain other criticisms levelled against the functioning of the IMF are given below:

- The IMF has **not enough resources** for immediate future. The resources are not sufficient to meet the future needs of its members. Unfortunately, the developed countries are not willing to increase the quota of the Fund.
- According to the rules of the IMF, it deals only with those imbalances in payments which arise out of current trade transactions. So, **the Fund has limited scope**.
- The quotas of the various member countries have **not been fixed on any scientific basis**. These quotas have been fixed keeping in mind the economic and political interest of the US and the UK.
- Another criticism against the Fund is that **it discriminates in favour of** certain countries in its day-to-day functioning. It gives special concessions to **developed countries** while neglecting the genuine interests of backward and developing nations. No action is taken against the western countries when they flout the directives of the Fund. It is on account of this discriminatory treatment that the new nations of Africa have referred to the Fund as the "Rich Men's Club". In January 1984, the IMF succumbed to the pressure from the USA and West Germany and started paying, with effect from 1st May 1984, higher interest on the money is borrowed from the rich countries and charged more for the loans it made to the developing nations.
- Another **failure** of the fund is that it has not been successful in persuading member countries **to eliminate exchange controls** and other restrictions on foreign trade.
- It has **not succeeded in bringing stability in exchange rates**. The exchange rates of different countries have been changing despite the existence of the Fund. This was due to the absence of any sanction or force behind the regulations of the IMF.
- The objective of the fund was to bring about a system of **free convertibility of currencies**, but unfortunately this objective **could not be achieved** in actual practice. Excepting the US Dollar, no other currency is freely convertible into any other currency.
- **The Fund has developed conditionalities** over the last 5 decades or so which a country has to fulfil for getting a loan from the Fund. With these conditions the fund exercises surveillance over the exchange rates, monetary, fiscal and related policies of the borrowing countries which makes a mockery of its policy of non-interfering in their internal economic affairs.
- The Fund has been playing only a secondary role rather than the central role in international monetary relations. It does not provide facilities for short-term credit arrangements. This has resulted in "swap" arrangements among the central banks of the Group of Ten of the leading developed countries. It provides short-term credit to tide over temporary disequilibria in their balance of payments. Such swap arrangements have led to the growth of euro-currency market, and has thus reduced the importance of the Fund.

- As pointed above, the sudden and unexpected East-Asian crisis in Philippines, South Korea, Thailand, Indonesia, and Malaysia put a question mark on the working of the Fund.

Friedman has blamed the IMF for global crisis because it has been the result of government's intervention in the market, both internationally through loans, subsidies or taxes, and externally through the IMF. When the Bretton Woods System collapsed in 1971, the member countries adopted the floating exchange rate policy and the fund's role of regulating the exchange rate ended. Prior to the 1995 Mexican crisis, the aim of the fund was to provide advice, information and loans to its members. But when the fund helped Mexico in a bailout package in its crisis of 1995, it acted as international lender of the last resort. Under it, the fund laid emphasis on close financial relations among banks, corporations and governments and to increase the operations of stock and bond markets to generate greater competition between domestic and international financial institutions. This policy led to the Asian and global financial crisis when there was successive decline in shares, bonds and currencies of these countries. The real beneficiaries were not the borrowing nations but the foreign banks who lent to these countries. When due to declining exchange rates, they started withdrawing their funds; there was a crisis in the borrowing countries. Thus, the IMF has been weak in controlling financial crisis. Schwartz suggests that it should be shut down and according to Friedman; it should be abolished as it did more harm than good.

As with many debates about international economics, it is not clear which side has the winning hand about the appropriateness of IMF policies. There are cases where one can argue that IMF policies have counterproductive, or only had limited success. For example, one might question the success of the IMF's involvement in Turkey given that the country has had to implement some 18 IMF programmes since 1958.

However, the IMF can also point out to some of its noted accomplishments, including its success in containing the Asian crisis, which could have rocked the global international monetary system to its core. The supporters give credit to the IMF for its debt handling of politically difficult situations, such as the Mexican peso crisis, and for successfully promoting a free market philosophy.

With several years' intervention of the IMF, the economies of Asia and Mexico recovered. Definitely they all averted the kind of catastrophic explosion that might have occurred had the IMF not stepped in.

The IMF cannot force countries to adopt the policies required to correct economic mismanagement. While a government may commit to taking corrective action in return for an IMF loan, internal political problems may make it difficult for a government to act on that commitment. In such situations, the IMF is caught between a rock and a hard place, because if it decides to withhold money, it may trigger financial collapse and it is the situation that the IMF seeks to avoid.

Despite these criticisms, the IMF has shown sufficient flexibility to mould itself in keeping with the changing international economic conditions.

- The IMF's surveillance over its members' economic and financial policies must be strengthened so that the institution can provide more effective early warnings when economic trouble looms so that countries will have more incentives to heed those warnings before trouble actually hits.
- The IMF needs to ensure more effectively that its lending to help resolve financial crises restores countries' access to capital markets and supports a revival of economic growth.
- It must ensure that its policy advice and financial support for low-income countries are appropriately directed towards helping those countries, emerging from poverty.
- The reform of the IMF must address the equity and effectiveness of the way the institution is governed. As the economic importance and role of different nations and regions ebb and flow, and as their dependence on the IMF for financing and advice differs, so should their role and influence within the IMF if the institution is to retain its political credibility.

3.3 World Bank

3.3.1 Introduction

The World Bank is a United Nations international financial institution that grants loans to developing countries for capital programmes. The World Bank is a part of the World Bank Group, and a member of the United Nations Development Group.

The World Bank's official aim is to reduce poverty. According to its Articles of Agreement, all its decisions must be directed towards a commitment to the promotion of foreign investment and international trade and to the facilitation of capital investment.

3.3.2 Establishment

International Bank for Reconstruction and Development (IBRD) or the World Bank is a sister institution of the IMF. Both the institutions came into existence at the same time as a result of Bretton Woods Conference held in 1944.

There are some fundamental differences in the objectives and functions of IMF and the World Bank. The objective of IMF is to remove the short-term disequilibrium in the balance of payments of the member countries by lending to them foreign currencies out of its own stock. The objective of the World Bank is to eliminate the long-term disequilibrium in the balance of payments of member countries by advancing long-term loans to them for development purposes.

The objective of the Bank is the reconstruction and development of the economies of the member countries. It is one of the world's largest sources of development assistance. It has extended assistance to more than 100 developing economies. Thus, it brings finance and ideas to the developing economies to improve living standards and eliminate the worst forms of poverty.

For each of its client, the Bank works in co-operation with governmental agencies, non-governmental organisations and the private sector to formulate assistance strategies.

According to Prof. John H. Williams, the World Bank is even more important than IMF. In his view, there would be hardly any need for the Fund if the World Bank were to perform its functions well.

The World Bank consists of 5 closely associated institutions; each institution plays a distinct role in the objective to fight poverty and improve living standards for people in the developing world.

The term World Bank refers to two of the institutions, namely- The International Bank for Reconstruction and Development (IBRD) and The International Development Association (IDA). The other institutions are – The International Finance Corporation (IFC), The Multilateral Investment Guarantee Agency (MIGA) and The International Centre for Settlement of Investment Disputes (ICSID).

All the five institutions have specialised in different aspects of development but they use their comparative advantages to work together towards a common goal, i.e., poverty reduction.

3.3.3 Principles of the World Bank

The principles on which the Bank functions to fulfil their mission are as follows:
(a) Fight poverty with passion and professionalism for lasting results.
(b) Help people to help themselves and their environment by providing resources, building capacity, sharing knowledge and for partnerships in the public and private sectors.
(c) Be an excellent institution and is able to attract, excite and nurture diverse and committed staff with exceptional skills who know how to listen and learn.

The principles of the Bank are client centric, working in partnership, accountable for quality results, dedicated to financial integrity and cost-effectiveness, inspire and innovative.

3.3.4 Objectives of the World Bank

In the Articles of Agreement, following are the objectives of the World Bank:
(i) To help in the reconstruction and development of member countries by facilitating the investment of capital for the productive purposes including the restoration and reconstruction of the economies devastated by war.

(ii) To bring about an easy transition from a war economy to a peace-time economy.
(iii) To encourage the development of productive resources in developing countries by supplying them investment capital.
(iv) To promote private foreign investment by means of guarantee or participation in loans and other investments made by private investors and when private capital is not available on reasonable terms, to supplement private investment by providing, on suitable conditions, finance for productive purposes out of its own capital funds raised by it and other resources.
(v) To promote long-term balanced growth of international trade and the maintenance of equilibrium in the balance of payments of member countries by encouraging long-term international investments.
(vi) To help in raising productivity, the standard of living and the conditions of labour in member countries.

The loans made by the Bank – directly or through guarantees – are intended for certain specific projects of reconstruction and development in member countries. Thus, the advances of the World Bank to member countries mainly are to help them lay down the foundation of sound economic growth.

The main focus of the Bank is to help the poorest people and the poorest country, but for all its clients, the Bank lays emphasis on the need for –

(i) Investing in people, particularly through basic health and education.
(ii) Protecting the environment.
(iii) Focus on social development including governance and institution-building, that would serve as key elements of poverty reduction.
(iv) Strengthening the ability of the governments to deliver quality services, efficiently and transparently.
(v) Supporting and encouraging private sector development.
(vi) Promotion of reforms to create a stable macroeconomic environment and thus encourage investment and long-term planning.

To reduce poverty and improve living standards in the developing world, the World Bank supports a wide range of programmes through its loans, policy advice and technical assistance. Over the past generation, more progress has been made in reducing poverty and raising living standards than during any other period in the history of developing countries.

3.3.5 Functions of the World Bank

World Bank performs the following functions:
(i) Granting reconstruction loans to war devastated countries.
(ii) Granting developmental loans to underdeveloped countries.

(iii) Providing loans to governments for agriculture, irrigation, power, transport, water supply, education, health, etc.
(iv) Providing loans to private concerns for specified projects.
(v) Promoting foreign investment by guaranteeing loans provided by other organisations.
(vi) Providing technical, economic and monetary advice to member countries for specific projects.
(vii) Encouraging industrial development of underdeveloped countries by promoting economic reforms.

3.3.6 Policies of the World Bank in their Lending Operations

The Bank, in its lending operations is guided by certain policies which have been formed on the basis of the Articles of Agreement.

(i) The Bank should properly assess the repayment prospects of the loans. For this, it should consider the availability of natural resources and existing productive plant capacity to exploit the resources, and study the nations' past debt record.
(ii) The Bank expects the borrowing country to mobilise its domestic resources and the Bank lends only to enable a country to meet the foreign exchange content of any project cost.
(iii) The Bank does not expect the borrowing country to spend the loan in a particular country only. In fact, the Bank encourages the borrowers to procure machinery and goods for the 'Bank financed projects' in the cheapest possible market consistent with satisfactory performance.
(iv) The Bank indirectly attaches special importance to the promotion of local private business.
(v) It is the Bank's policy to maintain continuing relations with borrowers. This is done to check the progress of projects and keep in touch with the borrowing countries' financial and economic developments.
(vi) As a matter of general policy, the Bank concentrates on lending for projects which are designed to contribute directly to productive capacity, and normally does not finance projects which are mainly of social character, such as education, housing etc. Most Bank loans have been made for basic utilities, like power and transport, which are prerequisites for economic development. Further, the Bank also emphasises upon the management of the projects.

3.3.7 Different Lending Operations

Traditionally, the World Bank has financed all kinds of capital infrastructure such as roads and railways, telecommunications, and ports and power facilities. Its development strategy emphasises on investments that can directly affect the well-being of the masses of poor people of developing countries by integrating them as active partners in the developing process. Recently, the Bank has stepped up its lending for energy development. Bank's lending for power, form the largest part of the Bank's energy programme, but commitments for oil and gas developments have shown the greatest increases.

(i) Structural Adjustment Lending: This lending supports programme of specific policy changes and institutional reforms in developing countries designed to achieve a more efficient use of resources, and, thereby would:

(a) Contribute to a more sustainable balance of payments in the medium and long term and to the maintenance of growth in the face of severe constraints;

(b) Lay the basis for regaining momentum for future growth.

(ii) Special Action Programme (SAP): The SAP established for a two year period, was composed of financial measures, combined with policy advice, to help countries implement adjustment measures and high-priority projects needed to restore credit worthiness and growth. According to the Bank's report, the SAP has been highly successful in meeting its objectives.

(iii) B-Loan and Export Credit: In January 1983, the Executive Directors authorised the establishment of a new set of financing instruments to help the Bank's borrowers increase and stabilise flows of private capital on approved terms by linking part of commercial bank flows to IBRD operations.

These instruments, which comprise the B-Loan pilot programme, include 3 options:

(a) Direct Bank participation in the late maturities of a B-Loan;

(b) Bank guarantee of the late maturities, with the possibility of release from all or part of its share; and

(c) Bank acceptance of a contingent (emergency) obligation to finance an element of deferred principal at final maturity of a loan with level debt-service payments with floating-rate interest and variable amounts of principal repayment.

The Board approved the fourth option, which was the prearranged sale of participants in Bank loans arranged on commercial terms.

Examples of different lending operations:

- **Education: INDIA: [1.2 billion $]:** The district primary education programme was begun in the early 1909s to achieve universal primary education. It is the world's largest education programme reaching 60 million children.

- **Health: INDIA: [142 billion $]** Tuberculosis is the largest single cause of adult illness and death from communicable disease. In 1997, India introduced tuberculosis control project and it covered approximately 525 million people.

- **Health: Brazil: [163 million $]** AIDS cause early in 1990s. Some 175 non-governmental organisations carried out more than 400 grassroots campaigns reaching half million people.

- **Infrastructure: Bangladesh: [135 million $]:** People living in rural areas are not connected with proper roads. They were facing difficulty in developing trade and getting medical aid. The World Bank rural roads and markets improvements and maintenance project improved 50 km.
- **Environment: Sri Lanka:** It tried to reduce dependency on costly improved petroleum projects. World bank supported project has helped Sri Lanka in developing vibrate private industry involved in the production and delivery of renewable energy. It provided credit to individual entrepreneurs, NGOs and village cooperation.
- **Economic growth - Mozambique: [40 million $];** Mozambique was one of the poorest countries. World Bank helped through multilateral investment guarantee agency (MIGA) given guarantee to various investors and including Industrial Development Corporation (IDC).
- **Financial Services - Pakistan:** World Bank helped in establishment of Pakistan Poverty Alleviation Fund which provides micro-credits at concessional rate. It benefited **67500 borrowers.**
- **Debt Relief - 26 Countries:** IBRD and IMF have established debt relief programme called Heavily Indebted Poor Countries. It represents a commitment by the international committee to world together to reduce the debt of very poor countries.

3.3.8 Other Activities

The other activities of the IBRD include:

(i) Training: In 1956, the Bank set up a college, known as the Economic Development Institute (EDI) for training senior officials of the member developing countries. Its training material ranges from macro-economic planning, pricing, and development policies to the management of agricultural research, rural health care, industrial policy, energy policy, railway management etc.

(ii) Technical Assistance: Technical assistance has been an integral part of the Bank operation since its inception. It consists of two broad categories:

(a) Engineering-related, such as feasibility studies, engineering design, and construction supervision,

(b) Institution-related, such as institutional studies, management support and training.

Technical assistance include funds for supervision, implementation and engineering services, energy, power, transportation, water supply, industry, etc. It provides such technical assistance as short-term training, appointment of advisors for technology service on evaluation and monitoring panels, economic advice on project preparation.

(iii) Inter-Organisational Cooperation: The IBRD is also engaged in inter-organisational cooperation, that is, cooperation between the IBRD and other international organisations. For example, between IBRD and the UNESCO, the WHO, the GATT, the UNCTAD, the United Nations Environment Programmes, the ILO, the Asian Development Bank, etc.

(iv) Economic and Social Research: The Bank devotes roughly 3% of its administrative budget to economic and social research. Research activities are undertaken by the Bank's own research staff and also in collaboration with outside researchers. The results of completed research projects appear in articles in international economic journals, books, in World Bank Staff Working Papers, and its own journal, *Finance and Development*. The Bank also helps strengthen indigenous research capacity in member developing countries.

(v) Operations Evaluation: The Bank helps borrowers in the post-evaluation of their Bank assisted projects. It has set up the Operations Evaluation Department for this purpose. Projects reviewed are also subject to performance audit by this Department's staff.

(vi) Settlement of Investment Disputes: The Bank has set up the International Centre of Settlement of Investment Disputes (ICSID) between States and Nationals of other states. The Bank has successfully mediated in solving many international investment disputes such as the River Water Dispute between the India and Pakistan, and of the Suez Canal between Egypt and the UK.

To conclude, the Bank's overall performance must be judged not only by its lending operations but on its success in providing advice and technical assistance.

3.3.9 Critical Evaluation

The World Bank (IBRD) has been quite successful in achieving its principal goal of reconstruction and development. It helped in the reconstruction of Europe after its destruction in the Second World War. In the process of growth, it has been helping the developed and developing countries alike. It has been lending not only for infrastructural investment but also for raising the productivity and living standards of the poor people. Despite its positive role, certain criticisms are levelled against it. The quantity and composition of World Bank lending is clearly inadequate for the challenges it faces in developing countries.

(i) Interest Rate is High: It is criticised that the bank charges a very high rate of interest on loans, and also an annual commitment charge on undistributed balances and a front-end fee. Though a new procedure related to the cost of borrowing for calculating the interest rate and front-end fee has been adopted by the Bank, but still the interest rate continues to be high. Only a small portion of the total World Bank assistance is in the form of 'soft loans' (IDA credits). The major part of the World Bank lending to many developing countries like India is on commercial terms. This is one of the reasons for the increase in their debt-service problem. The IBRD lending rates now 'float' in line with the world market rates. This is a major shift from the Bank's original role of cushioning developing countries against fluctuations in market interest rates.

(ii) Share of Developing Countries in Bank's Capital is Inadequate: It has been argued that the Bank has failed to meet the financial needs of the developing nations fully. Its loans have hardly touched the fringes of the total capital requirements of developing countries economic and social uplift. Further, the Bank has not been successful in raising the productivity and living standards of the people in such countries. The poorest countries hardly receive 3.5% of the total loans.

(iii) Discriminatory Treatment: In its day-to-day functioning, the World Bank has been discriminating against the countries of Asia and Africa. As against this, the Bank has been quite indulgent to the countries of Western Europe. The countries of Asia and Africa, together, have the largest population, vast areas and unexploited resources, yet much larger amounts of loans have been received by the Western Europe with small population and not Asia and Africa. This is clearly indefensible. The loans to the member countries should be given strictly on merit and economic consideration.

(iv) Loans for Specific Projects Only: It is argued that the World Bank extends loans only for specific projects, not for the general development of these countries. Further, these countries need *untied* loans which they can use according to their plans of priority.

(v) Repayment in Foreign Currencies: Another objection is that the Bank insists upon receiving the repayment of the loan from the borrowing country in the currency in which it was extended to it. The developing countries find it difficult to comply with such conditions of the Bank.

(vi) Loans for Agriculture and Allied Occupations: World Bank extend loans to developing countries mostly for agriculture and other related occupations, not for heavy and basic industries. The loans extended to India, for example, were almost wholly for such activities as agriculture, irrigation, power and mining.

(vii) Partiality for Private Sector: The World Bank in its lending operations, has shown a clear bias in favour of the private sector. The President of the World Bank, A. W. Clausen, in his first address clearly said that the Bank would place greater emphasis on partnership with the private sector and incentives to private enterprises.

(viii) No Respect for the Sovereignty of Aided Nations: Another argument against the World Bank is that it often interferes with the sovereignty and decision-making process of the borrowing countries of the Third World. It often imposes policies and programmes on these governments much against their wishes – policies and programmes which are not politically and administratively convenient for them.

(ix) Size of the Fund: The availability of the funds depends on, inter alia, the willingness of the developed countries to contribute. It is pointed out that the US which is the largest contributor, is not only reluctant to increase its own contribution, but also reluctant to let other countries like Japan to do so since its own voting power would be correspondingly reduced. In other words, the quantity and composition of World Bank lending is clearly inadequate for the challenges it faces in developing countries.

The Bank may not have come up to the expectations of the developing countries. But, in evaluating its role, we should not ignore the limitations within which it has been functioning all these years. The Bank has certainly been instrumental in accelerating the pace of economic development in different countries of the world. If the capital resources of the Bank are made adequate, it will be in a much better and stronger position to render financial aid to the developing countries of the world.

Suggestions to make the IMF-World Bank more effective, especially for the developing countries:

(i) The contribution by the developed countries is the major source of funds for these institutions. Hence, dismantling the dominance of the developed countries in the management of these institutions is difficult. Only a change in the attitude of the developed nations can help achieve a smooth transformation.

(ii) The IMF should evolve into a World Central Bank.

(iii) There should be a substantial review of the SDRs and these additional SDRs should be allocated completely to the developing countries. An alternative to this would be to allow countries below a certain per capita income to have a larger reserve tranche at the IMF.

(iv) The developing countries taking World Bank loans have now to fall into one of the two groups:

(a) Country developed enough to afford the stiff terms demanded by the IBRD, or

(b) Poor enough to qualify for concessionary funds from the IDA.

Hence, it is suggested to create a new loan window – an Intermediate Assistance Facility (IAF) which could help countries ready to graduate from the extremely concessional IDA terms but not yet sufficiently strong to meet the tough terms of IBRD – such as India and Pakistan. This would enable the World Bank to focus its IDA resources on the long terms development of the least developed nations and the IBRD funds on the most creditworthy of the newly industrialising countries.

(v) The Bretton Woods Institutions have often focused more on the means of development i.e. GNP growth but have excluded human beings from their calculations. Thus, the suggestion is to refocus their work on human development if constructive contribution is to be done.

As Stiglitz points out, *"development is about transforming societies, improving the lives of the poor, enabling everyone to have a chance at success and access to health care and education. This sort of development won't happen if only a few people dictate the policies a country must follow. It also means that there must be broad participation that goes well beyond the experts and politicians. Developing countries must take charge of their own futures. But we in the West cannot escape our responsibilities."*

3.3.10 The World Bank and India

India, one of the founder members of the IBRD and IMF. It is one of the largest beneficiaries of the IBRD-IDA assistance. The Bank has been assisting India in its planned economic development by granting loans, conducting field surveys, rendering expert advice, sending missions, study teams, and training Indian personnel at the EDI. The World Bank has been assisting India in such projects as development of ports, oil exploration including the Bombay High and gas power projects, aircrafts, coal, iron, aluminium, railway modernisation, technical assistance etc.

Until China became a member of the World Bank in 1980, India was the largest beneficiary of the World Bank assistance. Now, there are a larger number of beneficiaries than India.

In 1997, the total World Bank assistance to India amounted about 5% of the total Bank assistance.

Over the years, the roles of the World Bank and the IDA almost reversed as regards its assistance to India. In 1974-75, of the total IBRD-IDA assistance to India, IDA accounted to $3/4^{th}$ and the World Bank for $1/4^{th}$. But in 1998, the World Bank accounted for nearly $2/3^{rd}$ and IDA about $1/3^{rd}$ of the total aid. This decrease in the share of soft loan naturally increases India's debt burden.

India's share in the IDA's global credit has declined over the years. Until 1979-80, IDA's assistance to India accounted for, on an average, about 40% of its total aid. Thereafter there was decline in this share.

Apart from the financial crunch to India, China's entry into the World Bank has seriously affected the fund flow to India. Although the World Bank aid to India is very large in absolute terms, yet the per capita aid has been low. India, with about a third of the world's poor needs a substantial increase in the concessional finance to accelerate the programmes of poverty alleviation and economic development.

3.4 UNCTAD

3.4.1 Introduction

Established in 1964 as a permanent intergovernmental body, the United Nations Conference on Trade and Development (UNCTAD) (French Conférence des Nationsunies sur le Commerce et le Développement (CNUCED)) came into force.

UNCTAD deals with trade, investment, and development issues and is the principle organ of the United Nations General Assembly. The organisation's goals are to: "*maximise the trade, investment and development opportunities of developing countries and assist them in their efforts to integrate into the world economy on an equitable basis.*"

The conference ordinarily meets once in four years; the permanent secretariat is in Geneva.

The conference ordinarily meets once in four years; the permanent secretariat is in Geneva. Formulating policies relating to all aspects of development which includes trade, aid, transport, finance and technology is the main goal of UNCTAD. To conceive and implement the Generalised System of Preferences (GSP) is one of the principal achievements of UNCTAD. Special tariff concessions to such exports are necessary to offer so as to promote exports of manufactured goods from developing countries, is often discussed in UNCTAD. Keeping this in mind, the developed countries formulated the GSP scheme under which manufacturers' exports and some agricultural goods from the developing countries enter duty-free or at reduced rates in the developed countries. Imports of the same items from developing countries would enjoy a competitive advantage, since imports of such items from other developed countries are subject to the normal rates of duties.

UNCTAD came into force in 1964 to resolve the concerns of the developing countries over the international market, great disparity between developed nations and developing nations and multi-national corporations. It was established so as to provide a forum where developing countries could talk about their worries relating to the economic development. The organisation grew from the view that existing institutions like GATT (now replaced by the World Trade Organisation, WTO), the International Monetary Fund (IMF), and World Bank were not properly organised to handle the particular problems of developing countries.

3.4.2 Objectives of UNCTAD

The objectives of UNCTAD are:

(a) To eliminate the trade gap between the developing and developed countries and also to reduce the gap, and
(b) To fasten the rate of economic growth of the developing world.

3.4.3 Functions

The main functions of the UNCTAD are:

(i) To promote international trade between developed and developing countries with a view to accelerate economic development.
(ii) To negotiate trade agreements.
(iii) To formulate principles and policies on international trade and related problems of economic development.
(iv) To make proposals for putting its principles and policies into effect.
(v) To function as a centre for a harmonious trade and related documents in development policies of governments.
(vi) To review and facilitate the coordination of activities of the other U.N. institutions in the field of international trade.

3.4.4 Activities

The important activities of UNCTAD include:

(a) Technical elaboration of new trade schemes;

(b) Research and support of negotiations for commodity agreements; and

(c) Various promotional activities designed to help developing countries in the areas of trade and capital flows.

3.5 Agreement on Textiles and Clothing (ATC)

3.5.1 Introduction

ATC is essentially designed to correct a long standing inconsistency in the multilateral trading system. International trade in textiles and clothing had been excluded from the normal rules and disciplines of the GATT from 1961 onwards. The system was first incorporated in a so-called Short-Term Cotton Arrangement ("STA"), followed by a Long-Term Arrangement ("LTA") and, later, by the Multi-Fibre Arrangement ("MFA"). The MFA continued until the WTO Agreements came into effect on 1 January 1995.

While GATT rules prohibited the use of quantitative restrictions to provide protection to domestic industries, the system allowed the use of such restrictions. To be the Most Favoured Nation (MFN) of the GATT, it required that equal treatment be given to all countries and the system permitted the burden of the restrictions against imports from such countries. An obvious departure from the basic principles of the multilateral trading system constituted a major distortion in international trade, more so as restrictions were applied mainly on imports from developing economies. It also meant an obstacle to the normal development of trade.

The removal of such distortions and the further liberalisation of trade was the principle aim of the Uruguay round. It was hence agreed that negotiations should be undertaken to bring about the reintegration of the textiles and clothing sector into the same mainstream of multilateral rules as for any other industrial sector.

3.5.2 Purpose of ATC

The main objective of the ATC was to integrate the textile and clothing sector into the normal disciplines and rules of the GATT. "Integration" *is the act of unifying or ending the difference in treatment.* Hence, it implies the elimination of those practices from the sector which did not conform to the normal rules of the GATT.

In order to determine the practices which did not conform to the rules of the GATT, and which therefore constitute the context of the ATC, reference to Paragraph 2 of the Preamble to the ATC recalling the April 1989 Decision of the Trade Negotiations Committee can be helpful. That Decision specified that integration of the sector will cover the phase-out of restrictions under the Multi-fibre Arrangement and other restrictions on textiles and clothing not consistent with GATT rules and disciplines. The decision stipulated that:

(a) Substantive negotiations will begin in April 1989 in order to reach agreement within the time-frame of the Uruguay Round on modalities for the integration of this sector into GATT, in accordance with the negotiating objective;

(b) Such modalities for the process of integration into GATT on the basis of strengthened GATT rules and disciplines should inter alia cover the phasing out of restrictions under the Multi-fibre Arrangement and other restrictions on textiles and clothing not consistent with GATT rules and disciplines, the time-span for such process of integration, and the progressive character of this process which should commence following the conclusion of the negotiations...

Thus the context of the ATC demonstrates that the object and purpose of "integration" is the phase-out of restrictions on textile and clothing products that were maintained under the Multi-fibre Arrangement and any other restrictions that were not consistent with GATT rules and disciplines. Although the April 1989 Decision of the Trade Negotiations Committee also referred to "other restrictions not consistent with GATT rules and disciplines" in addition to restrictions under the multi-fibre agreement, such other restrictions were actually rather rare. Therefore the main purpose of the ATC is the phasing out of restrictions applied under the MFA. These restrictions were applied by major developed countries, almost exclusively, on imports from developing countries and economies.

3.5.3 Main Provisions of ATC

The main objective of the ATC was to bring an end to the system of restrictions that were being applied by developed countries on textile and clothing imports from the developing countries as these restrictions moved away from some of the principles of GATT.

A framework was laid out where this objective would be achieved in a gradual and systematic manner in a period of 10 years. The principal elements of the framework are explained below.

1. Product Coverage

The ATC put forward a list of products to which it applies. The list is based on the Harmonised Commodity Description and Coding System Nomenclature (the so-called HS), and defines particular products at the six-digit level of the HS.

In general, the products covered are those in Section XI (Textiles and Textile Articles) of the HS, excluding however natural fibres such as raw cotton, jute, silk, etc. In addition, the list includes products from outside Section XI defined under some HS lines or part lines. In all, the list consists of 781 full lines at the 6-digit level of the HS, and another 14 lines of which only certain portions are covered by the ATC. This extensive product coverage that has been at the root of concerns about the so-called "back-loading" of the integration process.

2. The Integration Process and its Mechanics

The second, and the central element of the ATC framework relates to its integration process. Pursuant to this, each importing Member is required to notify and integrate products from the list covered by the Agreement, in accordance with the following schedule 2:

- **As of 1 January 1995:** Products that accounted for at least 16 per cent of the Member's imports in 1990, in volume terms.
- **As of 1 January 1998:** Another at least 17 per cent.
- **As of 1 January 2002:** A further at least 18 per cent.
- **As of 1 January 2005:** All remaining products.

Article 9 of the ATC provides:

This Agreement and all restrictions under there shall stand terminated on the first day of the 121st month that the WTO Agreement is in effect, on which date the textiles and clothing sector shall be fully integrated into GATT 1994.

There shall be no extension of this Agreement.

Once a particular product is integrated, all quota restrictions on its imports from WTO Members are terminated. Integration also means that the importing country is henceforth bound to observe full GATT rules and disciplines with respect to that product.

The Agreement left the actual choice of products for integration in the first three steps (i.e., from January 1995, 1998 and 2002 respectively) at the discretion of the importing Member concerned, the only condition being that the list at each stage should include a mix of products from all four subsectors, (i.e., tops and yarns, fabrics, made-up textile products, and clothing).

In actual implementation, the importing restraining countries took full advantage of this discretion and the extensive product coverage as follows:

(i) First, the list of products covered by the Agreement included a significant number in which trade was never restricted under the MFA. According to estimates, in the case of the EU, such non-restrained products accounted for some 42 per cent of total imports. In the case of the United States, the comparable figure was about 40 per cent. The percentage for Canada was even higher.

All these countries chose to include the un-restrained products in their integration schedules notified for the first three steps. Consequently, they avoided integrating products in which trade was actually restrained.

(ii) Second, since they had discretion on the choice of products, they also elected to first take up mostly tops and yarns, fabrics or made-up textile products, with as little as possible from clothing items in which developing countries have the most comparative advantage due to the labour intensive nature of the processes required in their manufacture and, on which quota restrictions have been most pronounced.

Thus, while the obligation in terms of fulfilling the mechanics of integrating the required minimum percentages might have been met, the same cannot perhaps be said of the realisation of the object and purpose of the Agreement. This is why widespread concerns have been voiced about the process of implementation, in so far as the realisation of the central objective of the ATC is concerned.

3. Increases in Quota Growth Rates

We now talk about the quota growth rates. Under this element, the Agreement stipulated that, until the relevant products are integrated, the levels of quota restrictions on those products should be increased according to the following formulae:

As of 1 January 1995: All annual quota growth rates, which existed in respective bilateral agreements prior to the ATC, be increased by a factor of at least 16 per cent.

Thus an annual growth rate of 6 per cent should be increased to 6.96 per cent; 5 per cent to 5.80 per cent; 4 per cent to 4.64 per cent; 3 per cent to 3.48 per cent; 2 per cent to 2.32 per cent; 1 per cent to 1.16 per cent.

As of 1 January 1998: The annual growth rates resulting from the above formula should be increased further by at least 25 per cent.

As of 1 January 2002: The rates resulting from the above (i.e. 1998) should be increased by at least another 27 per cent.

In actual practice, under MFA bilateral agreements, there existed a wide range of growth rates, the average being between 3 per cent and 5 per cent. They also varied in each of the three restraining countries. Consequently, quota levels have increased from their pre-ATC levels. However, the average overall increase in access (particularly for the main traded products) has not been significant enough to eliminate the restrictive effect of quotas.

4. Transitional Safeguard

The fourth part of the ATC takes into consideration the transition period necessary to apply a specific transitional safeguard mechanism. Article 6 of the Agreement lays down the procedures and conditions under which an importing member can introduce new restrictions on imports of particular products.

Article 6 points out that the transitional safeguard should be used as carefully as possible, and should be constant with the provisions of the Article and with the effective implementation of the process of integration.

Members recognise that during the transition period it may be necessary to apply a specific transitional safeguard mechanism (referred to in this Agreement as "transitional safeguard"). The transitional safeguard may be applied by any Member to products covered by the Annex, except those [products] integrated into GATT 1994 under the provisions of Article 2...

Even in cases where the importing and exporting countries concerned agree that the situation called for the establishment of a restraint, the TMB is required to determine whether the restraint is justified in accordance with the provisions of Article 6. Any transitional safeguard actions that are made must be reviewed by the Textile Monitoring Body (TMB).

5. Supervision of Implementation

The ATC did not feel the need to foresee a Committee to review and consult on the implementation of the agreement on a regular basis, unlike the other agreements negotiated in the Uruguay Round. It instead created a body known as the Textile Monitoring Body (TMB) to supervise the implementation of the ATC and most importantly examine all measures taken under the ATC and their conformity with its provisions on a regular basis.

In order to oversee the implementation of this Agreement, the Council for Trade in Goods shall conduct a major review before the end of each stage of the integration process. To assist in this review, the TMB shall, at least five months before the end of each stage, transmit to the Council for Trade in Goods a comprehensive report on the implementation of this Agreement during the stage under review, in particular in matters with regard to the integration process, the application of transitional safeguard mechanism, [etc.,]... The TMB's comprehensive report may include any recommendation as deemed appropriate by the TMB to the Council for Trade in Goods.

In the light of its review, the Council for Trade in Goods shall by consensus take such decisions as it deems appropriate to ensure that the balance of rights and obligations embodied in this Agreement is not being impaired.

6. Other Miscellaneous Provisions

The Agreement also contains provisions for preferential treatment in access for small suppliers, for the administration of restrictions, and for the prevention of circumvention of the Agreement. Members should also take such actions as may be necessary to stand by the GATT rules and disciplines, in order to achieve access to the markets and to make sure the application of policies following the fair and equitable trading conditions, subsidies and countervailing measures and the protection of intellectual property rights.

3.6 Generalised System of Preferences (GSP)

The Generalised System of Preferences (GSP) is a scheme designed by the UNCTAD to encourage exports of developing countries to developed countries. The scheme states that the developed countries must grant duty concession on imports of specified manufacturers and semi manufacturers from the developing countries.

In the year 1968, in New Delhi, a resolution was adopted at the UNCTAD-II, that introduced GSP, which is the result of the realisation that temporary advantages in the form of generalised arrangements for special tariff treatment for developing countries in the market of developed countries may assist developing countries to increase their export earnings and so contribute to an acceleration in the areas of their economic growth.

Many countries such as USA, Japan, Norway, New Zealand, Finland, Sweden, Hungary, Switzerland, Australia, Canada, Australia, Bulgaria, and Poland including the EEC countries have introduced the GSP.

The GSP is applicable only for a period of 10 years from its institutions by the preference granting countries and it is subject to certain strict limitations. The GSP is available only to developing countries.

Each scheme has a safeguard clause or an escape clause to protect the sensitive sectors in its economy. Keeping in view its local production base and certain other factors, the preferential rates of duty allowed on the import of manufacturers and semi manufacturers and processed agricultural products differ in schemes in different developed countries as each country has brought out its own GSP.

The following conditions need to be satisfied in order for an item to be qualified:

1. The GSP list must include the product;
2. Under the GSP, the country which exports the items should be declared as a beneficiary country;
3. The value added requirements/process criteria must be complied with;
4. From a GSP beneficiary country to the GSP donor country, a product should be imported;
5. A certificate of origin in form 'A' duly filled in and duly signed by the exporter and it must be sent to the buyer/importer and should be duly certified by a designated Government authority;
6. If the import of the GSP item in question is subject to a quota/ceiling, the quota/ceiling of the import from the GSP beneficiary countries has so far not been exhausted in EEC countries. This is known as the competitive need clause.

3.7 Global System of Trade Preferences (GSTP)

Among the developing countries, expansion of trade is viewed as an important feature of economic cooperation among developing countries (ECDC).

Though since 1968, the UNCTAD authorised a scheme of trade preference, it was not until 1979 that the group came up with an action plan for collective self reliance . However it took an additional three years for the group to adopt a programme of Global System of Trade Preferences (GSTP).

In July 1985, a group of 77 countries held a conference in New Delhi where they resolved to complete the first round of negotiations by May 1, 1987 on GSTP. The agreement reached at the Conference included:

- across the board tariff preference margin of 10 per cent
- the removal of reduction of non tariff barriers

- selection of specific sectors and products where trade preferences could be extended
- trade creating production sharing and marketing arrangements.

The delay in coming with a good GSTP, shows the lack of unity, which was missing from the developing countries. The Generalised System of Preferences (GSP), designed by the major industrialised countries to give tariff concessions in favour of developing countries to facilitate easier access for the latter's exports to the former, particularly of manufacturers and semi-manufactures, came into being much faster than the GSTP. These countries form an extremely heterogeneous lot with great diversities in levels of development and industrialisation trade regimes and in the least of all, approaches to development. Though the GSTP may be effective, it can only be one way of promoting out South-South financial and monetary cooperation, new payment arrangements and joint ventures in production and marketing. Due to these factors developing countries have made very little progress in the past decade. They should show a unity of purpose and sense of urgency and only then will the South-South trade prosper.

3.8 International Commodity Trading and Agreements

3.8.1 Introduction

International Commodity Agreements (ICA's) are essentially multilateral instrumentalities of governmental control that support the international price of individual primary commodities, especially through such arrangements as export quotas or assured access to markets. Commodity study groups should be differentiated from international commodity agreements, as the international commodity agreements lack in operation responsibility; from international cartels of a nongovernmental character; and from the Combined Food Board (1942–1945) or the International Materials Conference (1951–1953).

The definition also did not include the following points:

(1) Bilateral bulk-purchase agreements;
(2) Plans for a commodity reserve currency;
(3) Measures for the reduction of tariffs or nontariff restrictions against the international movement of goods or services;
(4) Multilateral control arrangements governing the market outlets for manufactured products, such as the International Cotton Textile Agreement negotiated in 1961;
(5) Proposals for international food reserves;
(6) Arrangements for sectoral integration, in the pattern of the European Coal and Steel Community or the Common Agricultural Policy of the European Economic Community.

The most important agreement of the 1920s was the Stevenson Rubber Scheme, implemented by the British and Dutch governments on behalf of their respective colonial territories in Malaya and the Netherlands East Indies.

Agreements for wheat, sugar, tin, coffee, and olive oil have been successfully negotiated since the end of World War II. The International Wheat Agreements (IWA) of 1949 and 1953, and the postwar International Sugar Agreements (ISA) are examples of two forms of commodity agreements. Floor and ceiling prices were established for sugar and enforced essentially by regulating the permissible exports of member countries; the sugar agreement stated that the stocks with the exporter should not exceed or fall short of the percentages of export quotas stated. For wheat, a different approach was taken where importers agreed to accept stated quantities if the price fell to a minimum level and the exporters agreed to provide the stated quantities whenever the price was at the contract ceiling.

The wheat agreement was to be essentially inoperative, at the prices which were between the floor and ceiling.

In The Tin Agreement, a buffer-stock agency:

(a) had to purchase,

(b) might purchase,

(c) could not purchase or sell without specific authorisation,

(d) might sell,

(e) was required to sell.

The agreement also provided for imposition of export controls after buffer accumulations exceeded specified amounts.

The USA avoided agreements on industrial raw materials which fluctuated in demand and only very recently has participated in which it was the predominately the producer. In the case of sugar (of which the United States remains a net importer), it has acted more in a producer than in a consumer capacity; too large a differential between domestic prices and those prevailing abroad would embarrass the continuation of the domestic sugar-control system.

3.8.2 Prerequisites for Negotiation

The following points are the prerequisites which are to be met if an international commodity conference to form into an agreement:

(1) **Inelastic Demand:** Supporting the market price of any individual commodity is certain to have immediately and sharply adverse effects if substitutes are available. The existence of synthetic rubber explains the complete lack of any postwar agreement for the natural product; restrictive agreements for individual oilseeds are ruled out by the existence of a considerable list of alternative seeds, as well as by competition from butter; but sugar has lent itself to a continuous succession of agreements since 1937.

(2) **Distress Price Levels:** As is best illustrated by the breakdown in negotiations for a revised sugar agreement in 1951 and for a cocoa agreement in 1963, exporting countries are not prepared to accept the necessary compromises unless prevailing prices are extremely low.

(3) **Reasonably Stable Market Shares:** Since export quotas generally divide up markets proportionately to the national shares prevailing in some base period, difficulties arise whenever there are either abrupt or longer-term shifts in the proportions contributed by various producing countries.

(4) **Mixed Producer–consumer Interest:** The longest-lived agreements currently in effect involve commodities concerning which the major industrial countries have rather mixed motives. Hence UK is interested in the low prices of sugar as an importing country; but the United Kingdom does not wish world sugar prices to fall to disastrous levels. The new agreement for coffee reflects some mutuality of producer and consumer interest within the major importing countries: no domestic sources of supply exist, but the temperate zone industrial nations are broadly concerned for the well-being of less developed countries in tropical regions of Latin America and Africa, which supply most of the world's coffee exports.

3.8.3 Obsolete Principles Versus Realities

To benefit the consumer, especially, in the chapter of the Havana Charter dealing with intergovernmental commodity-control agreements were provisions purporting by:

(a) equal representation for importing and exporting countries;

(b) participation by all countries "substantially interested" in the particular commodity;

(c) the check reins of publicity in the form of an annual report;

(d) the assurance of increasing market outlets for supplies originating in the regions of most efficient production.

A huge gap separates the principles underlying these provisions from the actual realities of the agreements which were negotiated in the post war period. The U.S.S.R. still votes as an exporting country, in the the International Sugar Agreement and the International Wheat Agreement, even though it is known as an heavy duty importer of both commodities. USA in the present age, imposes a ceiling on international tin prices by regulating the rate at which tin disposals are made out of that nation's strategic stockpiles, even though not a member of the ITA. Membership of a host of nations in present-day international commodity agreements may merely complicate the processes of administration and decision making, while in at least one instance—the decision of the United Kingdom *not to affiliate* with the IWA of 1953— the absence of a major wheat-importing country may have had a salutary effect in moderating the exercise of oligopolistic power.

The Organisation of Petroleum Exporting Countries (OPEC), which was established in 1960, violates the Havana Charter provisions requiring consumer representation. It follows a process of collective bargaining not with the importing countries but with the marketing and producing companies which are controlled by the advanced industrial countries namely the UK, USA, the Netherlands and France. An internal system of prorationing in the United States, on behalf of domestic producing groups, has already and inevitably given rise to a system of import controls, and a strong case can be made for having import quotas enforced by a multilateral, rather than a unilateral, instrumentality. Though Germany, Italy, and Japan are major consumers and importers of petrol, they have very little direct control over petroleum supplies. The petroleum-exporting countries include relatively wealthy members of the less developed world, while poorer members are heavily dependent on petroleum imports, also argues for a degree of restraint in the exercise of bargaining power by the OPEC.

3.8.4 Economic Effects

The international commodity agreements suffer from various limitations that characterise all efforts to support artificially the market position of individual commodities. Price targets which tend to be set too high often tend to be underestimated and the cost structures tend to be built up so that any set back to the producer is just passing by. For the agreements to last, it is not necessarily a virtue and in the case of sugar has been achieved only by making inoperative the key provisions governing export quotas during periods (especially of high prices) when agreement on market shares has proved impossible.

It has been argued that stabilisation of the price paid for only a portion of world export sales tends, broadly, to destabilise the price of the remainder. An important consideration is the inelasticity of demand in the stabilised portion of the market relative to that in the destabilised sector. Thus, the assurance of adequate supplies of sugar to the United States and of wheat to the United Kingdom, under successive international agreements or national control programmes, has tended, on balance, to be stabilising.

It is generally true that prices in national markets tend to fluctuate less widely than those of commodities sold without protection in residual "free" markets, it by no means follows that free market prices as a group are necessarily less stable than prices of primary commodities subject to world market conditions. While sterling-area producers are dominant exporters of all three, and the foreign-exchange reserves of the sterling area accordingly tend to fluctuate in keeping with their current market strength or weakness, none has been governed by an agreement in the postwar period. The fact moreover that the price swings which are experienced by these commodities have been reversible has led the major exporting countries to introduce various devices, that do have the effect of "stabilising" producer income from year to year. This approach represents an adjustment toward living with instability.

Controls over the market price of individual commodities have undesirable side effects, politically as well as economically. The severity of export quotas imposed under the tin agreement appears to have a long-term effect on productive capacity; when export restrictions on tin were relaxed, output failed to revive in step with a strong recovery in consumption, and, accordingly, this commodity provides a classic example of the irreversible supply curve.

3.8.5 Current Pressures Favouring Agreements

The number of international commodity agreement has been tending to multiply and there are some good reasons for this trend to continue. The USA for one has moved from opposing these agreements to one where it is being accepted. These agreements though, tend be favoured more by the less developed countries so as to raise their foreign exchange which is earned by the major exports. The French authorities have supported the international market sharing arrangements in Europe. The German Federal Republic, as the major importer of agricultural commodities within the European Economic Community, favours agreements as instrumentalities for maintaining a place for overseas suppliers within the Common Market. The United Kingdom, which has until recently relied on a policy of cheap food imports together with a programme of direct payments to its domestic agricultural producers, has begun to develop a series of agreements with major overseas suppliers of grain and meat. International commodity agreements have considerable appeal to all external suppliers favourably impressed with the short-term advantages, and prepared to overlook the longer-run disadvantages, of having market outlets assured on a quota basis.

3.8.6 Alternatives

Other alternatives have been introduced other than the international commodity agreements for transferring of purchasing power to less developed countries who barely have any earnings. Some of these alternatives such as proposals for a commodity-reserve currency, serves as the ends of foreign aid and international monetary "reform" at the expense of undermining the role of the price system as the major instrument of economic management in free-enterprise societies. Others have the major advantage of leaving the price system largely unaffected as the allocator of economic resources. Finally, the International Monetary Fund has made available for compensating shortfalls in export proceeds of less developed countries, when those shortfalls arise for reasons not within the control of the country experiencing the balance-of-payments difficulties. Such an approach has the important virtue of taking into account fluctuations in export volume rather than responding exclusively to variations in commodity prices.

Points to Remember

- During the closing years of the Second World War, an international monetary conference was held at Bretton Woods in the USA. This conference was held in 1944, to prepare a plan to root out the economic causes leading to the outbreak of the war. This plan is known as the Bretton Woods Plan.
- **The Bretton Woods Plan** was divided into two parts: the establishment of the International Monetary Fund (IMF) and the setting up of the International Bank for Reconstruction and Development (IBRD), i.e., the World Bank.
- The main **objectives of IMF** are to alleviate the problems of international liquidity (to help the member countries meet their balance of payment deficits), and to achieve international monetary and macroeconomic stability.
- **WTO** is a more powerful and effective organisation than GATT. It has a more effective dispute settlement mechanism.
- Similar to GATT, under WTO too developing countries, particularly least developed countries are accorded a number of concessions and favours. They are allowed longer period to fulfil the liberalisation commitments.
- WTO calls upon the developed countries to grant special preferences to imports from developing nations.
- **World Bank – IBRD** – was established to help the reconstruction and development of various national economies by providing long-term capital assistance.
- World Bank is one of the world's largest sources of development assistance.
- At the beginning of May 2008, the IBRD had 185 countries as members.
- India, one of the founder members of IBRD and IMF, is one of the largest beneficiaries of the IBRD-IDA assistance.
- **UNCTAD** is the principal organ of the United Nations General Assembly dealing with trade, investment, and development issues. The organisation's goals are to: "maximise the trade, investment and development opportunities of developing countries and assist them in their efforts to integrate into the world economy on an equitable basis."
- ATC is essentially designed to correct a long standing anomaly in the multilateral trading system.
- **The Generalised System of Preferences (GSP)** is a scheme designed by the UNCTAD to encourage exports of developing countries to developed countries. Under this scheme, developed countries grant duty concession on imports of specified manufacturers and semi- manufacturers from developing countries.

- **International Commodity Agreements (ICA's)** are essentially multilateral instrumentalities of governmental control that support the international price of individual primary commodities, especially through such arrangements as export quotas or assured access to markets.

Questions for Discussion

1. Explain the objectives and functions of the World Bank.
2. Give the background against which the IMF was established.
3. What were the main objectives of IMF?
4. Explain the objectives and functions of IMF.
5. Give the difference between GATT and WTO.
6. Explain the objectives and functions of WTO.
7. Discuss the objectives and functions of UNCTAD.
8. What are the provisions in Agreement on Textile and Clothing (ATC)?

Multiple Choice Questions

1. _____ was replaced by the _____ on 1st January 1995.
   - (a) GATS, WTO
   - (b) WTO, GATT
   - (c) GATT, WTO
   - (d) IMF, GATT

2. Globalisation refers to :
   - (a) Lower incomes worldwide
   - (b) Less foreign trade and investment
   - (c) Global warming and their effects
   - (d) A more integrated and interdependent world

3. _____ is only a legal agreement and it is not an institution but _____ is a permanent institution.
   - (a) GATT, WTO
   - (b) WTO, GATT
   - (c) WTO, IMF
   - (d) IMF, GATT

4. The WTO was established to implement the final act of Uruguay Round agreement of _____
   - (a) MFA
   - (b) GATT
   - (c) IMF
   - (d) UNO

5. WTO stands for :
   (a) World Technology Association
   (b) World Time Organisation
   (c) World Trade Organisation
   (d) World Tourism Organisation

6. The main promoter of trade liberalisation was :
   (a) GATT (b) NAFTA
   (c) IMF (d) WTO

7. GSP stands for :
   (a) Generalised System of Promotion
   (b) Generalised System of Preferences
   (c) Goods System of Preferences
   (d) Generalised Scene of Preferences

8. ATC is essentially designed to correct a long standing anomaly in the multilateral trading system
   (a) True (b) False

9. International commodity agreements (ICA's) are essentially multilateral instrumentalities of governmental control that do not support the international price of individual primary commodities
   (a) True (b) False

10. IMF stands for :
    (a) International Money Fund
    (b) International Monetary Fraud
    (c) International Monetary Fund
    (d) International Manly Fund

ANSWERS

| 1. (c) | 2. (d) | 3. (a) | 4. (b) | 5. (c) |
| 6. (a) | 7. (b) | 8. (a) | 9. (b) | 10. (c) |

Project Questions

1. What trading organisation represents the international trade objectives of developing countries? How do the concerns of developing countries differ from those of the industrialised, developed countries?
2. How far has India benefited by becoming a member of WTO?

Chapter 4...

Multinational Corporations and their Involvement in International Business

Contents ...

4.1 Multinational Corporations
    4.1.1 Introduction
    4.1.2 Meaning of Multinational Corporations
    4.1.3 Stages in the Formation of Multinational Corporations
    4.1.4 Characteristics of MNCs
    4.1.5 Terminology
    4.1.6 Objectives of MNCs
    4.1.7 Involvement of MNCs in International Business
    4.1.8 Types of Multinational Corporations
    4.1.9 Importance of MNCs
    4.1.10 MNCs around the World
    4.1.11 Advantages of MNCs to Host Countries
    4.1.12 Disadvantages of MNCs to Host Countries
    4.1.13 Advantages of MNCs to Home Countries
    4.1.14 Disadvantages of MNCs to Home Countries
    4.1.15 Code of Conduct
    4.1.16 Recommendations of the United Nations
4.2 International Investment Issues
    4.2.1 Technology Transfer
    4.2.2 Transfer Pricing
    4.2.3 Regulating of Foreign Investment
    4.2.4 Rationale Behind Regulation
    4.2.5 Modalities of Regulation in Host Country
    4.2.6 Modalities of Regulation in Home Country
- Points to Remember
- Questions for Discussion
- Multiple Choice Questions
- Project Questions

Learning Objectives...

- To understand the meaning and features of Multinational corporations
- To discuss the terminologies related to MNCs
- To study the role and importance of MNCs in developing countries
- To learn the arguments for and against MNCs
- To be able to explain the issues related to foreign investment involving technology transfer, pricing and regulations
- To understand the concepts of international collaborative arrangements and strategic alliance

4.1 Multinational Corporations

4.1.1 Introduction

The process of economic integration has hastened considerably in the last two decades. The three main channels of globalisation, trade, foreign direct investment (FDI) and the international transfer of knowledge and technology have developed very vigorously. International trade has grown stronger than world output. The degree of openness has exceeded the pre World War, 'One record level' in many countries. Multinational Corporations (MNCs) stand at the centre of all of these developments.

Multinational Corporations (MNCs) have become very large and powerful. Some, for example, are worth more than the entire GDP of a number of countries. So MNCs can have vast impact, for good and for ill, on the countries they do business in, especially if those countries are small and/or poor.

This chapter aims at giving an idea of the growing role of Multinational corporations (MNCs). It will give an insight into the important characteristics of different organisational models of international firms. It studies the positive and negative aspects of MNCs.

4.1.2 Meaning of Multinational Corporations

Multinational Corporations (MNCs), also known as Multinational Enterprise, Transnational Corporation (TNC), Global Corporation, International Corporation (or firm, enterprise or company) etc. have been regarded as *"the most important and most visible innovation of the post-war period in the economic field."*

Although the multinational corporation took birth in the early 1860s it was only after the Second World War that multinationals have grown rapidly. In the early days, the U.S. was the home of most of the MNCs. Now there are a large number of European, Japanese and other Asian multinationals.

The concept of multinational has several dimensions. In fact, there is no single criterion that can define the multinational; hence there is no single universally agreed definition of the term multinational corporation.

Some of the definitions given below are based on the different criterion –

Definition on the Criterion of Size: The term MNC implies massive proportions. But, massiveness is related to many factors like market value, sales, profits and return on equity, which yield varying results and determine the largest multinationals.

However, the extent of internationalisation does not depend on the size. Indeed, many small firms are much more global than the larger ones. Equally important is to be pointed out that firms below certain size are normally excluded from the definition of multinational.

Definition on the Criterion of Structure: Structural requirements for definition as an MNC include the number of countries in which the firm does business and the citizenship of corporate owners and top managers.

Definition on the Criterion of Performance: This definition depends on such characteristics as earnings, sales and assets. These performance characteristics indicate the extent of the commitment of corporate resources to foreign operations and the amount of rewards from that commitment.

Definition on the Criterion of Behaviour: This is an abstract measure of multinationalisation and it refers to the behavioural characteristics of top management. Globalisation is a mindset that reflects the global orientation of the company.

According to an **ILO** report, *"the essential nature of the multinational enterprises lies in the fact that its managerial headquarters are located in one country (referred to as "home country") while the enterprise carries out operations in a number of other countries as well ("host countries")"*. It implies *"a corporation that controls production facilities in more than one country, such facilities have been acquired through the process of Foreign Direct Investment. Firms that participate in international business, however large they may be, solely by exporting or by licensing technology are not multinational enterprises"*.

Being international or multinational is a matter of degree. Further, globalisation is not a one-dimension concept, and thus it is essential to employ a single-variable measure to characterise the concept of internationalisation.

An **MNC** *is an organisation that engages in production or service activities, through its own affiliates, in several countries, maintains control over the policies of those affiliates and manages from a global perspective.* With a global perspective, top managers allocate resources and co-ordinate activities to take the best advantage of favourable business conditions throughout the world.

4.1.3 Stages in the Formation of Multinational Corporations

A Multinational Enterprise passes through the following stages:

(a) Products are exported to foreign nations.

(b) Sales organisations are set-up abroad.

(c) License use of Patents and technology to foreign firms that make and sell the MNCs goods.

(d) MNCs provide foreign production facilities substantial autonomy; however it reserves some important decisions for the home office.

(e) MNCs do provide foreign production facilities but important decisions like product design, marketing and finance are made at the home office.

(f) Decentralises authority throughout the company so that functions at home and abroad are done by executives from different nations.

Any multinational enterprise does not pass through the above mentioned stages in a sequential manner. The employees – whether the top management or down the line in production activity – should possess a global mindset. It means the willingness to accept the best idea or practice, no matter where it originates from.

4.1.4 Characteristics of MNCs

The important features and characteristics of MNCs are:

1. Area of Operation: MNCs operate in many countries with multiple products on a large scale and may undertake both manufacturing and marketing activities. Mostly MNCs from developed countries dominate in the world markets.

2. Origin: The development of MNCs dates back to several centuries, but their real growth started after the Second World War. While majority of the MNCs are from developed countries like USA, Japan, UK, Germany and other European countries, in recent years MNCs from countries like Korea, Taiwan, India, and China are operating in the world markets.

3. Comprehensive Term: The term MNC is a general comprehensive term and includes international and transnational corporations. The term global corporation is also included in the list of MNCs.

4. Profit Motive: MNCs are necessarily profit oriented and do not take much interest in the social welfare activities of the host country.

5. Management: Normally the parent company works like a holding company and guides its subsidiary companies by way of policies and directions in day to day operations.

6. Manufacture and Marketing Activities: MNCs undertake both manufacturing and marketing activities and while most are predominantly engaged in hi-tech and consumer goods industries, a large number of them are also engaged in pharmaceutical, petrochemicals, engineering, and consumer goods.

7. Quality Consciousness: MNCs are quality and cost conscious. To implement these concepts most MNCs are managed by professionals and experts with their own organisation culture and systems.

8. Branding Strategies of MNCs in International Markets: In the present global scenario MNCs need to set up effective branding strategies in order to be competitive. Different strategies, depending on the structure of the company and the products offered, are used.

4.1.5 Terminology

There is a debate about what to call a company, whose business ranges across national borders, tying together home and host countries through corporate policies and practices- MNCs, TNCs, MNEs, Global Corporations, International Corporations. We discuss below these various terms.

1. **Multinational Corporation (MNC):** These companies operate in multiple countries and thus some experts define such companies as an MNC or Multinational Corporation. This term is quite popular and seems to be the most generic name to describe corporations operating around the world.

2. **Multinational Enterprise (MNE):** When the international giants are state-owned enterprises, rather than by corporations, the term used for such companies is Multinational Enterprise or MNE. This term has entered the vocabulary of international business.

3. **Transnational Corporation (TNC):** Because companies 'transcend' or operate across national borders, some experts prefer the term Transnational Corporation or TNC. The United Nations favours this term and has created a Research Centre for the study of Transnational Corporations.

4. **Global Corporation:** This term seems to have first been used to describe a small number of companies, whose business was conducted in dozens of nations (perhaps more than 100 nations). For example, Nestle is truly global in this sense as the scope of its operations extends to more than 150 countries around the globe. Therefore, this term is often applied to companies doing business in several areas of the world- Europe, Latin America, Asia-Pacific and North America.

The term TNC (used to mean the same thing as MNC and similar terms) as given in UN's World Investment Report is – TNCs are incorporated or unincorporated enterprises comprising parent enterprises and their foreign affiliates. A **Parent Enterprise** is defined as an enterprise that controls assets of other entities in countries other than its home country, usually by owning **a certain equity capital stake**. An equity capital stake of 10% or more of the ordinary shares or voting power for an incorporated enterprise or its equivalent for an unincorporated enterprise is considered as a threshold for the control of assets. This percent varies, for example, in Germany and U.K., the threshold is a stake of 20% or more.

Characteristics of International Companies at a glance

Organisational Characteristics	Multinational	Global	International	Transnational
Configuration of assets and capabilities	Decentralised and nationally self-sufficient.	Centralised and globally scaled.	Sources of Core Competencies centralised others decentralised.	Dispersed, interdependent and specialised.
Roles of Overseas Operations	Sensing and exploiting local opportunities.	Implementing Parent Company Strategies.	Adapting and Leveraging parent company strategies.	Differentiated contributions by national units to integrated worldwide operations.
Development and diffusion of knowledge	Knowledge developed and retained within each unit.	Knowledge developed and retained at the centre.	Knowledge developed and retained at the centre and transferred to overseas units.	Knowledge developed jointly and shared worldwide.

Reproduced from Christopher A Bartlett and Sumantra Ghoshal, Managing Across Borders, Boston, and Harvard Business School Press 1998.

4.1.6 Objectives of MNCs

Profit maximisation is the fundamental goal of an MNC. The MNCs and its subsidiaries have the following objectives:

(a) Manufacturing in countries where it finds greatest competitive advantage.

(b) To buy and sell their products anywhere in the world to take advantage of the most favourable price to the company.

(c) To achieve greater sales.

(d) To obtain a high and increasing return on invested capital.

(e) To take advantage, throughout the world, of changes in labour costs, productivity, trade agreements and currency fluctuations.

(f) To undertake expansion or contraction based on worldwide competitive advantages.

(g) Maintain and improve technological and other company strengths.

(h) To maintain control of important decisions.

(i) Encounter fewer barriers in host nations.

4.1.7 Involvement of MNCs in International Business

MNCs play an important role in the economic development of underdeveloped countries.

1. Filling Savings Gap: The first important contribution of MNCs is their role in filling the resource gap between the targeted or desired investment and domestically mobilised savings. For example, to achieve a 7% growth rate of national output when the required rate of savings is 21% and when the savings that can be domestically mobilised is only 16% then there is a 'saving gap' of 5%. If the country can fill this gap with foreign direct investments from the MNCs, it will be in a better position to achieve its target rate of economic growth.

2. Filling Trade Gap: The second important contribution relates to filling the foreign exchange or trade gap. If the MNCs are able to generate a positive flow of export earnings a reduction or removal of the deficit in the balance of payments can be achieved.

3. Filling Revenue Gap: The third important contribution of MNCs is filling the gap between targeted governmental tax revenues and locally raised taxes. By taxing MNC profits, LDC governments are able to mobilise public financial resources for development projects.

4. Filling Management/Technological Gap: The fourth important contribution is that multinationals not only provide financial resources but also provide needed resources including management experience, entrepreneurial abilities, and technological skills. These skills are transferred to their local counterparts by means of training programmes.

MNCs also bring with them the most sophisticated technological knowledge about production processes while transferring modern machinery and equipment to their subsidiaries. Such transfers of knowledge, skills, and technology are desirable and productive for the recipient country.

5. Other Beneficial Roles: MNCs also bring several other benefits to the host country.

(a) Domestic labour benefit in the form of higher real wages.

(b) Consumers benefit by way of lower prices and better quality products.

(c) Investments by MNCs will also encourage more domestic investment. This is brought about by ancillary units that are set up to supplement the industries of the MNCs.

(d) MNCs expenditures on research and development (R & D), though limited is bound to benefit the host country.

Apart from these there are indirect gains through the realisation of external economies.

4.1.8 Types of Multinational Corporations

1. **Ethnocentric:** These types of MNCs have a strong orientation towards the home country and key posts are allotted only to employees from the home country.

2. **Polycentric:** Opposite to ethnocentric, polycentric type of MNCs have strong orientation towards the host country. In this scenario a few key people are nationals and the rest are from the host country.

3. **Regiocentric and Geocentric:** These MNCs are concentrated in the whole world and they select the best employees on an international level.

4.1.9 Importance of MNCs

The establishment of multinational companies has proved a blessing all over the world. Some of their roles are as follows:

1. **Transfer of Capital and Technology:** The multinational companies transfer investment and, advanced technology to developing countries by establishing branches and subsidiaries. Thus developing countries like Nepal get the benefits of advanced technology and capital investment through such companies.

2. **Mass Production:** With the help of advanced technology MNCs can produce quality goods and products at cheaper prices. This leads to an increase in consumption as production of more units reduce costs.

3. **Increase in Employment Opportunity:** Multinational companies require a large number of skilled as well as unskilled employees for operational activities. This provides employment opportunities to the people of the host country as a result of which economic standards of society are improved.

4. **Increase in Government Revenue:** A multinational company is a large scale business paying large amount of duties, income tax, VAT, etc. to the government. Thus government revenues are increased due to the presence of such companies.

5. **Research and Development:** R & D practices are very important in this competitive world. A multinational company conducts several research and development activities to meet international standards of its products and services. Such programmes are beneficial to society as they help to develop better equipment, quality products and advanced technology in production.

6. **Good International Relation:** A multinational company recognises the country in the international market. It creates a harmonious relationship between the parent company and subsidiary countries.

4.1.10 MNCs around the World

The position of MNCs in global economy is outstanding. Today, there are more than 82,000 MNCs around the world, controlling over 810,000 affiliates.

The following table shows the ranking of MNCs according to the Fortune 500 list:

Table 4.1: Gives the World's Largest Corporations

Rank	Company	Country	Industry	Revenue in USD
1	Wal-Mart	United States	Retail	$476.3 billion
2	Royal Dutch Shell	Netherlands United Kingdom†	Petroleum	$459.6 billion
3	Sinopec	China	Petroleum	$457.2 billion
5	ExxonMobil	United States	Petroleum	$407.7 billion
6	BP	United Kingdom	Petroleum	$396.2 billion
7	State Grid Corporation of China	China	Power	$333.4 billion
8	Volkswagen	Germany	Automobiles	$261.5 billion
9	Toyota	Japan	Automobiles	$256.5 billion
10	Glencore	Switzerland	Commodities	$232.7 billion

4.1.11 Advantages of MNCs to Host Countries

The preface to the ILO report on Multinational Enterprises and Social Policy observes, "for some, the Multinational Companies are an invaluable dynamic force and instrument for wider distribution of capital, technology and employment; for others they are monsters which our present institutions, national or international, cannot adequately control, a law to themselves with no reasonable concept, the public interest or social policy can accept."

MNCs have played a significant role in the development of poor countries. Be it transfer of technology, introducing best management practices, improving quality of life of people, helping in improving the productivity, the contribution of MNCs has been praiseworthy. MNCs, it is claimed, help the host countries in the following ways:

(i) MNCs help to increase the investment level and thereby boost the income and employment in the host country.

(ii) MNCs help to increase industrial and economic activities of host country.

(iii) Domestic industry gets sophisticated management technique.

(iv) MNCs help to reduce import and favourable effects on balance of payment.

(v) Improves the competitive ability of domestic business due to competition.

(vi) Domestic consumers have the advantage of consuming a variety of goods and services.

(vii) MNCs earn foreign exchange by exporting to the other neighbouring countries.

(viii) Maximum utilisation of natural resources of the host country.

(ix) MNCs help to increase competition and break domestic monopolies.

(x) The MNCs enable the host countries to increase their exports i.e. provide greater access to international markets and decrease their import requirements, thus help to build their foreign exchange reserves.

(xi) MNCs kindle a managerial revolution in the host countries through professional management and the employment of highly sophisticated management techniques.

(xii) They provide products and services that raise the standard of living of the people in the host countries.

(xiii) The Transnational Corporations (TNCs) have become vehicles for the transfer of technology, particularly to the developing countries.

(xiv) They work to equalise the cost of factors of production around the world.

(xv) MNCs provide an efficient means to integrating national economies.

(xvi) They encourage the development and spin-off of new industries. The enormous resources of the multinational enterprises enable them to have very efficient research and development systems. Thus, they make a commendable contribution to inventions and innovations.

(xvii) MNCs also stimulate domestic enterprise because to support their own operations. The MNCs may encourage and assist domestic suppliers.

(xviii) They assume investment risk that might not otherwise be undertaken by the developing country.

(xix) MNCs mobilise capital for productive purposes from less productive areas.

Naturally, MNC managers and their defenders respond that many of the criticisms of their behaviour are only partially true at best. It is pointed out by defenders that at times domestic business in developing countries may engage in more harmful practices, then why single out only the MNCs? Despite their alleged shortcomings, they say, MNCs significantly influence positively the host governments to achieve their national aims.

4.1.12 Disadvantages of MNCs to Host Countries

MNCs are criticised, particularly by developing countries, on grounds like low wages, exploitation of labour, depletion of resources and abuse of human rights.

It may be recollected that the MNCs main goal is to earn money. They are operating in any country and in any form with the only objective of earning profit and not to indulge in philanthropic activities.

In particular, developing countries nurture the following grievances against the MNCs.

1. **Self-Interests are Primary:** When the interest of MNCs clash with the needs of host countries, it is the MNCs which must compromise its interest for the satisfaction of the host nation. However, in practice, this is not so. For example, Coca-Cola's self-serving fights in countries where its subsidiaries are located. In Mexico, the company is trying to stop a plan to levy 20% tax on soft drinks. In India, the company silenced an NGO which revealed that the soft drink contained pesticides. Food companies entice children with sugary cereals that are bad for their teeth.

2. **Costly Damages Inflicted with Impunity:** Examples can be cited to draw home this point. Firstly, the infamous Union Carbide that had leakage of deadly gases at Bhopal and killed more than 20,000 instantly and injuring 100,000 people. The company paid only a paltry amount of $ 500 per person. Dow Chemical has bought the Bhopal plant, taking all of Union Carbide's assets but assuming no liability. Second example is of OK Tedi, gold and copper mine in Papua, New Guinea. The company dumped 80,000 tonnes of contaminated material daily, for 12 years, into the OK Tedi and Fly Rivers and it extracted for itself some $ 6 billion worth of ore.

3. **Encourage Bribing:** MNCs justify bribery as it adds to their bottom-line. Mining and oil companies often reduce the cost of acquiring natural resources by bribing government officials for concessions. Because, it is much cheaper to pay a government official a large bribe than to pay market price for oil or some other natural resource. In U.S., for instance, bribing has been banned. But this has been replaced by contributions to political parties. Companies like GE, Microsoft and Disney and many others have invested $ 150 million in political parties and campaigns for US federal candidates between 1991 and 2001, and enjoyed $ 55 billion in tax breaks in three years alone.

4. **Worst Hit is Marginal and Small Firms :** Thousands of small firms in developing countries have closed their shutters because of the competition from large MNCs. Corporate giants like Wal-Mart believe in buying cheap and at such low rates that they can drive small firms to bankruptcy. Its strict policy against formation of unions implies that its workers are often low-paid and their low wages force down wages at competitor organisations. In this way the entire workforce is affected.

5. **Environmental Degradation:** Many nations are becoming more concerned about the impact of MNCs on their environment. Environmental concerns are rapidly moving higher in the list of priorities throughout the world, even the Least Developed Countries.

6. **Impact on Society:** MNCs affect the local ways of thinking with their introduction of habits, behaviour and ethical values, new products, management styles, more money, technology etc. The introduction of jeans, movies, western attitudes towards women, work habits shift cultures towards Western values. In short, the ethical fabric of the society of a host country is often denoted by undesirable and corrupt practices of MNCs. A report of the UN highlighted many such practices such as unfair competition and restrictive trade practices, rigging of bids and many market distortions. They also resorted to devious means to increase their profits.

7. **Interference with Economic Goals:** This can occur in many ways. For instance :

    (a) The multinational company may wish to locate a plant in an area of prosperity when the host country would prefer its location in an underdeveloped region.

    (b) Further, since MNCs typically do their R & D at home, host countries become technologically dependent on the MNCs for innovation and invention.

    (c) The MNCs are able to attract bank loans that could have been available for local business.

    (d) Though LDCs need investment in infrastructure, but MNCs are hardly known for developing this sector.

    (e) The host country may also lose control over its own economy, as some actions of the MNCs may not be consistent with what is desired by the host country.

8. **Imperialism:** Many LDCs feel relegated to the role of supplying raw materials and cheap labour because they are denied the technology to develop into industrialised nations. As such, many of awakening nations look on foreign managers with distrust as the embodiment of not easily forgotten exploitative colonialism.

9. **Symbol of Frustration:** Many of the LDCs are governed by some form of dictatorship that is antagonistic to the free market mechanism governing decision-making of the MNC. Many LDCs insist on being partial owners of undertakings set up by MNCs. And, in situations of social upheaval, a host country may nationalise the assets of a company even without paying compensation. The anger against MNCs often forces them to leave a host country.

10. **Technology:** The technology brought in by MNCs is hardly suitable to LDCs. Such technology is highly capital intensive but developing nations need a labour intensive one. The technology is highly expensive also. The MNCs charge exorbitantly in the form of fee and royalty, which put a severe strain on the foreign exchange reserves. There are instances of "technology dumping" wherein MNCs use obsolete technology. MNCs tend to make the industries in developing countries permanently dependent on foreign expertise and technology.

4.1.13 Advantages of MNCs to Home Countries

MNCs in the home country have the following advantages.

1. MNCs create opportunities for marketing the products produced in the home country throughout the world.
2. They create employment opportunities to the people of the home country both at home and abroad.
3. They give a boost to the industrial activities of the home country.
4. MNCs help to maintain a favourable balance of payment in the home country.
5. The home country can also get the benefits of foreign culture brought by the MNCs.
6. Optimum utilisation of natural resources and conservation of the countries' scarce resources like petroleum resources in the USA.

4.1.14 Disadvantages of MNCs to Home Countries

1. MNCs transfer capital from the home country to various host countries thus causing an unfavourable balance of payment.
2. MNCs may not be able to create employment opportunities for the people of the home country if they adopt a geocentric approach.
3. As investments in foreign countries are more profitable, MNCs may neglect the home country's industrial and economic development.
4. MNCs may neglect industrial development of home country as the transnational companies follow the secular approach. MNCs may exploit the natural resources resulting in excessive exploitation of natural resources.

4.1.15 Code of Conduct

It is widely felt that there must be a code of conduct to guide and regulate the MNCs.

1. According to the **Brandt Commission,** the main elements of an international regime for investment should include framework that would allow developing nations and TNCs to benefit from direct investment on terms contractually agreed upon. Home countries should not restrict investment or the transfer of technology abroad and should avoid from other restrictive practices like export controls not restrict current transfers like profits, royalties and dividends, or the repatriation of capital, so long as they are on terms which were agreed when the investment was originally approved or subsequently negotiated.
2. Co-operation by government in their tax policies to monitor transfer pricing and to eliminate the resort to tax havens.

3. Fiscal and other incentives and policies towards foreign investment to be harmonised among host developing nations, to avoid the undermining of the tax base and competitive positions of host countries.

4. Legislation promoted and co-ordinated in home and host countries in order to regulate the activities of TNCs in matters such as ethical behaviour, disclosure of information, restrictive business practices, anti-competitive practices and labour standards.

5. An international procedure for discussions and consultations on measures affecting direct investment and the actions of TNCs.

4.1.16 Recommendations of the United Nations

The Code of Conduct for MNCs, drawn by the Commission on TNCs, set up by UN's Economic and Social Council, requires MNCs to-

- Respect the national sovereignty of host countries and observe their domestic laws, regulations and administrative practices.
- Not interfere in internal political affairs or in inter-governmental relations.
- Respect human rights.
- Adhere to host countries' economic goals, development objectives and socio-cultural values.
- Not engage in corrupt practices.
- Disclose relevant information to host country governments.
- Apply good practice with regard to payment of taxes, restrain from involvement in anti-competitive practices, consumer and environmental protection and the treatment of employees.

The **OECD Code of Practice** (1976) for MNCs, declares that they should contribute positively to economic and social progress within host nations. Its main provisions were that MNCs should:

- Contribute to host countries science and technology objectives by permitting the rapid diffusion of technologies.
- Provide full information for tax purposes.
- Consider the host nation's Balance Of Payments objectives when taking decisions.
- Not behave in manners that would restrict competition by abusing dominant positions or market power.
- Avoid unfair discrimination in employment and provide reasonable working conditions.

- Regularly make public significant information on financial or operational matters. Host countries should possess the absolute right to nationalise foreign-owned assets within their frontiers, but must pay proper compensation.

The demand by developing countries that the Code becomes legally binding was rejected by the UN General Assembly, at the behest of economically advanced countries.

4.2 International Investment Issues

4.2.1 Technology Transfer

Technology transfer can be of the following types:

1. The international transfer of technology from the R & D or engineering department to the manufacturing department of a firm based in a country is covered by technology transfer.
2. Technology transfer also includes the transfer of technology from a laboratory of a MNC in the host country to the laboratory in another.
3. It also includes the transfer of technology from a research consortium supported by many firms to one of its members.

In simple terms, *technology transfer is a process that permits the flow of technology from a source to a receiver.*

The source: owner or holder of knowledge such as an individual, company or country.

The receiver: is the beneficiary of the transferred technology.

International technology transfer takes place via:

- trade,
- foreign direct investment,
- joint ventures with local partners,
- simple technology licensing, although in the latter case, some tacit knowledge probably also needs to be transferred.

A risk factor revolves around the foreign firm that many local firms imitate their products thereby taking away some of their profits, so the presence of enforceable IPRs should encourage all these activities. In fact, **Edith Penrose** goes as far as to argue that for developing countries *"the only economic advantages to be gained from granting foreign patents lies in the possibility that in one way or another such grants will induce the introduction of foreign technology and capital".*

Imitation risk is at the highest when the host country has the power to adopt and imitate such technology, which is usually found in middle income countries than in low income countries. This risk is further increased, if technologies require local adaptation in order to fit local needs and regulatory requirements and standards. If there is a strong IPR protection, foreign firms prefer to license technologies so that amount of technology transfer is less. This decision may also be influenced by the ability of foreign firms to enforce license contracts. However, it is also conceivable that stronger IPRs increase the incentives for firms to exploit IPRs themselves instead of licensing out. It is likely that these relationships differ by industry and type of activity, i.e., manufacturing or distribution.

Parties in the Transfer Process

International technology transfer has both:

- horizontal
- vertical dimension, each with its own elements.

There are three basic elements in technology transfer:

- Home country
- Host country
- Transaction

The vertical dimension of technology transfer refers to the issues specific to the nation state, or to the industries or firms within the home and host countries.

Home Country's Reactions to Technology Transfers

Home countries always have anxiety about the transfer of their technology. Their main concern is that establishment of production facilities by MNCs in subsidiaries abroad lessens their export potential. They also argue that due to some of the MNCs import from their subsidiaries, the volume of imports of the home country tends to increase. Since there is a decrease in exports and increase in imports, this balance of trade tends to be unfavourable to the home country and also technology transfer tends to affect unfavourably the competitive advantage to the home country. Often there are labour unions in the home country who oppose the technology being transferred stating that the jobs that are created from this new technology benefits the host country citizens.

Host Country's Reactions to Technology Transfers

The subject of technology transfers is highly sensitive, often evoking strong reservations against it from the host country citizens. Based on economic and social factors, there are some criticisms against the technology transfer.

Economic implications: Economic implications include :

- payment of fee,
- royalty,
- dividends,
- interest,
- salaries to foreign technicians,
- tax concessions resulting in loss to the national exchequer.

The above need to be paid to the transferring country and hence proves to be an expensive affair to the host country. Apart from the above payments to be made, the supplier also extracts payments through other techniques such as over pricing and buying intermediates at high prices. Tie-up purchases and restriction on exports, and charging excessive prices are some of the malpractices involved.

Often the technology that is being transferred is not suitable for the developing countries. The technology that is developed is, designed to produce the types of goods that a rich country needs and to do so by methods, which are appropriate to resources endowment of developed nations, mainly for industrial countries. Technologies tend to be designed for the production of high-quality sophisticated goods on a large scale, using a higher capital and high level professional skills in place of cheap labour and which replaces the natural resources by synthetics. This is of no interest to the developing countries.

Social implications: More than the economic implications, it is the social and cultural implications of the technology transfer which are more serious. There is a transfer of culture from the exporting country along with the technology transfer. Take for example Indians who work for these firms, they get accustomed to the Western attitudes, behaviours, food habits, and dress. Have you thought why this is so? This is due to the fact that we not only import technology from the Western countries but the Indians who work in firms using such imported technologies gets influenced and accustomed to the skills, concepts, policies, practices, thoughts and beliefs. Many times one can see that some voluntary organisations in the country campaign against these cultural invasion.

Apart from the above there are other social problems like congestion, pollution, urbanisation and depletion of natural resources.

Apprehension of technology importing countries may be justified but it does not mean that the host countries should be denied the benefits of new technologies. It is upto the host countries to minimise the unfavourable effects and take maximum benefit from the imported technologies. Figure 4.1 contains the basic plan.

- Identify and set entry conditions for **new** and/or existing foreign investors.
- Reserve certain sectors for local producers.
- Specify performance requirements from MNE: affiliates.
- Try and eliminate restrictions on use **of technology** supplied by MNEs.
- Limit **technology** payments (royalties) to foreign firms.
- Improve understanding of costs and **benefits of technology:** improve negotiating abilities.
- Solicit competitive bids from alternative **technology** suppliers.
- Encourage MNEs to sell **technology** on contractual basis.
- Limit duration **of technology** contracts.

- Encourage indigenous production of **technology.**
- Encourage market structure most conducive to an efficient inflow and dissemination of **technology.**
- Impose training obligations on MNEs.
- Give more incentives to MNEs to set up R & D facilities in **host countries.**
- Encourage development of state-owned enterprises (as in Brazil and India).
- Provide fiscal and other incentives to encourage privately financed R & D to the point where its marginal social **benefits** equate with its marginal costs.
- Reconsider macro-economic and macro-organisation policies so as to remove structural distortions in cross-border **technology** markets.
- Encourage development of clusters of supporting or related activities and also interaction between universities, cooperative research associations and private firms.
- Support industrial restructuring and by general education and other policies facilitate the upgrading of indigenous human capital.
- Liberalise **technology** and other markets which distort terms of **technology** transfer and diffusion.

Fig 4.1 Steps to Maximise Benefits from Technology Transfer

Strategies before Host Countries:

Relating to transfer technology, the host country sets up the following plan:

- **A host country might do nothing towards technology transfer:** This attitude stems from atleast two assumptions. First, the host economy is strong and vibrant enough and is capable of absorbing technology. Second, the economy and the government are incapable of evolving policies towards the import of technology.
- **A Government might specify performance requirements for foreign investors:** The performance requirements include indigenisation of production processes, adding to the exchange reserves and creating jobs to locals.
- **A host government might limit the amount of inward investment:** FDI (along with technology) is permitted by the Government of India upto 24%, 26%, 49%, 51% and 74% in different sectors of the country.
- **A Government could discourage restrictive clauses on technology transfer:** Technology transfer by MNCs can freely transfer technology to their subsidiaries who are situated in the host countries
- **A government might limit certain sectors** to domestic ownership and throw open other sectors for overseas technology.

- **A Government might influence terms and conditions of the technology transfer:** The host country invites FDI, but uses caution to think about the extent and type of technology it will need to serve its long term goals.

- **A Government might encourage indigenous technological development:** Sometimes the host government will motivate to do the R & D in the domestic market instead of importing the technology.. This is known as import substitution and is used when local capabilities are weaker and the overall coordination of policies to improve competitiveness is not likely to succeed. The emphasis of this strategy is to encourage exports and upgrade skills in the import-substituting industries.

- **The host government might encourage cross-border collaborative R & D:** Investment in R & D is so expensive that strategic alliances prove beneficial to alliance partners. Competition from MNCs might also encourage governments to engage in cross-border technological cooperation. The purpose of this 10 year research programme was to target the R & D intensive sectors of the IT industry, where the challenge from US and Japanese forms was intense.

- **The government might also obtain technology knowledge through other means:** The recipient country may buy technology in the open market by-passing the conventional routes. There are two advantages for the host country:
  - ✓ technology may be available at much cheaper rates and terms
  - ✓ dependence on MNCs for technology is minimal

Stages in the Transfer Process

There are five different stages in the transfer of technology between countries:

1. Assignments, including sale and licensing agreements covering all forms of industrial property including patents, inventor's certificates, utility models, industrial design, trade marks, service names, and trade names.

2. Arrangements, covering the provision of know-how and technical expertise in the form of feasibility studies, plans, diagrams, models, instructions, guides, formulations, service contracts and specifications, and for involving technical, advising and managerial personnel, personnel training and equipment for training.

3. This covers the provision of basic or detailed engineering design along with the installation and operations of the plant and equipment.

4. Acquisitions of machinery, equipment, intermediate goods and/or raw materials and any other purchases including leases so long as they are part of the transactions involving technology transfer.

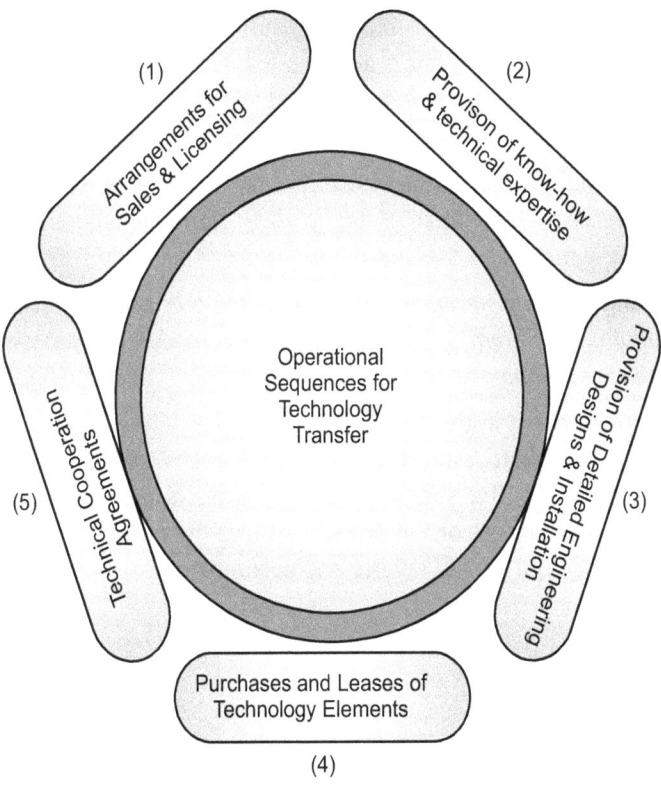

Fig. 4.2 : Operational Sequences for Technology Transfer

5. Industrial and technical cooperation agreements of any kind, including turn key agreements, international sub-contracting, as well as provision for management and marketing services.

There are different types of technology, each posing fundamentally different problems and demanding different solutions in the international transfer process.

Modes of Technology Transfer

Below are some of the modes of technology transfer:

1. **Internal R & D:** Technology acquisition via internal R & D consists of having a research and development group within the firm. The technology the firm uses is created by this team. This type of acquisition of technology enables an organisation to become more independent and stronger and has to its advantage to entail tax or other incentives. Some of the disadvantages of this type are high cost, risk of failure and long periods of time is required.

2. **Internal R & D with Networking:** This has almost the same pros and cons like the internal R & D. What differs between the two is the fact that the R & D teams make an intensive effort to keep up to date with the state of development of the

technologies which affect their products. During conference and trade shows, they network with technology creators and also follow technological developments which are published in papers, journals and magazines. They attend meetings, demonstrations and trade shows where competing products are on display.

The networking approach improves the firm's external technology acquisition capabilities. The R & D team is up to date with the different options that are available in the market.

3. **Reverse Engineering:** *Reverse engineering is the process of extracting knowledge or design information, from anything that is man-made. The process often involves disassembling something and analysing its components and workings in detail.*

This is quite common in the automobile and machinery industries. Companies first reverse their competitor's product to study the pros and cons before they design their own products. The strengths of the products are kept while a solution is created for the weakness of the product so that the new product is much between than the original. The pros of reverse engineering are:

- Less risky
- Less costly
- Less time to market
- It enables the development of a product that meets the competition in all its areas of strength and has a competitive advantage in the competitor areas of weaknesses

The **disadvantages** are:

- that it has potential to develop a me-too product
- There is also the possibility that the reverse engineering team does not properly understand the original design and the new product is actually poorer than the one studied.
- Legal risks are also involved by infringing on the patent rights of the owners of the original product.

Another Dimension of Reverse Engineering is the Reverse Brain Drain: The entrepreneurs and experts who have gained enough knowledge to set up enterprises in their country of origin is known as the reverse brain drain. China and Taiwan often vouch for such type of technology transfer.

4. **Covert Acquisition with Internal R & D:** In this type of technology acquisition, the firm finds out the technology developments which are being taken out by the competitors which are usually not open to the general public. By socialising with the competitor's employees and by talking to suppliers about the materials being sold to the competitors, many businesses get involved in this manner. The less careful

organisations often get involved in industrial espionage by using unfair means such as cameras, break and enter techniques to find out what is going on inside the competitor's plants.

Secret acquirement along with internal R & D is nearly the same as reverse engineering. It often results in a product that is the same. By adding value and solving technical problems, internal R & D can improve upon the products created by the competitors.

Costs, risks and time to market can be reduced. Risks of being sued and having a dishonest name for the firm are the drawbacks.

Covert Acquisition: When the product will be the exact copy of the competitor's product but without using internal R & D is known as covert acquisition. Since there are no development costs to recover, the firm can introduce it at a lower price, but apart from this price the product will have no changes from the original product. Those organisations who involve in such acquisitions have inferior products and will not be in a position to improve its products or deal with the technical problems the products may face along with high legal costs.

5. **Technology Transfer and Absorption:** This route is similar to internal R & D with networking. There is much more effort put into searching for, learning about, and translating, no-cost technology to the firm's applications is the only difference. Internal technical ability is necessary to understand the technologies found and to develop them into solutions for the firm's application.

   For process technologies, technology transfer and acquisition is most often used. An example would be where the firm finds a process technology that has been inverted by a government or educational institution, and applies the same to its own production line by acquiring components and attaching them to the existing equipment.

6. **Contract R & D**: Firms that lack the necessary facilities and expertise to conduct the required work but want to maintain control over the development, contract R & D is the best option. For those that need a specialised set of equipment or expertise for occasional short-term projects, Contract R & D is an excellent choice. This avoids the investment in these facilities and the on-going commitment to staff and would be underutilised. This allows a quick access to world-class personnel and facilities for specialised projects which would otherwise be out of reach to the company.

   Even though some firms have excellent R & D, they still prefer to choose on contracting out R & D projects. The two reasons being:
   - to maintain internal strength in technologies crucial to the firm's business
   - to occasionally contract R & D in core technology as well.

   This also helps the R & D team to be exposed to other environments.

The **advantages** of this route are:
- No investment in facilities,
- Low investment in staff.

The disadvantages are:
- No hands-on-knowledge in-house
- Difficulty in keeping information confidential.

7. **R & D Strategic Partnership:** On the same lines as contracting R & D is the R & D strategic partnerships. It consists of firms with a common need which will contract a research institution to conduct the research and work for them. By this way the firms share the risks and costs and create a situation where they learn from each other as well as from experts who conduct the research.

   The partners are usually competitors and hence the kinds of projects that are most favourable are competitive research. These projects are usually neither too risky nor very expensive for a firm to handle. Hence it would be beneficial for a firm to have a contract R & D or an internal R & D to translate the result of the applied research into a technology which the firm can use.

   R & D strategic partnerships can be initiated by:
   - one firm inviting others to join,
   - by informal group of firms,
   - by formulated association of firms in an industry,
   - or by the R & D institution itself.

   R & D strategic partnerships are becoming common with large companies in electronics/computers, automobiles, oil and mining etc.

   The **advantages** of this route of technology acquisition are:
   - shared risks,
   - reduced cost,
   - possibility of learning from others.

   The **disadvantages** are:
   - Need to share knowledge with others,
   - The necessity of adopting research results to own applications.

8. **Licensing:** The major benefit of licensing is a significant reduction in time to market relative to other forms of technology acquisition that require development. The acquiring firm shares the financial risks of acquiring the technology with the provider as the bulk payment is in the form of royalty.

A frequent argument against licensing is that the license might become a competitor's. Hence a simple relationship between the licensor and licensee should exist. Licensing can be a versatile plan that allows taking ownership interest in the foreign venture. Along with this trademarks will be with the licensor and the licensee only has it for a limited term.

Among the **advantages** of licensing technologies are:

- costs
- risks are less than internal R & D and time required to commercialise is less.

The **disadvantages** are:

- exclusivity may be lost,
- internal capability may not be developed.

9. **Purchasing:** Purchasing is a common and effective external technology acquisition. This is done by buying a piece of production machinery with embedded technology. A quick method of technology transfer as the technology is ready to use. The providing firm can also provide implementation support in the form of set-up and training. The costs will be lower than developing the technology because the providing company is generally in the business of providing the machines containing the technology to many users thereby spreading the development costs over several customers. It is low risk because the equipment has been proven to be technically competent and there are already users to evidence the machine's capability.

In this form, do not overlook the costs of internal activities such as time spent on training or the disruption of the present production during the installation of new machinery. It is also sold to many buyers so the question of it being exclusive is lost and there could be resistance from employees with the acquiring company.

There is yet another form of purchasing the technology – to pay for the know-how behind the technology and the right to use it in the firm's application. This is very similar to licensing, except it is a one-time purchase rather than an ongoing relationship.

10. **Joint Venture:** A partnership between two firms, one with a technology and another with market access is known as joint venture. It can take the form of the creation of a new firm with each of the partners owning shares in the new firm in proportion to the value of their contribution to the new firm. In this case, production facilities are installed in the new firm with the partners bringing technology and market know-how along with capital investment into the new firm. The distribution of marketing of the product may use the system that the firm with market access has in place, or that firm's know-how may be used to create a dedicated system for the new firm.

This is pretty similar to licensing. A contractual agreement describing who provides with what and how the expenses will be shared is formed between the providing and acquiring firms. The main difference between this and licensing is the fact that the technology provider has an expanded relationship with the acquiring firm. Joint decisions about production and marketing even though the acquirer actually produces the product and provides to the market are made.

The **advantages** are:

- both firms learn from each other.
- The technology can be implemented immediately, as it is already proven.
- risk involved is less and there are possibilities of learning from the provider of technology

The **disadvantages** are:

- either company cannot make decisions on its own,
- the partners have to agree on any major issue.
- Market risks are high and there are no chances of developing technical strengths.

11. **Acquisition of a Technology Rich Firm:** The final form of external technology acquisition is the acquisition of a firm that has know-how, which the acquiring firm desires. When one firm has a technological innovation that is affecting another company's innovation, the second company negotiates to purchase the entire company. This can result from a defensive action or it can be deliberate strategy to acquire technology.

The **advantages** are:

- short time to market,
- low risks,
- probability of buying good image.

The **disadvantages** are:

- possibility of acquiring negative baggage,
- merger problems.

Though the routes of technology acquisition are comprehensive, there is one which is not considered which is personnel and that includes:

- employment of nationals by foreign firms;
- employment of foreign technicians;
- migration of trained personnel;
- internal training produces the product and provides it to the market.

The advantage is that both firms learn from each other. The disadvantage is that either company cannot make decisions on its own, the partners have to agree on any major issue.

4.2.2 Transfer Pricing

Transfer pricing means *the determination of the 'prices' at which an MNC moves goods between its subsidiaries in various countries*. The ability to engage in transfer pricing at artificially high or low prices is an important feature of a centralised MNC. Take for example an MNC which gets raw materials from one country uses them as raw materials in another country and finally assembles it in a third country and ends up selling in a fourth country. The governments of the extraction, production and assembly countries will have sales or value added taxes; while the production, assembly and finished goods countries will impose tariffs on imports of goods. The government of the extraction country receives no revenue from sales taxes because the MNC's subsidiary in that country is selling its output to the same MNC's subsidiary in the production country at a price of zero. The only tax the MNC pays is a sales tax in the last country in the chain.

Transfer pricing, at unacceptably low values has been a major problem for many developing nations. Sometimes, therefore, the government of the country in which an MNC operates will insist that a government official shall decide the price at which the MNC exports its output, and not an employee of the MNC itself. The government makes sure that the host country gets a proper amount of sales tax. Similarly, importing countries might impose quantity-based instead of price-based import duties to make sure reasonable revenue from taxes on imports of an MNC's goods.

Apart from tax considerations, transfer prices need to be practical so that the profitability of the numerous international operations may be reviewed. Some points to set the transfer price are:

- The price at which the item could be sold in the open market (this is known as 'arms length' transfer pricing).
- Political negotiations between the units involved (a high or low transfer price can drastically affect the observed profitability of a subsidiary). Note the problems that arise if the 'buyer' happens to be the head office of the firm.
- Cost of production or acquisition.
- Acquisition/ production cost is a profit markup (note the problem here of deciding what constitutes an appropriate profit markup).
- Senior management's perceptions of the value of the item to the firm's overall international operations.

The solution that should be adopted should be such that maximum profit is made and the best facilitates the parent firm's control has over subsidiary operations.

Some of the problems faced while setting a suitable transfer price are:

(a) Possible absence of competition in local markets at various stages in the supply chain. Thus a 'market price' in such ill areas may be artificially high in consequence of the lack of local competition

(b) Disparate tax rates and investment subsidy levels in various countries.

(c) Executives in operating units deliberately manipulating the transfer price to enhance the book value of a subsidiary's profits.

(d) Differences in the accounting systems used by subsidiaries in different countries.

(e) If a price is set at too high a level the 'selling' unit will lie able to attain its profit targets too easily (at the expense of the 'buyer') and lead perhaps to idleness and inefficiency in the selling.

(f) There might not be any other product directly comparable to the item in question, again making it difficult to establish a market price.

4.2.3 Regulating of Foreign Investment

FDI is regulated both at the national and international levels. At the national level, the host country provides various incentives but this does not mean the government loosens its control. A lot of checks take place so that maximum advantage is reaped. At the international level it is the WTO that regulated the FDI under the aegis of TRIMS.

4.2.4 Rationale Behind Regulation

Host-country Perspective: We have seen earlier that there are certain benefits that can be obtained by the host country from the FDI inflow. Some of them are:

- Availability of scarce foreign exchange,
- Improvement in the balance of payments,
- Accelerated rate of economic development through warranted rate of investment,
- Through the creation of economic linkages.

These are the features that help for the adoption of a good FDI inflow policy by the government of the host country. FDI also checks often as it produces negative impact on the host economy, such as deterioration in its balance of payment on account of larger imports, payment of dividend and other fees, and continued dependence on the imported technology. The subsidiary sources its inputs either from the parent unit or from a third country unit of the firm, FDI inflow fails to help build what Porter calls a "cluster". The developmental impact on the FDI is very little. When such types of sourcing takes place, transfer pricing is common. This means over-invoicing of imports of the subsidiary, which in turn channels out scarce foreign exchange from the country and entails upon the balance of payments. The host government will first always push for the local sourcing.

Again, it is true that a high tariff wall motivates tariff-jumping FDI. It happens in cases where demand for the product is price-inelastic and local substitutes are not available, Consumers are then forced to bear the price rise. In order to avoid such a situation, host country governments often encourage FDI inflow through lowering of tariff.

Domestic producers face tough competition from foreign manufacturers along with the consumers in the host country that are affected through tariff-jumping FDI. They ask the government to put some sort of restriction on foreign investors so that the domestic market can be sheltered. The host country government controls the operation of foreign investors through economic as well as defense and national security. The US government puts prohibitions on foreign investment in air transport, coastal shipping, commercial fisheries, communications and energy resources.

When foreign ownership results in extraterritorial application of laws and the regulatory mechanism of the firm's home country to its activities in the host country, the host country government does not relish it and imposes certain restrictions.

The US anti-trust law is applicable not only to the US owned firms but also to foreign-country firms. Developing countries do not like use of inappropriate technology or technologies that do not help develop local skills by foreign firms.

Home Country Perspective: It is also the home country government that regulates FDI on, both, economic and political grounds. It encourages investment abroad when such investment is beneficial to the home country. But when foreign investment outflow is not conducive to the economy, the home country government imposes restrictions on it. FDI is also encouraged/restricted depending upon the political relationship with the host country.

4.2.5 Modalities of Regulation in Host Country

There are different tools for regulating FDI:

1. **Ownership:** In 1973, in India, when the government proposed to restrict FDI, the Foreign Exchange Regulation Act was amended to limit the equity owned by foreign investors to 40 per cent in 1973. Again when it tried to encourage FDI in 1991, the ceiling was removed and hence now foreign investors have 100% equity in an Indian enterprise.

2. The government opens different sectors of the domestic economy for FDI. In 1991, in India, when the purpose came to restrict FDI, it is not allowed in many sectors of the domestic economy. In 1968 and again in 1973, the Indian government limited scope for FDI inflow.

3. The government restricts the repatriation of dividend, royalty, and other fees to the home country. Instead it bought into force the balancing requirements where the foreign enterprise has to export a certain amount of its product, which could balance its payments for imports or other payments.

4. The host government provides financial incentives and infrastructural facilities to foreign investors in order to attract such investment.

The financial incentives normally include:

- Tax or tariff incentives.

The infrastructural incentives include:

- Free or subsidised provision of land, electricity, transport, and so on.

In India, foreign investors get such facilities if they operate on export processing zone/special economic zone.

4.2.6 Modalities of Regulation in Home Country

The home country government intends to encourage FDI outflow, it provides insurance cover to the investors against political risk in the host country. Sometimes it grants loans to the investors for investment abroad or guarantees loans provided by financial institutions. It puts pressure on the host country government to relax restrictions, if any. When the home country government intends to restrict FDI outflow, it withdraws the facilities given to the investors and increases the tax rates on profits earned. It imposes outright sanctions that prohibit making any foreign investment.

Points to Remember

- **MNCs** are business enterprises that carry transactions across countries. MNCs are the most active players in international business.
- The MNCs are also known as MNEs, TNCs, Global Corporations, and International Corporations.
- TNCs have been spreading and growing across the globe very rapidly. Although the MNCs from the developed nations still dominate the scene, more and more MNCs are emerging from the developing countries.
- **Multinational Corporation** has no universally acceptable definition.
- Firms that participate in international business, however, large they may be solely by exporting or by licensing technology are not multinational enterprises.
- With liberalisation, MNCs have been spreading fast in the developing countries, with China hosting the largest number.
- Several Indian companies too are emerging as global players. MNCs are criticised, particularly by developing countries, on several grounds.
- **Criticisms of MNCs:**
  - ✓ Self interest are primary
  - ✓ Costly damages inflicted with impunity
  - ✓ Encourages bribing

- ✓ Worst hit are the marginal and small firms.
- ✓ Interferes with economic goals
- ✓ Social disruption
- ✓ Environmental degradation
- ✓ Imperialism
- ✓ Frustration and antipathy
- ✓ Technology.

- **In support of MNCs:**
  - ✓ Provide employment.
  - ✓ Raise national product and productivity.
  - ✓ Help build foreign exchange resources.
  - ✓ Introduce and develop new technical skills.
  - ✓ Introduce new managerial techniques.
  - ✓ Encourage the development and spin-off of new industries.
  - ✓ Raise the standard of living of the people.

Questions for Discussion

1. What is an MNC? What are its salient features?
2. Examine the arguments for and against MNCs.
3. Discuss the involvement of MNCs in International Business.
4. Write short notes on :
   (a) Meaning of Multinational Corporation.
   (b) Code of conduct for MNCs.
   (c) Different patterns of MNCs.
5. Explain the issues related to foreign investment involving technology transfer, pricing and regulations.
6. Examine the concepts of international collaborative arrangements and strategic alliance.

Multiple Choice Questions

1. What does MNC stand for?
   (a) Multinational City
   (b) Multination Corporations
   (c) Multinational Corporations
   (d) Multination City

2. TNC stands for:
   (a) Transnational Corporation
   (b) Transport Corporation
   (c) Transnational Community
   (d) Transnation Corporation

3. A Parent Enterprise is defined as:
   (a) an enterprise that controls debts of other parties in countries other than its home country, usually by owning a certain equity capital stake
   (b) an enterprise that controls assets of other entities in its home country, usually by owning a certain equity capital stake
   (c) an enterprise that controls assets of other entities in countries other than its home country, usually by owning shares
   (d) an enterprise that controls assets of other entities in countries other than its home country, usually by owning a certain equity capital stake

4. Which is a type of a MNC?
   (a) Ethnocentric
   (b) Polycentric
   (c) Regiocentric
   (d) All the above

5. A partnership between two firms, one with technology and another with market access is known as:
   (a) Purchasing
   (b) Licensing
   (c) Joint Venture
   (d) Strategic R & D

6. The determination of the 'prices' at which an MNC moves goods between its subsidiaries in various countries is known as:
   (a) Transfer pricing
   (b) Purchasing
   (c) Licensing
   (d) None of the above

7. The most common route for investments by MNCs in countries around the world is to:
   (a) set up new factories
   (b) buy existing local companies
   (c) form partnerships with local companies
   (d) both (a) and (b)

8. Where do MNCs choose to set up production?
   (a) Cheap goods
   (b) Cheap labour resources
   (c) Economic sustainability
   (d) None of these

9. MNE stands for:
   (a) Multinational Enterprise
   (b) Multinational Employee
   (c) Multination Enterprise
   (d) Multination Entrepreneur

10. Investment made by MNC is called:
    (a) Mutual investment
    (b) Inter-government investment
    (c) Portfolio investment
    (d) Foreign investment

ANSWERS

| 1. (c) | 2. (a) | 3. (d) | 4. (d) | 5. (c) |
| 6. (a) | 7. (c) | 8. (b) | 9. (a) | 10. (d) |

Project Questions

1. You are the International manager of an Indian business that has just developed a revolutionary new personal computer that can perform the same functions as existing PCs but costs only half as much to manufacture. Several patents protect the unique design of this computer. Your CEO has asked you to formulate a recommendation for how to expand into Western Europe. Your options are (a) to export from the United States, (b) to license a European firm to manufacture and market the computer in Europe, or (c) to set up a wholly owned subsidiary in Europe. Evaluate the pros and cons of each alternative and suggest a course of action to your CEO.

2. In your opinion what has been the contribution of MNCs towards the development of developing countries?

Chapter 5...

Regional Economic Groupings in Practice

Contents ...

- 5.1 Regional Economic Grouping
    - 5.1.1 Introduction
    - 5.1.2 Types of Regional Economic Groups
    - 5.1.3 Objectives of Regional Integration
    - 5.1.4 Advantages of Regional Integration
    - 5.1.5 Disadvantages of Regional Integration
- 5.2 Regionalism Vs. Multilateralism
    - 5.2.1 Multilateralism
    - 5.2.2 Regionalism
- 5.3 European Union (EU)
    - 5.3.1 Introduction
    - 5.3.2 Origin
    - 5.3.3 Objectives of the EU
    - 5.3.4 Development of the EU
    - 5.3.5 Organisational Structure
    - 5.3.6 Structure and Functioning of European Commission (EC)
    - 5.3.7 India – EU Trade
- 5.4 North American Free Trade Agreement (NAFTA)
    - 5.4.1 Introduction
    - 5.4.2 Evolution and Structure of NAFTA
    - 5.4.3 Salient Features of NAFTA
    - 5.4.4 Functions of NAFTA
    - 5.4.5 Impact of NAFTA
    - 5.4.6 Structure and Functioning of NAFTA
- 5.5 Regional Economic Cooperation
    - 5.5.1 The Southern China Growth Triangle
    - 5.5.2 Low-Cost Sourcing
- 5.6 Emerging Developments and Other Issues
    - 5.6.1 Ecological Concerns
    - 5.6.2 Countertrade

5.6.3 IT and International Business
- Points to Remember
- Questions for Discussion
- Multiple Choice Questions
- Project Questions

Learning Objectives ...
- To understand the basic objectives and functions of the following Regional Economic Groupings:
    - European Union (EU)
    - North American Free Trade Agreement (NAFTA)
- To study the concepts of regionalism and multiculturalism
- To learn the emerging developments and other issues related to international business including
    - Growing concern for ecology
    - Counter trade
    - IT and international business

5.1 Regional Economic Grouping

5.1.1 Introduction

Regional Economic Groups are the associations of countries situated in a particular region whereby they come to a common understanding regarding rules and regulations to be followed while exporting and importing goods among them. They have liberal rules for member countries with a separate set of rules laid out for non-members. The European Union (EU), North American Free Trade Agreement (NAFTA), The Association of South-East Asian Nations (ASEAN), South Asian Association for Regional Cooperation (SAARC) are groups popularly known as trading blocs.

The idea behind creating trading blocs is to reduce or eliminate unnecessary trade barriers between member states, and to allow the free movement of goods, services, labour and capital. However, non-members of trading blocs face financial and non-financial restrictions on their exports to these blocs, such as tariffs, quotas and even restrictions. In today's scenario it is difficult for any country to survive outside one of these blocs as the world is into expanding groups of trading nations by promoting free trade among them, and at the same time restricting it to those countries outside of their blocs.

Regional Economic Integration represents an agreement among countries within a particular geographic region, i.e. an *economic bloc*, to reduce and ultimately remove tariff and non-tariff barriers to the free flow of goods, services, capital and labour. Neighbouring countries tend to ally with each other because of their proximity to one another and because of their similar regional tastes. This brings about ease of establishing channels of distribution and a willingness to cooperate with one another for the greater benefit of all allied parties.

5.1.2 Types of Regional Economic Groups

1. **Free Trade Area (FTA):** A free trade area is an economic bloc in which all barriers to trade are abolished among member countries. However each member country maintains its own independent external trade barriers beyond the bloc.

2. **Customs Union:** A customs union is an economic bloc in which all barriers to trade are abolished among member countries. However common external barriers are levied against non-members.

3. **Common Market:** A common market is an economic bloc in which all member countries face no barriers to trade. Common external barriers are levied against non-members and restrictions on the internal flows of capital and labour are abolished.

4. **Economic Integration:** Economic integration, i.e. an economic union, is an economic bloc in which all barriers to trade and flows of capital and labour within the bloc are enjoyed by the member countries. They establish common external trade and investment barriers; harmonise commercial, monetary and fiscal policies; establish a common currency and establish a political structure to deal with economic issues.

5. **Economic Union:** It is more advance level of integration. Apart from satisfying the conditions of the common market, it achieve some harmonised national economic policies, through a common central bank, unified monetary and fiscal policy, etc. example: European Union (EU).

Free trade area	Free trade among members				
Customs union	Free trade among members	Common external commercial policy			
Common market	Free trade among members	Common external commercial policy	Free factor mobility within the market		
Economic union	Free trade among members	Common external commercial policy	Free factor mobility within the market	Harmonised economic policies	
Economic integration	Free trade among members	Common external commercial policy	Free factor mobility within the market	Harmonised economic policies	Super-national organisational structure

Fig. 5.1: Types of Regional Economic Groups

5.1.3 Objectives of Regional Integration

1. To pursue economic benefits from achieving a more efficient production structure by exploiting economies of scale. This can be done through spreading fixed cost over larger regional markets, increased economic growth from foreign direct investment, learning from experience, etc.
2. To obtain non-economic objectives such as strengthening political ties and managing migration flows.
3. To ensure increased security of market access for smaller countries by forming regional trading blocs with larger countries.
4. To improve members' bargaining strength in multilateral trade negotiations or to protect against the slow pace of trade negotiation.
5. To promote regional infant industries because these industries cannot be viable without protected regional market.
6. To prevent damage to their trading strength due to further trade diversion from third countries.

5.1.4 Advantages of Regional Integration

1. Less chance of conflict and war.
2. Larger markets and customer base allows businesses within member countries to exploit economies of scale.
3. Freedom of movement of goods and people.
4. Increased global significance.
5. Improving environmental and social conditions.
6. The promotion of democracy and liberalisation.
7. The elimination of protectionism increases trade, leading to a more efficient allocation of member state resources.
8. More concentration on specialised industry.
9. Optimum utilisation of resources.

5.1.5 Disadvantages of Regional Integration

1. Loss of sovereignty, independence, and national identity.
2. Loss of national power in favour of an even bigger government.
3. Increased competition leading to unemployment in some domestic industries.
4. Loss of border control and the increased risk of smuggled goods and people.
5. Uniform laws don't account for cultural differences.
6. The elimination of trade barriers among the member states may divert trade away from more efficient non-member states that are disadvantaged by the protectionism they still face.

5.2 Regionalism Vs. Multilateralism

5.2.1 Multilateralism

Multilateralism means involving two or more nations or parties. It is represented by the efforts on liberalisation of international relations, and was started when the GATT was signed and developed into broader fields of trade in services, investment, agricultural products, public procurement, and intellectual property rights with its more sophisticated successor - World Trade Organisation (WTO).

A **multilateral agreement** is defined as a *binding agreement between three or more parties concerning the terms of a specific circumstance*. The agreements usually occur between three individual parties or agencies but the terms mostly refer to multilateral agreements between several countries. The agreements result in a common ground between the various participants involved in the issue concerning them at present. Multilateral agreements lessen the trade barriers between the parties involved and hence increase the economic integration between the parties. It is a successful method of liberalising trade in an interdependent global economy.

The agreement is usually complex in nature and allows many countries to join in. The General Agreement on Tariffs and Trade, (GATT) now administered by the World Trade Organisation, is a treaty in which subscribers commit to individual levels of tariffs for trade with other countries.

Robert Keohane defined Multilateralism as: *"the practise of coordinating policies in groups of three or more states."*

Multilateralism, according to **Ruggie** (1992), *can be seen as a deep organising principle of post-war international life* with three defining characteristics:

1. **Indivisibility** of the system is a whole in which the actions of one party affect all parties and each party acknowledges its allegiance to the single whole. It is indivisible in that it permits an extremely dense and far-reaching network of trade links and of intergovernmental contacts and is viewed as having an existence separate from all the individual trade links between participants, and in that its separate existence is seen as valuable.
2. **Generalised** rules of conduct interactions between parties are governed by widely recognised general principles, rather than ad hoc or particularistic interests.
3. **Diffuse reciprocity** of all parties expects to gain from the system, but do not demand precise reciprocity from every separate transaction. Reciprocity is diffuse in that governments do accept individual actions that appear not to be in their immediate interests, but it is generally accepted that, overall, every country has to gain.

Often Multilateralism is said to be the method where countries get together and solve their problems in an interactive and cooperative manner.

Looking at Ruggie's definition of multilateralism, the concept of regionalism weakens multilateralism as it goes against the MFN. The definition also tends to be destructive as it aggravates the situation where the parties focus more on some links than others. One way is to make sure that regionalism follows generalised rules where all agree and it should not prevent some links having strong stand than the others. The former merely recognises that the world trading system is imperfectly multilateral, while in practice the latter depends on whether governments shift their focus from general to particular trade relations.

5.2.2 Regionalism

Regionalism in international trade policy refers to the economic integration between two or more countries based on formal agreements. The most commonly used definition of a regional free trade agreement is an agreement among countries within a specific geographical region. The concept "regional" refers to a limited number of countries, as mentioned above, and is used to set it apart from multilateral liberalisation, which includes all member states of the WTO. Its objectives are to eliminate barriers to trade and facilitate the cross-border movement of goods and services among the signatories. The WTO also requires regional trade agreements to reduce tariffs between countries, but does not allow these countries to increase tariffs on countries which do not participate, according to the Harvard University. When tariffs are reduced, it allows people to buy goods from other countries at lower prices and the trading partners allow conditions that are suitable for both the parties.

Regionalism does not necessarily refer to unions of countries in specific regions, although this is often the case, but also to trade agreements among countries on different continents. According to the **Inter-American Development Bank**, *Regional trade agreements regulate more than one half of global trade.* Examples of some famous regional trade agreements include the European Common Market and the North American Free Trade Agreement.

5.3 European Union (EU)

5.3.1 Introduction

In recent years, a large number of trading blocs have emerged. These exist in all parts of the world. The number of regional trade agreements rose from less than 25 in 1990 to more than 90 in 1998. These range from huge regional trading blocs like EU to small and loose agreements between groups of small countries.

5.3.2 Origin

The European Economic Community (EEC), also known as the European Common Market (ECM) or the European Community (EC) and now as European Union (EU) is by far the most successful of the regional economic integration schemes.

It was formally established by the Treaty of Rome in 1957. But the efforts in this direction can be traced to 1951 when the European Coal and Steel Community Agreement was signed in Paris. The EEC originally comprised of six nations-Belgium, France, Republic of Germany, Italy, Luxembourg and Netherlands. As of now, EU has 27 members and some more are expected to join.

The Treaty of Rome required every member country to:
- Eliminate tariffs, quotas and other barriers on intra-community trade.
- Adopt a common policy on agriculture, transport and competition in industry.
- Free movement of productive factors, to be allowed, within the community.
- Form a common internal tariff on their imports from the rest of the world.
- Policies on taxation, monetary and social security to be harmonised.

In 1973 the EEC was expanded with the inclusion of U.K., Denmark and Ireland. In 1981 Greece joined the community. In 1986, the membership of EC rose to number 15 when Spain, Portugal, Austria, Finland and Sweden joined.

A detailed programme for attaining a single integrated market was set forth by the EC's executive body in June 1985 in a White Paper entitled 'Completing the Internal Market'. This programme envisaged the unification of the economies of the member nations into a single market by removing all border barriers to trade and mobility and by unifying the economic policies and regulations. This was described as Europe 1992 (EC 1992).

The White Paper listed 300 specific areas where it was intended to eliminate the physical, technical and fiscal hurdles to an integrated market of a genuine European Community (free movement for goods, services, persons and capital was intended).

Following were the hurdles that were to be removed:
- Border control.
- Different taxation systems.
- Controls on mobility of capital.
- Limitations on the mobility of people and their right to establishment.
- Differing regulations of services.
- Different product regulations and standards.
- Protectionist public procurement policies.
- Difference in legal framework for business.

With a population much larger than that of the US and a GDP close to that of the US and higher than that of Japan, the EC is the largest market in the world. Some observers regarded the EC-1992 as the "EUROPEAN FORTRESS" or "FORTRESS 92". It meant that henceforth exports from non-member countries to the EC would have to encounter a mounting barrier. However, the EC officials maintained that the Fortress Europe was a senseless story. They argued that the single European market would boost the world trade and growth.

It is true, however, that the real objective of the single market is to boost the competitiveness of European industry and its rivals, mainly the USA, Japan and South-East

Asian countries. It meant that the benefits of liberalisation would not be extended to non-EC nations in a unilateral and automatic manner. Non-members who want to sell their goods and services in Europe would have to provide EU with reciprocal access to their national markets.

The total membership of the EU, with effect from May 1, 2004 became 25 with the nations namely Estonia, Lithuania, Poland, Czech Republic, Slovak Republic, Hungary, Slovenia, Cyprus and Malta joining in Bulgaria and Romania joined in 2007, taking the number of members of EU to 27. There are already indications of other countries to join the Union in future.

At present The European Union (EU) comprise 28 member states, which are party to the founding treaties of the union and thereby subject to the privileges and obligations of membership. The European Union (EU) comprises of nations namely Austria, Belgium, Bulgaria, Croatia, Cyprus, Czech Republic, Denmark, Estonia, Finland, France, Germany, Greece, Hungary, Ireland, Italy, Latvia, Lithuania, Luxembourg, Malta, Netherlands, Poland, Portugal, Romania, Slovakia, Slovenia, Spain, Sweden and United Kingdom.

5.3.3 Objectives of the EU

(i) Elimination of customs duties among member states.
(ii) Elimination of obstacles to the free flow of import and/or export of goods and services among member nations.
(iii) Free movement of capital and people within the union.
(iv) Establishment of common custom duties and united industrial/commercial policies regarding countries outside the community.
(v) Common laws to maintain competition throughout the community and to fight monopolies or illegal cartels.
(vi) Acceptance of common agricultural policies, transport policies, technical standards, health and safety regulations and educational degrees.
(vii) Common measures for consumer protection.
(viii) Regional funds to encourage the economic development of certain countries/regions.
(ix) Greater monetary and fiscal co-ordination among member states and certain common monetary/fiscal policies.

5.3.4 Development of the EU

Since the signing of the EU's founding treaty, the EU has been engaged in enlargement and deeper integration. After creating a customs union, the EU has now achieved something approaching a single market among all its members and has recently introduced a fledgling monetary union between 11 of its members. The EU has also been establishing formal links with countries and trading blocs beyond its borders. The EU is not aiming at mere economic integration but by economic integration it aims at achieving political union.

The economic benefits from this huge trading block are substantial.

- There will be gains from eliminating the transaction costs associated with border patrols, customs procedures and the like.
- Economic growth will be boosted due to economies of scale which will be achieved when production facilities become more concentrated.
- There will be gains from more intense competition among EU firms. Firms that were monopolistic in one country will now be subject to competition from firms in other country.

Firms operating in Europe will enjoy substantial benefits.

(i) These firms will gain as their operations in one country can now be freely expanded into others.

(ii) Their products may be sold freely across borders.

(iii) The free movement of capital allows these firms to sell securities, raise capital and recruit labour throughout Europe.

(iv) Firms will enjoy substantial economies of scale in production and marketing.

(v) The most interesting development for firms operating in the EU is the dynamic potential of the single market and economic and monetary union.

(vi) A large competitive market like EU will encourage efficiency and innovation prompting the reorganisation of companies, industries and markets.

(vii) It has to restructure the European industry.

Firms from non-member countries also gain from the EU. Well-established US based MNCs such as H. J. Heinz will be able to reap the benefits of the new economies of scale. For example, earlier 3M plants turned out different versions of its product for various markets. But, now the 3M plant in Wales makes abrasives and tapes for all Europe and enjoys economies to scale.

Many MNCs are developing Pan-European strategies to exploit the emerging situation i.e. they are standardising their products and processes to the greatest extent possible without compromising local input and implementation.

EU benefits as the enlargement of EU by 10 more members will boost economic growth and create jobs in both the old and new member states. In other words, the increased membership is expected to strengthen the EU's role in world affairs, foreign security, trade policies and other fields of global governance. It is also expected that the quality of life will improve as the new members adopt EU policies on environmental protection and the campaign against drugs and illegal immigration. Thus, EU will be enriched through increased cultural diversity, interchange of ideas and improved understanding of other people.

5.3.5 Organisational Structure

The EU is made up of multiple bodies and institutions. The below figure lists the important bodies and institutions:

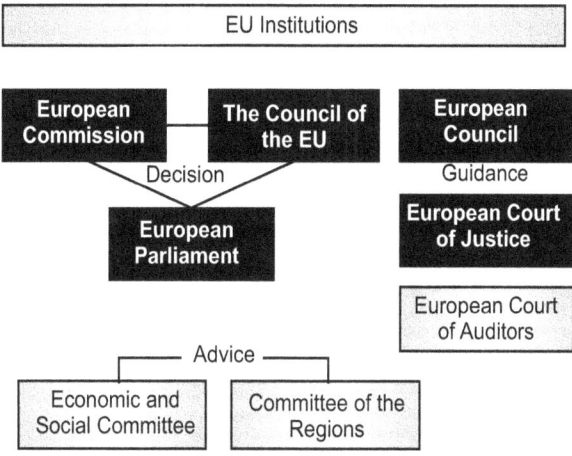

Fig. 5.2: EU Institutions

1. **European Commission:** The European Commission acts as the executive of the European Union, and it is the only body that may propose new legislation. There are 28 commissioners representing one from each member state. Each member is taken on board by consulting with the Parliament as well as the member states, although the commission's main purpose is to represent the European view as a whole, rather than the perspectives of individual member states. After every 5 years, a new commission is appointed. The Commission is divided into departments, each of which is responsible for proposing new legislation and policies in a given area. A major role is played by the Commission in implementing and enforcing EU directives and regulations and it represents the EU in international negotiations.

2. **Council of the European Union:** The main legislative body of the EU, along with the Parliament is The Council of the European Union, also known as the Council of Ministers. The Union is also made up of 28 members, one representing each member state and each one is assigned specific issue areas. The main responsibilities are:

- Passing laws (often, but not always, in conjunction with Parliament),
- Coordinating economic, foreign, and criminal justice policy,
- Making treaties.

Those member states that have a bigger population can receive more votes, but most decisions need to be passed by the majority vote, which requires a minimum of 260 (out of total 352) votes.

3. European Parliament: The European Parliament mainly has an advisory role but with the introduction of the Treaty of Maastricht (1993) it soon became an important legislating partner to the Council. The Parliament consists of 785 members, who are directly elected by the population of the member states once every five years. The main responsibilities are:
- To pass laws in conjunction with the Council
- Adopt or reject the EU budget.

It does not initiate the legislation but it can ask the European Commission to do so. It is responsible for holding the Commission politically accountable, and members of Parliament may question Commissioners regarding various policies. Parliament also has the power to dismiss the Commission by adopting a motion of censure.

4. European Court of Justice: The major judicial body of the EU is the European Court of Justice. There are 28 judges, again each one appointed by a member of state in consultation with the other member's states for 6 years term. Cases are typically decided by smaller chambers of judges, and the Court is assisted by advocates-general who present the issues of law in the case. The ECJ chooses cases that come from the EU law but it is not limited to the disputes about the application of treaties, disputes about interpretation or the failure to implement the EU legislation. It may decide cases arising between member states, EU institutions, businesses, and individuals, and its decisions are binding.

5. European General Court (formerly Court of First Instance): The European General Court is the lower court to the ECJ. Though it was created with limited jurisdiction in 1989, its jurisdiction got expanded to cover most issues that can be decided by the ECJ in 2001. The Court of First Instance does not decide cases brought by the member states. The Court's decisions are subject to appeal to the ECJ, and like the ECJ, it is made up of at least 28 judges, each one selected by a member state.

6. European Central Bank: The European Central Bank is responsible for issuing the Euro as well as with the setting and implementing monetary policy.

5.3.6 Structure and Functioning of European Commission (EC)

The first real supranational organisation is the European Commission, having no international or domestic political equivalent.

Composition of the Commission

As of November 2005, EU consists of 25 members who are suggested by the governments of the member states and are appointed for a 5 year term. At the present time it also needs a vote of appointment by the European Parliament before it can be sworn in. The commissioners need to act independently in the interest of the Community and not as negotiators for their states. 20,000 official staff support them which is divided in to 24 director general (e.g.: agriculture, transport etc.) and niche services which are also split into departments and directorates.

Functions of the Commission

The Commission's main tasks can be summarised under four headings.

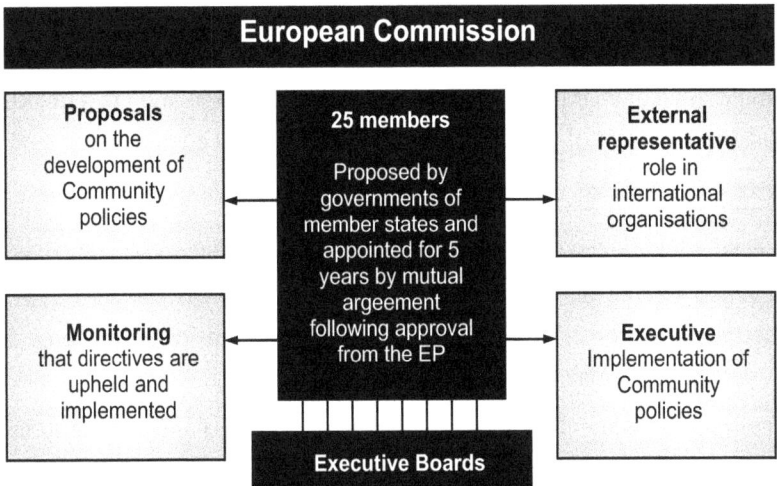

Fig 5.3: European Commission

1. **Proposals for Developing Union Policies:** Right of initiative: Based on the proposal from the Commission, each decision has to be taken by the Council. The Commission's task is to act as an engine of integration drawing up proposals for the development of Community policy. The Commission gets considerable influence in the legislative procedure by the right and authority to determine the EU's agenda, to submit proposals at a particular juncture and to link differing initiatives.

2. **Guardian of Treaties:** Whenever violations are identified, the Commission can appeal to the European Court of Justice and the Commission is also responsible for monitoring the application of treaty provisions and decisions made by other EC institutions.

3. **Executive Authority:** Executive authority for the implementation of Community policy: This includes as the implementation of EC policies as well as the administration of finances as well. Of course, this does not mean that the Commission is responsible for making sure that the countless number of decrees and guidelines are implemented in individual member states. This is carried out by the administrations in the member states or their regional sections. The Commission's main role is to supervise and monitor the actions being taken by the member states.

4. **External Representation:** The Commission represents the EU at the GATT negotiations and international organisations; this sometimes takes place together with the member states and/or the respective presidents.

Characteristics of the Commission

The Characteristics of the Commission are:

- Its distinct differentiation at a functional level.

- The fact that it represents a multi-national bureaucracy using an extensive system of committees (commitology) within which very close cooperation takes place both with the administrations of member states and with national and European associations.

5.3.7 India – EU Trade

India's stake with the EU is high. The country enjoys a multidimensional relationship with the EU, its largest trading partner, accounting for a quarter of its overseas trade. The EU is also the foremost investor in India and is a major destination for service providers, a vital technology vendor and a major contributor of development aid.

The Free Trade Agreement launched in 2007 enabled the EU and India to further increase their trade in goods and services as well as bilateral investment through trade and investment liberalisation.

The 2012 negotiations made substantial progress in bringing about improved market access for goods and services and achieving a meaningful chapter on government procurement and sustainable development among others.

India is an important trade partner for the EU and an emerging global economic power. The country combines a sizable and growing market of more than 1 billion people. The value of EU-India trade grew from € 28.6 billion in 2003 to € 72.7 billion in 2013. EU investment stock in India grew substantially reaching € 41.8 billion in 2012. Trade in commercial services quadrupled in the past decade, going from € 5.2billion in 2002 to € 22.5 billion in 2012.

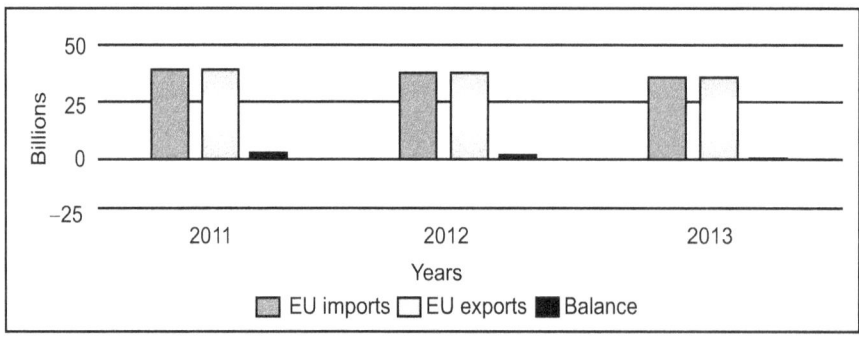

Fig. 5.4: EU-India "Trade in Goods" Statistics

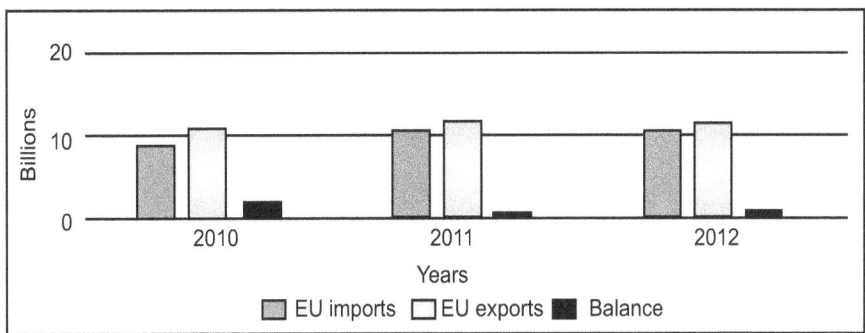

Fig. 5.5: EU-India "Trade in Services" Statistics

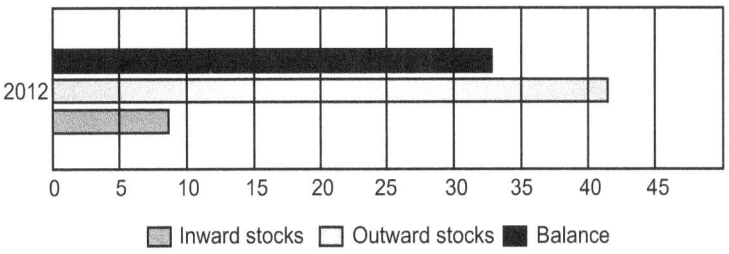

Fig. 5.6: Foreign Direct Investment

The largest trade partners, within the EU have been United Kingdom, Germany, Belgium and France.

India's exports include (to EU) textiles, jute, leather goods, polished diamonds, engineering goods, chemicals, marine products etc. **India's imports** include edible oils, dairy products, capital goods, optical instruments, aluminium and copper products, synthetic rubber, photo and cinematographic goods etc. India also receives technology, investment and development aid from EU countries.

The performance of India in relation to its exports is quite poor due to various factors such as lack of price competitiveness, poor quality image, bad reputation with respect to delivery schedules, poor export marketing skills, protectionist policy followed by the EU countries etc. This poor performance on exports front calls for corrective measures. The EU is a highly competitive market courted by about 100 trading nations and unless Indian competitiveness measures up to the international level, things will not be easy. But, India's achievement to overcome the fortress has not been very impressive, which countries like Japan and the South-East Asian countries have achieved to a certain extent. The positive factor that works as advantage for Indian exporters and for exporters of other countries is that henceforth they will need to deal with one set of rules and regulations when dealing with EU instead of the rules and regulations of each of the member country to which they want to export. Likewise, one currency (Euro) applies to most of the members of EU.

Benefits to India from Enlarged EU

- One great benefit is the replacement of the different policy and regulatory environments of the newly joined members by that of the uniform policy and regulatory environment of the Union and the reduction in transaction costs.
- There would be expansion of the market benefitting from the enlargement of the Union.
- Availability of new ports in the enlarged EU could reduce transportation costs.
- The enlarged EU may also spur joint ventures with Indian companies.
- The harmonisation of the tariff structures of the new members i.e. average weighted tariff of these countries will significantly come down to the benefit of the exporters to these markets.

Challenges to India

- As the ACs are labour abundant and low income countries, India may also face stiff competition due to temporary mobility of its natural resources, persons to EU and business outsourcing by EU to India.
- Many Indian products will have to face a stiff competition in the EU from the new members.
- The low labour cost in these nations could encourage EU firms to set up manufacturing bases there or source from there which can negatively affect Indian exports to EU because it would give rise to competition from these firms in other markets.
- Countries like Poland and Czech Republic, compete with India in selling textiles and apparel, footwear and leather, chemical compounds, iron and steel, auto parts etc. As per one estimate, India and Poland compete in EU market for 46 of the top 100 exports from India to the EU. In short, it is feared that the relative competitive advantage of many of India's exports to the EU (15) may be affected by the enlargement of EU.
- The Accession Countries (ACs) may even affect the FDI inflow to India. Poland, Hungary and Czech Republic compete with India in top 10 most attractive destinations for FDI.

Government may have to ease up its policy framework and the Indian businesses may have to reposition themselves to take full advantage of the opportunities posed by the expansion of the world's largest economic block.

To sum up, there are apprehensions expressed about the mighty EU. One of the main concerns of the US and Asian countries is that the EU will at some point impose new barriers on exports into the EU from non-member. Various indications are there to prove that the EU has adopted protectionist policies towards external trade. As for the less developing countries, they are benefitting from the EU, as the EU covers trade as well as aid. Increasing assistance is given to developing countries in general with less regard for political or strategic ties. In turn, the EU firms benefit from contracts relating to project assistance.

5.4 North American Free Trade Agreement (NAFTA)

5.4.1 Introduction

The North American Free Trade Agreement which came into effect on January 1, 1994 is an agreement signed by Canada, Mexico and the United States, creating a trilateral trade bloc in North America. It superseded the Canada–United States Free Trade Agreement between the US and Canada.

As of 2013 this trade bloc, in terms of combined purchasing power and GDP of its members, is the largest in the world.

5.4.2 Evolution and Structure of NAFTA

The United States signed its first free trade agreement (FTA) with Israel in the mid-1980, followed by a Free Trade Agreement with Canada in 1988 and in 1994 was the North American Free Trade Agreement i.e. NAFTA. It was expanded to include Mexico, making North America a giant free trade area. Thus, NAFTA came into being on January 1, 1994 comprising U.S., Canada and Mexico. This Agreement is an American counterpart to the EU, but the purpose of EU is economic and political integration whereas the purpose of NAFTA is purely economic.

NAFTA is more important because it is the largest trading bloc i.e. largest economic grouping as it encompasses the whole of the North America- combined population and total GNP greater than the 15 member EU (not the expanded EU). In future, NAFTA could further expand by adding more countries together such as North, Central and South America.

The Table 5.1 below gives us the data on NAFTA Members.

Table 5.1: Economic Indicators NAFTA (for 2013)

Countries	Population, Millions Persons	GDP (Official Exchange rate), Billions US Dollars	GDP per Capita, Thousands US Dollars	Inflation Rate, %	Unemployment Rate, %	Trade Balance, Billions US Dollars
Canada	34.6	1825.0	52.7	1.0	7.1	-12.3
Mexico	116.2	1327.0	11.4	4.0	4.9	0.2
USA	316.7	16720.0	52.8	1.5	7.3	1,348.0

The uniqueness of NAFTA is that it is not only the world's largest trading area but it combines two of the world's major trading nations with a large developing nation. Geographically, there is a strong logic to this trading area. The USA is Mexico's main export market and Mexico is one of the USA's main trading partners. However, many Americans fear that Mexico's low-wage economy will attract investment from the USA. This would result in unemployment when the companies relocate. Despite these fears, trade between the USA and Mexico has increased substantially since 1994.

The NAFTA aims at elimination of tariffs and agreement also extends to wide range of non-tariff barriers. It includes in areas of service, public procurement, foreign investment, intellectual property rights and environmental measures. NAFTA is not a custom union as members are free to set their own external tariffs and rules of origin, requiring a minimum 50% local content for cross-border trade in most products.

Although Canadian-Mexican trade was not considerable when the Agreement was signed but it was significant between US and the other two countries. The U.S. is the largest trading partner of both Canada and Mexico and Canada and Mexico are the first and third most important trading partners with the U.S.

It is expected that NAFTA will provide dynamic effects of economic integration. For example, U.S. and Canadian consumers are expected to gain from low cost agricultural goods. Further, Canada and U.S. also stand to gain from Mexico, which is a huge export market for the two countries.

5.4.3 Salient Features of NAFTA

The NAFTA seeks to eliminate all tariffs on products moving among the three countries and end other barriers to services and investment capital within North America.

Following are the areas covered by NAFTA:
- **(a) Trade Rules:** Safeguards, subsidies, countervailing and antidumping duties and health and safety standards.
- **(b) Market Access:** Tariff and non-tariff barriers, rules of origin and governmental procurement.
- **(c) Services:** Provisions to ensure trade in services (consulting, engineering, software etc.) that exist for trade in goods.
- **(d) Dispute Settlement:** Provides a dispute settlement that will be followed instead of countries taking unilateral action against any offending party.

- **(e) Intellectual Property:** All the three countries pledge to provide adequate and effective protection and enforcement of intellectual property rights, while ensuring that enforcement measures do not themselves become barriers to legitimate trade.
- **(f) Investment:** Establishing investment rules that will protect the interests of investors.
- **(g) Intellectual Property:** All the three countries pledge to provide adequate and effective protection and enforcement of intellectual property rights, while ensuring that enforcement measures do not themselves become barriers to legitimate trade.

A very significant feature of the NAFTA is that, while most free trade agreements have provisions only for the trade liberalisation, it includes labour and environmental standards. The labour standards were included due to the fear that U.S and Canada would lose jobs to Mexico due to Mexico's cheaper wages, poor working conditions and no stringent environmental enforcement. Similarly, environmental standards were included to push for an upgrade of environmental standards in Mexico and allow no room for lax in environmental standards.

5.4.4 Functions of NAFTA

The major functions of NAFTA are:
1. To eliminate trade barriers in various service sectors belonging to its member nations.
2. To reduce high Mexican tariffs and help promote agricultural exports.
3. To assist firms spanning the three nations to bid on government contracts.
4. To assure fair market value to investors by reducing risk and offering the same legal rights that are enjoyed by local investors.
5. To help investors to claim against a government by offering legal help.

5.4.5 Impact of NAFTA

NAFTA has achieved substantial trade liberalisation. The trade between the US and Canada and US and Mexico is substantial and has been rising fast. The two-way trading relation between the US and Canada is the largest in the world. Mexico is the second largest market for US exports, earlier it was Japan. Further, Mexico is the third most important supplier to the US market after Canada and Japan. As for Canada-Mexico trade, they are still marginal trading partners with each other. NAFTA is expected to provide the dynamic effects of economic integration. For example, Canadian and US consumers are expected to benefit from low cost agricultural products and also can count on the benefit from the large and growing Mexican market, which is a huge market for US products.

NAFTA has set an example of trade diversion. Many US firms have established manufacturing facilities in Asia to take advantage of cheap labour, and then ship products from there to the US. It is expected that NAFTA members will be able to use each other rather than the Asian nations as locations for trade investment. Such movement has already been started by US automakers Ford who have established manufacturing facilities in Mexico to serve the US market.

The creation of NAFTA is as significant as introduction of euro in Europe, China's metamorphosis into capitalism. The formation of NAFTA was seen as a bold attempt to demonstrate to the world the power and ability of free trade to convert a poor country into a developing nation. Thus, if there was litmus tests for globalisation i.e. how can globalisation have its positive impact on the economy, it was NAFTA.

It is already a decade since the agreement was signed and the member nations have several reasons to feel proud of bloc's achievements. American manufacturers, who were desperate to be relieved from Asian competition, rushed to Mexico to take advantage of low wages (which were $1/10^{th}$ of those in the US). Foreign investment almost flooded Mexico, rising at $12 billion per year during the last decade, which is three times than what India receives. As a result exports grew and Mexico's per capita income rose by 24% ($4000), nearly 10 times higher than the per capita income in China. The economy of the country at $594 billion is placed as the ninth largest in the world.

There have been divergent views on the benefits of NAFTA. One fear expressed is its **impact on employment**. It is the loss of jobs to both US and Canada in favour of Mexico. This loss results from the increasing location of manufacturing facilities in Mexico to benefit from low-wage labour there. From the point of view of Mexico, the integration may lead to massive restructuring of the economy and resultant unemployment. The reason is that the exposure of the Mexican firms to giant American and Canadian competitors.

Further, the **environmental** lobby has voiced concerns about NAFTA - they point to the sludge in the Rio Grande River and the smog in the air over Mexico City. They warn that Mexico could degrade clean air and toxic-waste standards across the continent.

Those who **fear loss of National Sovereignty** in Mexico have opposed to NAFTA. Critics in Mexico argue that their country will be dominated by the US firms that will not really contribute to Mexico's economic growth. Instead, US will use Mexico as a low cost assembly site, while keeping their high-paying, high-skilled jobs to border regions-or to the business that migrated to Mexico border (*maquiladora* industries). There is sharp criticism from the way the US firms located in Mexico treat labour, particularly union organisers. For example, in early 1994, Honeywell Inc was accused of firing employees, who tried to organise a union at a Mexican manufacturing plant where worker's average pay was $1.00 per hour.

Mexicans fear that the US is no more interested in their country and have a feeling that by joining NAFTA the Mexico's sacrifices made have exceeded the benefits that they are receiving. The hope of Mexico was that it would be America's biggest workshop. However, this honour has gone to China.

In Mexico, the policymakers believed that trade agreement would get them more benefits and signed trade agreements with 30 other nations, more than any other nation. Undoubtedly, consumers got cheaper and better quality goods. But local manufacturers for goods like toys, shoes, farmers of rice and corn are struggling to survive the competition from cheap imports. This perception in Mexico is spreading to other Latin countries. These countries after 15 years of open economy to trade and investment are showing signs of fatigue with the free market formula preached by the US and the IMF. This is an ironical situation. NAFTA which initiated the free trade movement, as catalyst for poor economies, spurred the Uruguay round of global trade arguments in the mid 1990s and setting the stage for China's entry into the WTO (metamorphosis of China into capitalism).

Let us understand the promises made and realities of NAFTA.

(a) **Promise:** In exports, Mexican made goods would compete successfully in the US.
   Reality: Exports have tripled, but only a handful of Mexican companies have been benefitted from the large gains.

(b) **Promise:** In terms of investment, foreign capital would flow across Mexico to capitalise on the nation's low wages.
   Reality: Foreign Direct Investment (FDI) averages $ 12 billion per annum, but it mainly goes to Border States.

(c) **Promise:** In terms of jobs, the agreement would create manufacturing jobs and raise Mexico's incomes.
   Reality: No doubt, 500,000 jobs have been created, but the peso *maquiladoras* crash has held down wages. *Maquiladora* industry or assembly plants are attracted by tax benefits, low costs and tax regulations.

(d) **Promise:** In relation to stability, NAFTA would force Mexico to maintain financial discipline and follow strictly the reforms.
   Reality: Mexico has not relapsed into protectionism: Sovereign debt is investment grade.

(e) **Promise:** As for Mexico's relation with US, Mexico and the US would forge an unbeatable partnership in a global economy.
   Reality: Although business/commercial links stay strong governmental relations have not been cordial.

5.4.6 Structure and Functioning of NAFTA

NAFTA's governance structure is simple and based on two institutions:
1. the Free Trade Commission (TFC)
2. the Secretariat.

1. The Free Trade Commission (FTC)

The Free Trade Commission (FTC) is the main or principal body of NAFTA and it supervises the performance and evolution of NAFTA. The other responsibilities include dispute settlement and it is also composed of the US Trade Representative, the Canadian Minister for International Trade, and the Mexican Secretary of Commerce and Industrial Development. The day-to-day work of the FTC is carried out by expert working groups and committees.

This authority was laid out in Article 2001 (2) of the NAFTA, which gave express power to the FTC to oversee, resolve, and supervise the work of "all committees and working groups established under [the NAFTA] Agreement".

The FTC also has implied power in Section 2001 (3) to *"establish, delegate, seek the advice of non-governmental groups and take other [unspecified] action".*

Every year these powers are implemented at the trilateral cabinet-level meetings as prescribed by Article 2001, or in the acts that review the national court decision affecting North American Trade.

The powers of the FTC are:
1. Technical,
2. Specific,
3. Obligatory.

There is no effective method of amending the NAFTA rules, and the FTC works in harmony. Lacking the ability to delegate power or vote by majority rule as a legislature might, the FTC suffers from a democratic deficit and this could damage its long-term legitimacy. If NAFTA is to be feasible, this minimal institutionalisation will need to be reformed in the future, the technical nature of NAFTA is in keeping with the functionalist approach.

2. The Secretariat

Organised on a national basis, with each member responsible for supporting its own staff, the Secretariat serves as an administrator for the FTC. Technically speaking, the secretariat assists the FTC, along with the dispute panels, committees, and working groups. There are separate national offices of the Secretariat in Mexico City, Ottawa and Washington. This decentralised structure does not mean the secretariat has any real power of its own through delegation from the FTC. It actually takes care of the day to day activities prescribed by Article 2002. *If the FTC directs it under Article 2002 (a)(c) to administer a trade dispute panel, it must adhere to the guidelines of Article 2012.* Due to this high level legal aspect, the secretariat is restrained from acting independently and just insures that real decisions are made by the FTC rather than at the discretion of secretariat staff. This low level of delegation limits the responsiveness of the secretariat to exogenous groups such as labour or environmental groups and guarantees that free trade and investor interests will be guarded vociferously.

The national secretariats are also complemented by a NAFTA Coordinating Secretariat (NAFTACS) based in Mexico. This trilateral secretariat was created on January 14, 1995. The central secretariat is to help administer labour and environmental issues that fall under

NAFTA. This body is not really active in reality due to the limited enforceability and tax regulation and is unequal in power to the investment and free trade lobbies. As interests clash, the US domestic opposition to NAFTA is great among the environmental and labour communities and will grow. This means that the international secretariat needs greater authority to overcome the narrow interests of business elites in each country, and thus endow NAFTA with democratic legitimacy.

5.5 Regional Economic Cooperation

The emergence of regional cooperation has been one of the most important developments in the world trade system. When the Cold War ended political tensions reduced between countries in Asia which increased vertical integration. Cities like Bangkok, Kuala Lumpur, and Singapore have been lifting their populations out of poverty in part through cooperative arrangements with neighbouring countries. Transnational economic zones have utilised the different endowments of the various countries of East Asia, exploiting cooperative trade and development opportunities. Information technology has improved linkages between economies and put remote regions in contact with the world.

1. The private sector provides capital for investment;
2. The public sector provides infrastructure, fiscal incentives;
3. The administrative framework to attract industry.

The means of enhancing economic development and providing economic security within the regions is what is considered by Regional cooperation. Trade among ASEAN members accounted for more than 23% of all trade by member nations in 1994, topping that of any of the group's major trading partners.

The Southern Growth Triangle, also known as SIJORI (Singapore, the Johore state of Malaysia, and Riau Province of Indonesia), was formed in 1989 and covers a population of about 6 million people. It attracted $10 billion in private sector investments during its first five years. This can be seen in other Asian countries too, encouraging economic development. There are currently four growth triangles which have been established since 1989 and they involve 11 countries. In East and Southeast Asia there eight growth polygons with additional triangles being planned. For example, Cambodia, Laos, Myanmar, Thailand, Vietnam, and China's Yunnan Province have been discussing ways to develop the Mekong area since 1992.

A competitive model to attract investment and technology is provided by regional cooperation. According to the secretary general of ASEAN, **Ajit Singh**, "*These growth areas will have to be flexible to change where necessary, innovative, and always attentive to the needs of the investors and the businessmen. They also have to be aware that they are* *competing with much larger countries such as China and India, whose capacities for attracting investors are much greater than their own"* Many large countries are watching the global economy and they now recognise their need to be a part of this fastest growing region in the world.

The growth triangles typically group remote regions of the nations involved in an effort to exploit complementary assets within the groupings. The governments of Brunei, East and West Kalimantan, and North Sulawesi of Indonesia; Sabah, Sarawak, and Labuan in Malaysia; and Mindanao and Palawan in the Philippines have given priority to expanding air and shipping routes within the East ASEAN Growth Area, another polygon. Where all parts of the polygon are at similar levels of development, growth is expected to be slower.

5.5.1 The Southern China Growth Triangle

Hong Kong, Taiwan, and the southern provinces of China comprise of The Southern China Growth area (Thant et al. 1994). China lags behind Hong Kong and Taiwan in economic development and also due to the fact it has a very huge population, growth in this triangle has enormous potential. This triangle was established with the encouragement of market forces and the private sector initiatives rather than the policy coordination among the countries. The PRC's economic reforms and open door policy initiated in 1978 laid the foundation for economic success in Guangdong and Fujian provinces. Establishment of China's first Special Economic Zone (SEZ) in 1980 provided for tax concessions, expanded land use rights, and simplified procedures for foreign investment. To reduce transaction costs and to provide greater access to the domestic as well as the world market, policies were designed for finance, trade and land use. For China, the triangle has provided exports, foreign exchange, and employment as well as access to the larger global economy. Policies formulated within the SEZs themselves have been even more liberal than those in other parts of the triangle.

Rapid economic growth and higher incomes have occurred in Guangdong and Fujian Provinces with materials and components from Taiwan's manufacturing sectors and the support of Hong Kong's advanced services sector. For Hong Kong and Taipei, the triangle has provided a means of implementing structural changes in manufacturing and export patterns at minimal cost. In spite of recent political posturing on the part of China, economic planners in Hong Kong and Taiwan are optimistic that economic logic will continue to drive regional integration.

5.5.2 Low-Cost Sourcing

Japanese and U.S firms are outsourcing production to low-cost contract manufacturers, as they seek to reduce the cost of their latest innovations. A growing number of low-cost parts and components suppliers can be found in China. Since China has a large pool of cheap labour and with minimum overhead too, the number of high quality vendors in China is increasing. This has led to joint ventures with companies from USA, Japan, Hong Kong, Taiwan and other Asian countries. The success of these firms is dependent upon providing competitive value in a timely manner.

Korea and Taiwan in 1980, provided the first step in the cost reduction chain by providing the most advanced process capabilities. With the establishment of global vendors like SCI and Solectron, Malaysia and Singapore became additional sources for contract manufacturing. Cost can be reduced today, by moving the production to cheap regions like China and the Philippines. Wong's Electronics in Hong Kong provides a three-step process for cost reduction that includes low-cost labour, low-cost sourcing, and low-cost production designs.

The home of lowest-cost manufacturing competitors in the electronics industry today are China, Thailand, Malaysia and Hong Kong. Since low-cost manufacturing countries generally lack the technologies required to become industry leaders, they must follow the technology trends as quickly as possible. OEM competitors from Taiwan and Singapore are being forced to open branch plants in China or other Southeast Asian countries to produce the most labour-intensive, cost-driven products.

5.6 Emerging Developments and Other Issues

5.6.1 Ecological Concerns

Many industries seek expansion not just limited to their own nation but to go international and seek new market for their products and services, in this globalisation era. In determining the competitiveness of products and goods on the international market, the environmental standards and norms play a significant role. Environmental responsibility is a vital component of a business strategy as it not only helps the environment, but it wins the trust of communities and gains the respect of the governments of the countries in which the business operates. Most of the businesses affect the environment by polluting, using resources and producing waste but they are however encouraged to improve their stand on environmental issues.

We may feel, the companies are going GREEN in this current age, however according to writer and green business strategist Joel Makeover, *"it represents a shift in how business is being done, born of a confluence of global challenges: energy and natural resource constraints, global security concerns, growing public health problems, and the spectre of disruptive climate change. And opportunities: a wealth of new enabling technologies that allow business efficiency to increase dramatically, dematerialising and detoxifying products and services along the way"*. The merging of economic and environmental interests may engender one of the biggest business transformations in decades, encouraged on by a societal imperative to bind the unparalleled power of the private sector to address the world's most pressing environmental problems.

Companies, whether big or small, have realised that going green can create new avenues of business value, increase in sales and reduced costs including reduced risk, increased ability to attract and retain talent, better quality and a good reputation. Not every company derives such benefits, but many have found ways to turn the emerging environmental ethic into a business opportunity.

During the second half of the twentieth century, enormous economic and population growth worldwide drove the impacts that threaten the health and the world — ozone depletion, climate change, depletion and fouling of natural resources, and extensive loss of biodiversity and habitat. During the 1990s, efforts by governments, NGOs, corporations and investors began to grow substantially to develop awareness and plans for investment into business sustainability.

Sustainable Business

If the business has adapted its practices for the use of renewable resources and holds itself accountable for the human rights and environmental impacts of its activities, then it is said to be sustainable. Some businesses want to operate in a socially responsible manner so as to protect the environment. Many profit-oriented corporations will forge an image of social responsibility through various public relations and marketing techniques; although this apparent image does not necessarily mean that they are sustainable.

Renewable Resources Investing

Triple Net investing (also known as Triple Bottom Line) refers to investing which includes financial bottom line, socially and environmentally-responsible investing. There is some controversy over the sustainability of triple net investing and whether it produces sufficient returns to be a sound principle for investing.

5.6.2 Countertrade

Countertrade *is a system of international trading that helps governments reduce imbalances in trade between them and other countries.* Countertrade can be the direct or indirect approach to exchange of goods for other goods instead of using currency. Countertrade is often used when a foreign currency is in short supply, or when a country applies foreign exchange controls, which are limits imposed on the availability of foreign currencies to importers for the purchase of foreign products. Developing countries use countertrade to control trade as a development technique.

5.6.3 IT and International Business

By utilising the latest advancements in information and communication technology, many businesses today are changing the way they do business. It is easier for businesses to communicate around the world today with the introduction of social media, smart phones, and tablet computers. It also helps them evaluate product performance and sales, and market and promote their products more effectively, all of which play an increasingly large role in international business.

In today's world, IT is shared largely through mobile devices as one can see smart phones, laptops, PDAs, etc. are being used in the workplace. These devices make it possible for companies to instantly share updates and new product releases not only within their company, but with affiliates, shareholders, colleagues and competitors anywhere in the world. International businesses have become extremely accessible, both to others in the business world and to customers due to the speed at which information can be shared via this type of technology.

The key to joining a global business community should be the minimum requirement of a company to show its online presence. Using social media like Facebook, Twitter, LinkedIn along with a website will allow companies to be abreast with their competitors and they can share information to their customers and also inturn get feedback for their products. Information technology helps international businesses by providing speedier and more reliable networking, marketing, advertising and research and development opportunities.

Since a company may be producing the same product on the other side of the world, International businesses face more competition than any other businesses. Information technology provides speed of communication that helps companies stay one step ahead of their competitors. In addition, more jobs are open to workers in an international business field. There is more interaction about employees in different countries for example, a worker in Japan can join a meeting in Delhi via video conferencing or a worker in Mumbai could sell products to a person in New York through online methods. Information technology is present in international business in several ways.

The Internet is possibly the most important facet, as most information is stored and shared globally thanks to this technology. Software and applications like Skype, VoIP (Voice Over Instant Protocol) and finance and productivity applications give businesses a faster, easier way to connect with others and organise their information. Smartphones like the BlackBerry and iPhone, as well as tablet computers and laptops, keep workers connected in any location, making their jobs more flexible and giving them access to information instantly.

According to a study at the Massachusetts Institute of Technology there are three ways a business worker can view this technology:
- as he makes the decision of whether to enter an industry,
- as he considers how to improve his business,
- as he considers how to get ahead of the competition.

Points to Remember

- WTO is a more powerful and effective organisation than GATT. It has a more effective dispute settlement mechanism.
- Similar to GATT, under WTO too developing countries, particularly least developed countries are accorded a number of concessions and favours. They are allowed longer period to fulfil the liberalisation commitments.
- WTO calls upon the developed countries to grant special preferences to imports from developing nations.
- The European Community (EC) is also known as European Union (EU).
- EU is by far the most successful of the regional economic integration schemes.
- The European Economic Community (EEC) was brought into being on January 1, 1958 by the virtue of the Treaty of Rome, 1957, had originally 6 member nations.
- By January 1, 1986, the expanded EC comprised of 15 nations.
- The programme of EC envisaged the unification of the economies of the member nations into a single market by removing all border barriers to trade and mobility and by unifying the economic policies and regulations.
- The unification of the EU is expected to produce great benefits for the member nations. It would lead to a restructuring of the economy of the EU. It would improve production, increase in income, employment and consumption and reduction in prices.
- With effect from May 1, 2004, the total membership of the EU increased to 25 and by 2007 it became 27.
- The EU is India's largest trading partner, accounting for nearly one-fifth of her trade.
- The EU has great potential as a market but India should pay attention to take advantage of this 'enlarging opportunity'.
- EU is the most advanced case of economic integration.
- The enlargement of EU by the accession of 10 new members is both a challenge and opportunity for India. As some of the new members are India's competitors, the enlargement of EU raises new challenges for India.
- NAFTA is North American Free Trade Agreement.
- It came into being on January 1, 1994, comprising United States, Canada and Mexico.
- The objective of NAFTA is purely economic.
- NAFTA has achieved substantial trade liberalisation.

- NAFTA, besides being world's largest trading area; it is unusual as it combines two of the world's major trading nations with a large developing nation.
- NAFTA covers various areas in relation to trade rules, market access, investment, intellectual property rights and dispute settlement.
- NAFTA has considerable impact on trade.
- The agreement is a decade old. The member countries have reasons to feel proud of the bloc's achievements.
- However, apprehensions are being voiced about the impact of NAFTA, such as loss of jobs, tax in environmental standards, loss of national sovereignty etc.
- Controversies notwithstanding, NAFTA has a logical rationale, in terms of both geographic trading importances.

Questions for Discussion

1. What are the types and advantages of regional groupings?
2. Describe the stages in the evolution of the European Union and the important features of the EU.
3. Write short notes on :
   (a) EC-1992;
   (b) India-EU trade.
4. Bring out the implications of EU on world trade.
5. List out the objectives of EU.
6. What are the benefits and challenges that India faces with enlarged EU?
7. Explain the evolution of NAFTA.
8. Discuss the areas that NAFTA covers in its agreement.
9. Examine the positive and negative impact of NAFTA.
10. Write a detailed note on NAFTA.
11. Explain the concepts of regionalism and multilateralism.
12. Discuss the emerging developments in International Business.

Multiple Choice Questions

1. What does NAFTA stand for?
   (a) North Asian Free Trade Agreement
   (b) North American Free Trade Agreement
   (c) North American Forced Trade Agreement
   (d) North American Free Trading Agreement

2. What does SAARC stand for?
   (a) South Asian Association for Regional Cooperation
   (b) South American Association for Regional Cooperation
   (c) South Asian Association for Regions Cooperation
   (d) South Asian Association for Regional Company

3. The types of Regional Economic groups are:
   (a) Free Trade Area
   (b) Customs Union
   (c) Common Market
   (d) All the above

4. Multilateral agreements occur between _____ countries.
   (a) 1
   (b) 2
   (c) 3
   (d) None of the above

5. The European Union (EU) was established in _____
   (a) 1959
   (b) 1957
   (c) 1960
   (d) 1958

6. The European parliament has _____ members
   (a) 28
   (b) 785
   (c) 29
   (d) 780

7. NAFTA is a trade agreement between:
   (a) U.S., Canada and UK
   (b) U.S., France and Canada
   (c) U.S., Canada and Mexico
   (d) U.K, U.S., Mexico

8. Who is NAFTA's principal body and oversees performance and evolution?
   (a) The Free Trade Commission (TFC)
   (b) The Secretariat

9. What comprises of the Southern China Growth area?
   (a) Hong Kong, Bangkok and the southern provinces of China
   (b) Hong Kong, Taiwan and the southern provinces of China
   (c) Hong Kong, Taiwan and the northern provinces of China
   (d) All of the above

10. The direct or indirect exchange of goods for other goods instead of currency is known as:
    (a) Foreign trade
    (b) Sales
    (c) International business
    (d) Countertrade

ANSWERS

1. (b)	2. (a)	3. (d)	4. (c)	5. (b)
6. (b)	7. (c)	8. (a)	9. (b)	10. (d)

Project Questions

1. How will NAFTA affect marketing opportunities for U.S. products in North America (The United States, Mexico and Canada)?

2. Should international businesses promote or fight the creation of regional economic integrations?

Case Studies

CASE STUDY – 1: Environmental Factors as Force Towards International Business

Balsara Hygiene Products Ltd., introduced in 1978 a toothpaste, Promise, with clove oil. This company had some fairly successful household hygiene products. By 1986, Promise captured a market share of 16 percent and became the second largest selling toothpaste brand in India. However, this position was toppled when Hindustan Lever introduced Close-Up gel, which appealed to the younger generation.

With the support of Export Marketing Finance programme and development assistance, Balsara entered the Malaysian market with *Promise* and *Miswak*.

The emphasis on the clove oil ingredient of the Promise brought in a good response in Malaysian market. Miswak also received a good response in the Muslim dominated Malaysia. Its promotion highlighted the religion. Miswak was a plant that had been used for centuries as a tooth cleaning twig. It had reference in Koran. The religious appeal in the promotion was reinforced by the findings of scientists all over the world, including Arabic ones, of the anti-bacterial property of clove and its ability to prevent tooth decay and protect gums.

Market intelligence revealed that there was a growing preference in the advanced countries for nature based goods. Balsara tied up with Auromere Imports Inc., Los Angeles. With intensive R & D Balsara developed a tooth paste containing 24 herbal ingredients that would satisfy the required parameters. Auromere was voted as the No. 1 toothpaste in North Eastern USA, in a survey conducted by the US Health Magazine, 1991. Various variants were introduced. A saccharine (sweetener) free toothpaste was introduced. Further, mint and menthol were taboo for users of homeopathic medicines, so a product free of such mint was developed. And, when the company realised that Auromere was not doing well in Germany due to the foaming agent used in the product, it developed a chemical free variant of the product.

In this way, Balsara used its environmental factors (Natural trust) to its advantage.

CASE STUDY – 2: Costa Rica using International Trade
About the Country:

Costa Rica is a Central American country of slightly more than 4 million people. It borders the Pacific Ocean and the Caribbean arm of the Atlantic. Its name "Rich Coast" refers to its fertile soil and bountiful biodiversity.

The World Bank classifies Costa Rica as upper middle income as it possesses features that can be associated with developed nations and some that we can associate with developing nations.

With a per capita Gross Domestic Product (GDP) of $ 12,500 (based on PPP in 2006), this country is highly dependent on agricultural goods, such as bananas, coffee, pineapples, and sugar, for its export earnings. The country has a high level of external debt, and its demographic features are - literacy rate of 96%, life expectancy at birth of 77.21 years, and fairly equitable distribution of income and has enjoyed a long history of democracy and political stability.

Four Historical Periods:

Like other countries, Costa Rica depends on International trade and factor-mobility policies i.e. strategies related to movement of goods, services, and production factors across borders, to pursue its economic objectives. In any country, these two policies are closely inter-twined with the nature and quantity of the goods that the country produces. Naturally, they also change over time, as both domestic and foreign conditions evolve, and they are politically sensitive, especially when it comes to the economic priorities and judgments of the nation's leadership.

Thus, like other countries, in Costa Rica also, these policies have evolved continuously. The four eras, in case of Costa Rica, is characterised by a particular set of policies regarding international trade and factor mobility.

1. 1800s to 1960: Liberal Trade- implies a policy of minimal government interference in trade and investment. In the latter part of the 1800s, most nations adopted policies of relative freedom from one country to another in relation to movement of goods, capital and people. Under the sway of liberal policies trade flourished and nations specialised in selling what they could best produce. Costa Rica was no exception, but it managed to adhere to this regime until the early 1960s. Costa Rican farmers specialised, first, in coffee and, later, after the development of refrigerated ships, in bananas as well. For most of the period, the country was well served by this liberal policy, mainly because coffee prices remained high. Several factors combined to convince Costa Rican leaders to **encourage diversified production** and **economic self-sufficiency**. These factors were: (a) trade disruptions occasioned by two world wars; (b) a drop in coffee and banana prices in relation to prices of manufactured goods, when new commodity producers (especially in Africa) entered world markets; (c) Latin American nations had insulated themselves from adverse international conditions, i.e. had less open global markets. As such, Costa Rica adopted policy of import substitution.

2. 1960 to 1982: Import Substitution- implies a policy of local production of goods and services that would otherwise have to be imported. In the early 1960s, Costa Rican authorities reasoned that if they limited imports, say by taxing them heavily, they would provide both Costa Rican and foreign investors with an incentive to produce more goods in the country for sale to Costa Rican consumers. They also realised that the Costa Rican market was too small to support investments requiring large-scale production. Further, Costa Rica joined with 4 other nations- El Salvador, Guatemala, Honduras, and Nicaragua- to form the Central American Common Market (CACM), which allowed goods produced in any member country to enter freely into the market of any other member. Under this arrangement, a company located in a member country would be in a position to serve a 5-country market rather than a one-country model. But the results were mixed. Costa Rica did diversify its economy. Although some foreign investment was attracted to the local manufacturing sector, most of it was for the Costa Rican market and not for the larger CACM market. So why was the strategy of import substitution, even coupled with regional trade agreement, less successful than CACM leaders had hoped?

It was simple, neither local nor foreign investors were convinced that the CACM was to last, and it turned out to be true. By the late 1970s, civil wars in El Salvador and Guatemala stifled those economies, and Nicaragua was committed to complete government control in all aspects, including trade; El Salvador and Honduras even went to war with each other. In some cases, import substitution led to increased exports. Costa Rica found new markets-local and export- for processed coffee and coffee seeds. Many economists began to worry that policies designed to protect local production were channelling the country's resources away from areas of production in which it had long been most efficient.

For example, Costa Rica had become nearly self-sufficient in rice production, but only because government policies kept lower-cost foreign-produced rice out of the market. The government managed to hold down consumer rice prices only by subsidising domestic producers. This was done by higher taxes on efficient industries that, in turn, found it difficult to expand as they were strapped for cash. On the other hand, some inefficient producers survived as they received subsidies and reaped benefits of high prices being paid by the consumers. Thus, Costa Rican policymakers concluded that the country must focus on the production of goods that could compete in international markets. In 1983, Costa Rica shifted to a policy of promoting exports.

3. 1983 to early 1990s: Liberalisation- of imports, export promotion, and incentives for foreign investments. The government began removing barriers to ensure that globally competitive companies and industries were to survive in the newly projected business environment. For example, rice imports rose substantially as the government removed the protective barriers that it had erected around domestic production. Further, policymakers decided to seek more outside capital and expertise to support economic reforms. And, it was the U.S. launched, by luck for Costa Rica, its Caribbean Basin Initiative, which allowed products originating in the Caribbean region (including Costa Rica) to enter the U.S. at lower tariff, or import-tax, rates than those originating elsewhere. To capitalise on this new opportunity, Costa Rica formed CINDE (a private organisation funded by the government and grants from the U.S. government). The purpose of CINDE was to aid in economic development, and one of its top priorities was attracting FDI. To increase CINDE's work, Costa Rica established an Export Processing Zone (EPZ) that allowed companies exporting finished output to import all inputs and equipment tax free. Government extended many facilities such as exemption from paying Costa Rican income tax for 8 years and allowed to pay at a 50% discount for the next 4 years. By 1989, 35 companies-mainly textile and footwear producers seeking to take advantage of Costa Rica's pool of inexpensive labour-had located in the EPZ. CINDE officials began to worry about 2 potential problems facing its ambitious new initiatives: (a) Costa Rica could not remain cost competitive in the type of products exported from EPZ as other nations, mainly Mexico, were benefitting from even lower U.S. tariffs. (b) Costa Rica's highly skilled and educated workforce was not being utilised to the best advantage by the types of industries attracted to the EPZ. CINDE officials decided to work with Costa Rican government to identify and attract investors who matched up better with Costa Rican resources.

4. Early 1990s to present date: Strategic trade and investment- implies a policy for the production of specific types of products and openness to imports. The approach that identifies and targets industries for global competition is known as strategic trade policy or an industrial policy. Costa Rican government took a close look at the characteristics of developing countries that were attracting significant amount of investments from abroad: a highly educated, largely English-speaking workforce, especially the availability of engineers and technical operators, political and social stability and relatively high levels of economic freedom, and a quality of life that would appeal to the managers and technical personnel that foreign investors would bring in to work in the facilities. Hence, the result was that in its targeted industries, Costa Rica should be able to compete on international market.

CINDE hired the Foreign Investment Advisory Service (FIAS) of the IFC (International Finance Corporation) to study the feasibility of attracting companies in these industries and the best means of attracting them to Costa Rica. The report of FIAS concluded that it was within Costa Rica's reach in attracting right number of the right companies. FIAS noted areas in which Costa Rica needed to improve, such as the protection of IPRs and English proficiency among technicians and engineers. In response to it, Costa Rica revised the curriculum for training mid-level technicians and set up Spanish-language training for the personnel brought in by foreign investors.

The progress was commendable. Setting out to attract investments in electronics and software, Costa Rica landed high-tech investors such as Reliability, Protek, Colorplast, and Sensortronics. The largest investment, however, has been by Intel. To attract the computer-ship giant, CINDE listed the questions and concerns that Intel might have; they were prepared to respond to them quickly and knowledgeably. They also involved top government and company leaders in meetings with Intel executives.

Since then, Costa Rica has turned its attention to medical devices, an area in which it has attracted investments by companies like Abbott Laboratories, Baxter, and Procter & Gamble. Although exports of coffee and bananas are still important to the nation's economy, but about 2/3rds of Costa Rica's exports have been manufactured goods, with high-tech products now constituting the backbone of the economy and export earnings.

Although largely an agricultural country, the Central American nation of Costa Rica has succeeded in diversifying its economy. Tourism is strong, as is technology. Puerto Limon, for example, is home to an oil refinery, and there's a petrochemical plant in nearby Moin. Intel operates a manufacturing and distribution centre in Heredia, east of the capital of San Jose.

CASE STUDY – 3: The Need to Define Proper Objectives

This is an issue not usually dwelt upon in market literature or forums and chat rooms, but success in Corporate FX (Foreign Exchange) Risk Management, or even speculative trading for that matter, often hinges upon :

- Defining your objective(s).
- Devising a plan or strategy to achieve the objective(s).
- Executing the strategy and very importantly, remaining focused on the objective.

Devising of a plan/ strategy and execution thereof are matters of expertise in market reading and dealing and are usually the more enchanting part of Risk Management or Trading. Rarely adequate attention is paid to the need to define proper **Objectives** for the risk management exercise. Even if the objectives have been properly defined, they are often forgotten in the heat of market activity. This leads to failure or underperformance in the big picture.

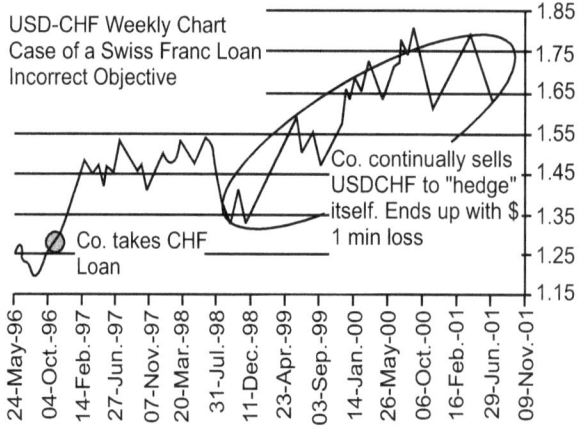

Fig. C.1

The Case of a Swiss Franc Loan :

A company with a Rupee Balance Sheet (take it as a USD Balance Sheet) contracts a Swiss Franc Loan at a USD-CHF rate near 1.25 towards the end of 1996, after which the Swiss Franc **weakens** to 1.45 by early 1997 and then trades in a range of 1.45-1.55 through the greater part of 1997-1998. It **strengthens** to about 1.35 by end of 1998.

The company accounts for the Loan in its books at 1.50 and wants to "earn back" the "loss between 1.50 and 1.35" through **"Hedging Operations"** which call upon it to sell USD-CHF in the Forward Market and earn Cash Profits on such Hedges, which will be booked in its Profit and Loss accounts.

Note, that **the focus is on CASH Profits/ Losses generated through "Hedges" and not on the VALUE of the Loan, which is a Balance Sheet item**.

The company starts its "Hedging Operations" near the epochal birth of the Euro.

As we all remember, 1999 was the year in which the Euro was born near 1.17against the Dollar and caused much anguish in the market by weakening throughout the year to end just above Parity. In the process it dragged the Swiss Franc down against the Dollar.

The company, to its dismay, found itself making Cash Losses on its "Sell USDCHF" hedges. To make up the initial losses, it sold more USDCHF in ever increasing larger amounts right through the year, trying to earn Cash Profits on interim bouts of Dollar weakness against the Swiss Franc. Huge Sell USDCHF trades were daily entered into for making a few pips profits, not realizing that the trades were all against the larger trend.

Its focus on the Cash Profit/ Loss made the company **overlook** the fact that the ongoing weakness in the Swiss Franc was decreasing the value of the Loan on its Balance Sheet.

In an attempt to first earn "hedging profits" and then to cover losses against the trend, it ended up with a **USD 1 million loss**, negating, to a large extent, the real Valuation Gain on its Balance Sheet.

Had its focus been on the Balance Sheet, the company would have stopped its "Hedging Operations" after the first few hedges made Cash Losses and proved that the market was actually reducing the value of its primary Loan exposure!

Sounds incredible? The moral of the story is that a lot of thought and deliberation should go into deciding upon **correct objectives** before commencing market operations. In a subsequent issue we shall take up the case of a company, which started out with the correct objectives, but lost its focus and underperformed as a result.

CASE STUDY – 4: Learn from your Mistakes – Pay Attention to Objectives, it Pays

The definition of proper **Objectives** is the first step in effective Corporate FX Risk Management.

Get the objectives wrong and you are most likely courting trouble.

Having set the correct objectives, the Risk Manager needs to keep them in mind after the 'Hedge' Strategy has been implemented, so as to not be led astray by the market. It pays immensely.

A conglomerate with a Rupee Balance Sheet had a large foreign currency loan book, 85% of which was denominated in US Dollars. The balance was in D-Marks, Yen and Sterling. Circa 1994-95, the Risk Manager decided to reduce the currency concentration risk and rebalance the loan basket using Currency Swaps. **The Objective was clearly defined as *Risk Diversification.***

It was decided to swap 10% of the Dollar loans into Yen. The Yen was chosen because interest rates were close to zero as compared to 6.50-6.75% on the USD 6-month Libor, giving a huge interest benefit. Further, the Yen was expected to weaken over a 3 year time frame. **The Swap took place in Jan-95 near 100 on the USDJPY Spot. (Japan Yen).**

Almost immediately thereafter, **the Dollar dived against the Yen**, to hit an all time low of 79.80 in April 1995. There were three months of intense agony. The company had never undertaken such a large foreign exchange deal. The Board was on the edge. Had the deal gone horribly wrong?

The Risk Manager reminded the Board that **the objective was Risk** Diversification and only 10% of the loan book had been put on the line. Further, the deal had a three year tenor. The market eventually turned around and the danger passed. The Swap came back into money. Now the Board was tempted to square off the trade and book whatever small profit was available. **Again the Risk Manager stuck to his guns, saying the Objective was long term Currency Diversification, not short term Trading Profits.**

The Board backed down and the Swap was allowed to run its course.

The Yen eventually touched 120 in 1997. The company booked a huge currency and interest rate gain of almost $17 million. Those who have been in the market through that period would appreciate how difficult it must have been to **steer** such a trade through to its end.

It is immensely commendable **that the Risk Manager did not waver from the Objective, neither in bad times nor in good times.**

The gains from the deal (which in itself was well conceptualized), was realized **by remaining focused on the objective**. (SOURCE : INTERNET).

CASE STUDY – 5: Based on Culture Risk.

McDonald and Hindu Culture :

McDonald's Corporation, everyday, on average, somewhere around the world 4.2 new restaurants are opened. By 2004, the company had 30,000 restaurants in more than 120 countries that collectively served close to 50 million customers each day.

One of the latest additions to McDonald's list of countries hosting the famous golden arches is India, where McDonald's started to establish restaurants in the late 1990s. Although, India has low per capita income, but the large and relatively prosperous middle class that estimated to number between 150 million and 200 million, attracted

McDonald's. India, however, offered McDonald's unique challenges. For thousands of years, India's Hindu culture has revered the cow. Hindu scriptures state that the cow is a gift of the gods to the human race. The cow represents the Divine Mother that sustains all human beings. Some 300 million of these animals roam India, everywhere, ambling down roads, grazing in rubbish dumps, and resting in temples- i.e. everywhere, except on your plate, for Hindus do not eat the meat of the sacred cow.

McDonald's is the world's largest user of beef. Since 1955, countless animals have died to produce Big Macs. Thus, how can a company whose fortunes are built upon beef enter a country where the consumption of beef is a grave sin? The alternative was to use pork instead. But, there are some 140 million Muslims in India, and Muslims do not eat pork. This leaves the company with chicken and mutton. McDonald's responded to this cultural food dilemma by creating an Indian version of its Big Mac- the "Maharaja Mac"- which is made from mutton. Other additions to the menu conform to local sensibilities such as the "McAloo Tikki Burger".

All foods are strictly segregated into vegetarian and non-vegetarian lines to match with the tastes and preferences in a country where Hindus are vegetarian. The Head of the company in India referred to as "reinvent ourselves for the Indian palate."

For a while, this seemed to work. Then in 2001 McDonald's was blindsided by a class-action lawsuit brought against it in the U.S. by three Indian businessmen living in Seattle. All the businessmen were vegetarians, and two of them were Hindus. They sued McDonald's for "fraudulently concealing" the existence of beef in McDonald's French fries. The company had said that it used only 100% vegetable oil to make the French fries, but the company soon admitted that it used a 'minuscule' amount of beef extract in the oil. McDonald's settled the suit for $ 10 million and issued an apology, which read," McDonald's sincerely apologise to Hindus, vegetarians, and others for failing to provide the kind of information they needed to make informed dietary decisions at our U.S. restaurants." The company pledged to do a better job of labelling the ingredients of its food and to find a substitute for the beef extract used in its oil.

However, the news travelled fast and the revelation that McDonald's used beef extract in its oil was enough to bring Hindu nationalists onto the streets in Delhi, where they vandalised one of the McDonald's restaurant, causing $ 45,000 in damage, shouted slogans outside of another outlet, picketed the company's headquarters; and called on India's prime minister to close McDonald's stores in the country.

McDonald's Indian franchise holders immediately issued information that they used oil which did not contain any beef extract. Hindu extremists responded to this information by stating that they would submit McDonald's oil to laboratory tests and check if the oil contained any beef extract.

However, the negative publicity seemed to have little impact on McDonald's long-term plans in India. The company continued to open restaurants, and by 2005 had 65 restaurants in the country with plans to open another 30 or more. When Indian customers asked why they frequented McDonald's restaurants, they noted that their children enjoyed the "American" experience, the food was of consistent quality, and the toilets were always clean.

Thus, understanding of other cultures and recognition of the differences enhances the cross-cultural communication. The truly global companies must come to grip the legal and moral atmosphere in which they operate.

CASE STUDY – 6: Managing the Challenges of WTO Participation.

Protecting the Geographical Indication for Darjeeling Tea :

This case study relates to the geographical indication (GI) protection of Darjeeling tea.

It tells the story of the unauthorised use and registration of 'Darjeeling and Darjeeling logo' by Japanese companies already registered in Japan by the Tea Board of India. The study also refers to the unauthorised use and attempted registration of the words 'Darjeeling and Darjeeling logo' by some other developed countries.

Problem :

India is the world's largest producer of tea, with a total production of 846 million kg in the year 2002, supplying about 31 per cent of the world's favourite hot drink. Among the teas grown in India, **Darjeeling tea offers distinctive characteristics of quality and flavour, and also a global reputation for more than a century.** Broadly speaking, there are two factors which have contributed to such an exceptional and distinctive taste, namely (i) geographical origin and (ii) processing. Thus Darjeeling tea has been cultivated, grown and produced in tea gardens in a well-known geographical area – the Darjeeling district in the Indian state of West Bengal – for over one and a half centuries.

Legal Backing :

Even though the tea industry in India lies in the private sector, it has been statutorily regulated and controlled by the Ministry of Commerce since 1933 under various enactments culminating in the Tea Act, 1953. The Tea Board was set up under this Act. A major portion of the annual production of Darjeeling tea is exported, the key buyers being Japan, Russia, the United States, and the United Kingdom and other European Union (EU) countries such as France, Germany and the Netherlands.

In order **to ensure the supply of genuine Darjeeling tea**, a compulsory system of certifying the authenticity of exported Darjeeling tea was incorporated into the 1953 Tea Act in February 2000. The system makes it compulsory for all the dealers in Darjeeling tea to enter into a licence agreement with the Tea Board of India on payment of an annual licence fee. The terms and conditions of the agreement provide, inter alia, that the licensees must furnish information relating to the production and manufacture of Darjeeling tea and its sale, through auction or otherwise. The Tea Board is thus able to compute and compile the total volume of Darjeeling tea produced and sold in the given period. **No blending with teas of**

other origin is permitted. Certificates of origin are then issued for export consignments under the Tea (Marketing and Distribution Control) Order.

Data is entered from the garden invoices (the first point of movement outside the factory) into a database, and the issue of the certificate of origin authenticates the export of each consignment of Darjeeling tea by cross-checking the details. The customs authorities in India have instructed, by circular, all customs checkpoints to check for the certificates of origin accompanying the Darjeeling tea consignments and not to allow the export of any tea as 'Darjeeling' without this certificate. This ensures the sale-chain integrity of Darjeeling tea until consignments leave the country.

Legal Protection at Domestic Level - CTM (Certification Trade Marks) Registration :

In order to provide legal protection in India the Tea Board of India registered the 'Darjeeling logo' and also the word 'Darjeeling' as Certification Trade Marks (CTMs) under the (Indian) Trade and Merchandise Marks Act, 1958 (now the Trade Marks Act, 1999).

GI Registration :

The Tea Board of India has also applied for the registration of the words 'Darjeeling' and 'Darjeeling logo' under the Geographical Indications of Goods (Registration and Protection) Act, 1999 (the Act) which came into force with effect from 15 September 2003, in addition to the CTMs mentioned above.

Under the Act :

(a) No person shall be entitled to institute any proceeding to prevent or recover damages for the infringement of unregistered geographical indications.

(b) A registration of geographical indications shall give to the registered proprietor and all authorized users whose names have been entered in the register the right to obtain relief in respect of infringement of the geographical indications. However, authorised users alone shall have the exclusive right to the use of the geographical indications in relation to the goods in respect of which the geographical indications are registered.

(c) A registered geographical indication is infringed by a person who, not being an authorised user thereof,

    (i) uses such geographical indications by any means in the designation or presentation of goods that indicates or suggests that such goods originate in some other geographical area other than the true place of origin of the goods in a manner which misleads the public; or

    (ii) uses any geographical indications in such a manner which constitutes an act of unfair competition including passing off in respect of registered geographical indications; or

    (iii) uses another geographical indication to the goods which, although literally true as to the territory, region or locality in which the goods originate, falsely represents to the public that the goods originate in the region, territory or locality in respect of which such registered geographical indications relate.

(d) The purpose of the GI Act is to create a public register, and

(e) The GI Act confers public rights.

Advantages of GI Protection at Domestic Level and Export Markets :

The reason for the need for additional protection for GI over and above the CTM has been set out by the chair of the Tea Board of India as follows :

- When CTM registration is not accepted in a jurisdiction where protection is sought, for example, France for Darjeeling;
- Because GI registration is necessary to obtain reciprocal protection of a mark mandate under EU Regulation 2081/92; and
- Registration gives clear status to a GI, indicating a direct link with geographical origin.

Quite apart from the aforesaid reasons the GI Act in India has also been enacted in order **to comply with its obligation under the Agreement on Trade-Related Aspects of Intellectual Property Rights (TRIPS)**, which requires WTO members to enact appropriate implementation legislation for GI.

Steps taken at International Level :

(a) **Registration of Darjeeling tea and Logo :** In order to protect 'Darjeeling' and 'Darjeeling logo' as GI, the Tea Board of India registered the marks in various countries, including the United States, Canada, Japan, Egypt, and the United Kingdom and some other European countries, as a trade mark/CTM. In this context it is relevant to note that on 3 August 2001 the UK Trade Registry granted registration of the word 'Darjeeling' as of 30 March 1998 under the UK Trade Marks Act 1994. The United States has also accepted the application of the Tea Board for the registration of 'Darjeeling' as a CTM in October 2002.

(b) **The appointment of the International Watch Agency :** In order to prevent the misuse of 'Darjeeling' and the logo, the Tea Board has since 1998 hired the services of Compumark, a World Wide Watch agency. Compumark is required to monitor and report to the Tea Board all cases of unauthorised use and attempted registration.

(c) **The Assistance of Overseas Buyers :** In order to ensure the supply of genuine Darjeeling tea, the Tea Board has sought the help of all overseas buyers, sellers and Tea Council and Associations in so far as they should insist on certificates of origin to accompany all export consignments of Darjeeling tea.

The Role Played by Local and External players :

(a) **The Tea Board of India :** The sole representative of tea producers in India, is responsible for the implementation of the government's regulations and policies. It is vested with the authority to administer all stages of tea cultivation, processing and sale (including the Darjeeling segment) through various orders issued by the government. It works in close co-operation with the

(b) **Darjeeling Planter's Association :** Which is the sole producers' forum for Darjeeling tea.

Both the Tea Board and the Darjeeling Planter's Association (DPA) have been involved at various levels in protecting and defending the 'Darjeeling tea' and 'Darjeeling logo'. The primary objects are (i) to prevent misuse of the word 'Darjeeling' for tea sold worldwide; (ii) to deliver the correct product to the consumer; (iii) to enable the commercial benefit of the equity of the brand to reach the Indian tea industry and ultimately the plantation worker; (iv) to achieve international status similar to champagne or Scotch whisky in terms of both brand and equity and governance/ administration.

The Tea Board of India assumed the role of complainant in making and filing opposition or other legal measures whenever cases of unauthorized use or attempted or actual registration of Darjeeling and Darjeeling logo were brought to its notice. Such legal measures are generally taken where negotiation failed. For instance, in February 2000 in Japan the Tea Board of India filed an opposition against Yutaka Sang Yo Kabushiki Kaisa of Japan for registration of the trade mark 'Darjeeling Tea' with the map of India, and against Mitsui Norin Kabushiki Kaisa for the use in advertising of the 'Divine Darjeeling' logo. These opposing parties defended the invalidation action filed against them.

Some disputes relating to Darjeeling tea have been settled through negotiation undertaken by the Tea Board of India with the foreign companies concerned, with the help of their respective governments. Thus, the Tea Board with the help of the Indian government continues to negotiate with France at various levels over the activities of the French trademark authorities. Moreover Bulgaria, Switzerland agreed to withdraw the legend 'Darjeeling Tea fragrance for men' pursuant to legal notice and negotiations.

In one of the cases in France, the Tea Board of India put the applicant Comptoir des Parfums (which advertised in March 1999) on notice, and drew its attention to the prior rights and goodwill in the name of Darjeeling as the GI for tea, and requiring it to withdraw its application voluntarily. Based on the correspondence, the applicant consented to the amendment of all specifications of goods by the addition of 'all those goods being made of Darjeeling tea or recalling the scent of Darjeeling tea'.

'The Tea Board of India feels that a partnership with the buyers in the major consuming countries such as Germany, Japan and the United Kingdom would be the only long term solution to the problem of possible passing off.'

Challenges :

The Tea Board of India has faced a series of hurdles, challenges and difficulties in the protection and enforcement of the word 'Darjeeling' and of the Darjeeling logo. Some of the major challenges faced by the Tea Board's effort to protect 'Darjeeling' and the Darjeeling logo in Japan, France, Russia, the United States and other countries are given below.

(a) Unauthorised use and Registration of Darjeeling Tea and Logo in Japan : In the first case the Tea Board filed an invalidation action against International Tea KK, a Japanese Company, over the registration of the Darjeeling logo mark, namely, Darjeeling women 'serving tea/coffee/coca/soft drinks/fruit juice' in the Japanese Patent Office (JPO) on 29 November 1996 with the trademark registration number 3221237. The impugned registration was made notwithstanding the registration in Japan of the identical Darjeeling logo mark by the Tea Board of India, with the trademark registration number 2153713, dated 31 July 1987. The Tea Board also filed a non-use cancellation action. On 28 August 2002 the JPO Board of Appeal held that the pirate registration was invalid because it was contrary to public order and morality. With regard to the Tea Board's non-use cancellation action, the JPO decided that International Tea KK had not furnished sufficient evidence to substantiate its use of registration and thereby allowed the appeal of the Tea Board.

In the second case, the Tea Board of India opposed the application for 'Divine Darjeeling' in class 30 (Darjeeling tea, coffee and cocoa produced in Darjeeling, India) filed by Mitsui Norin KK of Japan advertised on 29 February 2000. The opposition was mainly on three grounds, namely (i) 'divine' is a laudatory term and accordingly the mark for which protection is sought is merely 'Darjeeling', which is clearly non-distinctive; (ii) 'Divine Darjeeling' is misleading in so far as 'coffee and cocoa produced in Darjeeling' are concerned, all the more so because the district of Darjeeling does not produce coffee or cocoa; (iii) Darjeeling tea qualifies as a geographical indication under international conventions including TRIPS and ought to be protected as such in Japan, a member of TRIPS.

The JPO Opposition Board dismissed the invalidation action filed by the Tea Board of India primarily on the ground that the mark 'Divine Darjeeling' as a whole was not misleading or descriptive of the quality of goods. However, the non-use cancellation action succeeded, because the registered proprietor was not able to place on record adequate evidence to prove the use of the mark in Japan.

In yet another case the Tea Board of India brought an invalidation action against Japanese trade mark registration of 'Darjeeling tea' with a map of India in class 30 by Yutaka Sangyo Kabushiki Kaisa, on the ground that the registration was contrary to public order and morality. This action was rejected on the ground that 'the written English characters "Darjeeling tea" and the map of India for the goods of Darjeeling tea are used as an indication of the origin and quality of Darjeeling tea and will not harm the feelings of the Indian people'. However, the non-use cancellation action filed by the Tea Board succeeded, because the registered proprietor was not able to place on record sufficient evidence to prove the use of the mark in Japan.

A perusal of these decisions reveals that the JPO did not decide the contention of the Tea Board of India relating to the TRIPS Agreement, which requires WTO members to provide the legal means to prevent the use of a GI for goods originating in a geographical area other than the true place of origin in a manner which misleads the public to constitute an act of unfair competition. Indeed, non-disposal of the argument that the procedural guidelines of WTO be followed dilutes the effect of the TRIPS Agreement.

Other Examples of Defending GI Against Developed Countries :

France : While the Indian system protects French GIs, France on the other hand does not extend similar or reciprocal protection to Indian GIs. Thus, French law does not permit any opposition to an application for a trademark similar or identical to a GI, if the goods covered are different from those represented by the GI. The owner of the GI can take appropriate judicial proceedings only after the impugned application has proceeded to registration. The net effect of such a provision has been that despite India's protests, Darjeeling has been misappropriated as a trade mark in respect of several goods in class 25, namely, clothing, shoes and headgear. The French Examiner – even though he found evidence in favour of the Tea Board of India (i) on sufficient proof of use of 'Darjeeling' tea in France, and (ii) that the applicant had slavishly copied the name Darjeeling in its application – held that the respective goods 'clothing, shoes, headgear' and 'tea' are not of the same nature, function and intended use, produced in different places and sold through different networks. The Examiner also held that even if the applicant has slavishly copied the Tea Board's Darjeeling logo (being the prior mark), the difference in the nature of the respective goods is sufficient to hold that the applicant's mark may be adopted without prejudicing the Tea Board's rights in the name 'Darjeeling'.

In another case the Tea Board opposed the application against the advertised marks for Darjeeling in classes 5, 12 and 28 by Dor François Marie in France. The French Examiner rejected the Tea Board's opposition and held that the respective goods did not (i) have the same nature, function and intended use; and (ii) share the same distribution circuits. However, he held that although the applicant's mark constituted a partial reproduction of the Tea Board's prior figurative registration for the Darjeeling logo, the designated goods lacked similarity to that of the Tea Board's prior marks and the logo, therefore, may be used as a trade mark without prejudicing the prior rights of the Tea Board.

Russia : The Tea Board filed an application for unauthorised use by a company of the word 'Darjeeling'. This application was objected to on the ground of conflict with an earlier registration of the identical word by a company named 'Akorus'. The Russian Patent Office overruled the objection and accepted the application of Tea Board of India for the word 'Darjeeling'.

United States : The Tea Board is opposing an application filed by its licensee in United States to register 'Darjeeling nouveau' ('nouveau' is the French for 'new') relating to diverse goods and service such as clothing, lingerie, Internet services, coffee, cocoa and so on in respect of first flush Darjeeling tea. The registration application is under consideration even though 'Darjeeling' is already registered under US CTM law.

Other Countries : Quite apart from the above, in several cases the Tea Board of India opposed attempted registration and unauthorised use of the word 'Darjeeling' in Germany, Israel, Norway and Sri Lanka before the Patent Office of the country concerned.

Costs of Protection and Enforcement for the Industry and the Government :

Another major challenge faced by the Tea Board of India relates to legal and registration expenses, costs of hiring an international watch agency and fighting infringements in overseas jurisdictions. Thus during the last four years the Tea Board of India has spent approximately US$200, 000 for these purposes. This amount does not include administrative expenses including the relevant personnel working for the Tea Board, the cost of setting up monitoring mechanisms, software development costs and so forth. It is not possible for every geographical indication right holder to incur such expenses for protection. Further, like overseeing, monitoring and implementing GI protection, the high cost of taking legal action can prevent a country from engaging a lawyer to contest the case, however genuine and strong the case may be. Moreover, a lack of expertise in the proper handling of highly complex legal language is another challenge to be met.

Lessons for Others :

The Tea Board of India appears to be not satisfied with the policy as well as the approach of the patent authority in Japan and France. In order to deal with the situations described above, India, along with several other member countries of the WTO, wants to extend the proposed register for GI to include products or goods, other than wines and spirits, which may be distinguished by the quality, reputation or other characteristics essentially attributable to their geographical origin. The main advantage would be to develop a multilateral system of notification and registration of all geographical indications. In this connection, a joint paper has recently been submitted to the Two's TRIPS Council.

The Doha Ministerial Declaration under paragraphs 12 and 18 also provides a mandate for the issue of providing a higher level of protection to GIs to products other than 'wines and spirits' to be addressed by the TRIPS Council. According to the Tea Board, (i) extension of protection under Article 23 for products other than wines and spirits is required where no legal platform exists to register a GI or a CTM which is a TRIPS obligation, for example Japan; (ii) once the scope of protection is extended it would not be necessary to establish the credentials/reputation of a GI before fighting the infringement of similar 'types', 'styles', or 'look-alikes'; and (iii) additional protection would rectify the imbalance created by the special protection of wines and spirits

The experience in defending GI in France, the United States and Japan further strengthens the Tea Board's perspective on the subject. Despite a registration of 'Darjeeling' as a GI in France, the Tea Board was unsuccessful in defending it because French law does not permit any opposition to an application for a trade mark, similar or identical to a GI. Likewise, India's efforts to protect 'Darjeeling' in Japan did not succeed because the prefix 'Divine' has not gained currency in the Japanese language.

From the experiences described above it is felt that it is high time to evolve a rule that (i) no application for registration of a GI of the same or similar goods or products or even similar type, style or look-alike already registered in that country be ordinarily entertained by the competent authority of the country concerned. (ii) Further, the GI status and apprehended or actual violation of GI should be published at both domestic and international levels. (iii) adequate steps should be taken to evolve rules and procedures for GI or CTM registration in all the member countries of the WTO. This would prevent conflict to a great extent. (iv) Finally, a vigilance cell should be established to check the violation and misuse of the GI of any product.

CASE STUDY – 7: Starbucks

Howard Schultz's idea with Starbucks in the mid 1980s was to create a chain of Coffee house with a product differentiation of speciality "live coffee", service or customer intimacy with an "experience", and "third place" to add to their work and home alternatives.

STARBUCKS is a dominant multinational coffee house chain based in the United States. Starbucks is the largest Coffee house company in the world, with 7,521 company-owned and 5,647 licensed stores in 40 countries, making a total of 13,168 stores worldwide. Starbucks sells drip brewed coffee, espresso based hot drinks, other hot and cold drinks, snacks and items such as mugs and coffee beans.

Starbuck's Brand Image :

It is a dominant speciality coffee brand. Growth rate is 40% since it got public, serving 20 million unique customers and opening three stores a day and spending nothing on advertising.

Objective :

(i) To establish Starbucks as the most recognised and respected brand in the world.
(ii) To bring differentiation in the product.
(iii) To be unique in ways that are valuable to a wide range of customers.

Growth Strategies:

(i) In 1991, Starbucks became the first privately owned company to offer a stock option programme to all of their employees.
(ii) Higher employee satisfaction leads to lower turnover rates, which in turn leads to lower employee training costs, which leads to greater profits.
(iii) Starbucks serves the community- both local and abroad.
(iv) This provides Starbucks with plenty of good publicity.
(v) Starbucks also takes great interest in suppliers' well-being.

Factors that contributed to Starbucks success :

(i) Experimental branding strategy.
(ii) Customer service.
(iii) High quality coffee
(iv) Product variety.

Starbuck's Value Proposition :

(i) To create an "experience" around the consumption of coffee, an experience that people would weave into their lives.
(ii) To create an uplifting experience in "customer intimacy".
(iii) To create an "ambience" based on human spirit, sense of community, and the need for people to come together.

Controllable Elements :

(a) **Technological Development :** Starbucks card, for example, the Company has created the opportunities to improve customer service, shorten lines and make a customer's visit at Starbucks quicker and more convenient.

(b) **Placement :** (i) People socialise, read, study or just enjoy the music while drinking their coffee. (ii) Modifying coffee shops to make their stores unique that will create an appealing atmosphere. (iii) They focus on having plenty of comfortable seating so that people feel welcome.

(c) **Advertising :** Successful in advertising on a local level rather than to the nations as a whole. The company advertises through print medium, as Starbucks target market tends to be educated people.

(d) **Research & development :** (i) R&D of new and exciting products like four-cup thermal coffee-maker. (ii) "Double shot" espresso beverage. (iii) Starbucks Card is a wonderful convenience tool for customers that can serve as great gifts, reduces time spent.

Uncontrollable Elements :

(a) **Economic Factor :** In normal price variation, the demand for coffee is price inelastic. When coffee prices show increases, consumers reduce their consumption. Net revenues increased from $ 1.3 billion in fiscal year **1998** to $ 1.7 billion in fiscal year **1999**, due to company's store expansion. The company experienced certain level of cannibalisation of existing stores by new stores as store concentration.

(b) **Sociological Factors :** The company made outlines to make sure that its effect on the environment is positive. These principles are stated as:

(i) Understanding environmental issues.
(ii) Developing innovative solutions to bring about change.
(iii) Striving to buy, sell and use environmentally friendly products.
(iv) Recognising that responsibility towards our environmental future.
(v) Instituting environmental responsibility as a corporate value.
(vi) Measuring and monitoring our progress for such project.

(c) **Demographic Factors :**

(i) People aged 15-64 make up the largest percentage of the population, and will have greater control of the market. This implies that the most important target markets for Starbucks are people within this age group.
(ii) Two largest ethnic groups in the United States are White (83.5%) and Black (12.4%).
(iii) The ethnic background is important to a company because it influences tastes, trends, perceptions, values and beliefs of an individual.
(iv) Per capita purchasing power parity of $ 36,200 suggests that Americans can buy speciality coffee drinks from an expensive, quality-intensive organisation such as Starbucks.

(d) Legal Issues :

(i) Companies challenging the status of Starbucks California store managers and assistant managers as exempt employees under California wage and hour laws.

(ii) Threats could include a change in import laws. A change in status quo as far as imports go could greatly affect numerous areas of production for the company.

Risks and Solutions :

(1) RISK- Market Threat.

Solution : Starbucks must push to be the first mover :

(a) Innovate new products to stay ahead of such competitive tactics.
(b) Should become alert towards competitive market.
(c) McDonalds entered into a coffee agreement with Diedrich coffee.
(d) Starbucks could respond by acquiring Diedrich coffee.
(e) It could be a subsidiary that specializes in catering to the food service industry.

(2) RISK- Depends on overseas growth to maintain annual 20% revenue.

Solution : Marketing campaign to draw customers from Churchill.

Another option could be to use Starbucks incredible purchasing power to acquire Churchill.

(3) RISK- Offering only one product.

Solution : The Company could demonstrate Product Market diversification through research.

Bring environmental changes and make sure to entice as many people as possible into their stores. For example, Starbucks could start line of Children's fruit drinks and "yummy" milkshakes which would help bring families into the store.

Corporate Strategy :

Starbucks' Corporate strategy establishes itself as the premier purveyor of the finest coffee in the world.

- The firm principles of the Company are its maintenance of a proven work environment for every staff member in its retail stores.
- It upholds diversity and promises Starbucks persists to be profitable.
- Starbucks Corporation purchases and roasts high quality whole coffee beans and sells them, along with fresh, rich-brewed coffee, Italian-style espresso beverages, cold blended beverages, a variety of pastries and confectionaries, coffee-related accessories and equipment, and a line of premium teas, primarily through its company-operated retail stores.
- In addition to sales through its company-operated retail stores, Starbucks sells coffee and tea products through other channels of distribution.
- Starbucks through its joint venture partnerships produces and sells bottled Frappucino Coffee drink and a line of premium ice-creams.
- The Company's objective is to establish Starbucks as the most recognised and respected brand in the world.

Key drivers to future growth :
- Expanding core retail opportunity worldwide.
- Continue to innovate.
- Expanded customer base.
- Leveraged Starbucks brand in other products and channels.

Delivering on Service :
- Training hard skills and soft skills.
- Hundreds of combinations of drinks in their portfolio.
- Removing non-value added tasks.
- Introduction of automated espresso machines.

Parameters to measure service performance- "Basic service" to measure by service, cleanliness, product quality, speed of service. And, provide "Legendary Service".

Expansion.
- Owned close to 1/3rd of America's coffee bars.
- Coffee consumption was on the rise.
- Eight states in U.S. without a single company operated Starbucks.
- It was far from reaching saturation levels in many existing markets.
- New products were launched on regular basis.
- Product development process to take 12 to 18 months.
- Partner acceptance.
- Starbucks' stored value Cards.
- T-mobile hotspot wireless internet service.

Problems :
1. Lacked a strategic marketing group. New stores cannibalised existing store sales, but Starbucks did not see that as an important issue.
2. Very little image or product differentiation between Starbucks and competing chains.
3. The newer customers were younger, less educated, in lower income brackets, had less frequent visits, and had a different perception of Starbucks.
4. Concern had been expressed that Starbucks had lost the connection between satisfying their own customers and growing the business.
5. Starbucks wanted to serve the customer within 3 minute time window.
6. Starbucks wanted more handcrafted time consuming choices for consumers.
7. Starbucks sees them as selling innovative products.

Improving Profitability in Japan :

Starbucks improve profitability in Japan in the following ways :

- Encouraging domestic competition and greatly expanding the market for coffee chains.
- Introducing a dynamic decision-making style and corporate governance policies.
- Focussing on job creation and staff retention through stock options and by promoting a Japanese style "family" atmosphere.
- Finding a partner with similar corporate values and complementary strengths, and helping it grow much faster.
- Adding a unique dimension to the local coffee culture by offering a non-smoking environment.

Rediscovering the Starbucks customer :

- By focussing on building the image and introducing new products.
- By relaxing the labour hour controls in the stores to add an additional 20 hours of labour, per week, per store, at a cost of an extra $ 40 million per year.

Evaluations :

(a) Redefine their marketing strategies starting with a proper research and evaluation of what customer wants.

(b) Analyze the customers and potential customers through their speciality sales to see the impact upon current or potential retail sales in stores.

(c) Research those customers who do not frequent Starbucks, or who have never been inside a Starbucks store.

(d) Create a centralised marketing department which can attempt to coordinate all marketing efforts.

(e) Analyse the innovative sales to determine the effect on labour costs to determine if the sales support the costs and the potential decrease in the time available to quickly serve the customer.

(f) Concentrate new store openings in areas that would not cannibalise existing sales.

(g) Advertise more to establish the branding of Starbucks.

(h) Quick term to fix to add more employee hours to reduce wait time, although this should be allocated according to an established need per store.

(i) Separate service customers with customised orders from those which will require less time, such as customer just wanting coffee.

The Starbucks appears to consider competition as minimal, and they are somewhat insulated, this thought is either entertaining idea or is a strategic mistake, it should evaluate on.

CASE STUDY – 8: MARUTI SUZUKI INDIA LIMITED (MSIL)

International Marketing strategies.

MSIL is into manufacturing and after-sales service of passenger cars and sports-utility vehicles.

Maruti Udyog Limited (MUL) was established in 1981 through an act of Parliament, as a government company with Suzuki Motor Corporation (SMC) of Japan holding 26% stake. Suzuki was an obvious choice because of its unparalleled expertise in small cars. It had the following objectives to achieve:

- Modernisation of the Indian Automobile Industry.
- Production of vehicles in large volumes.
- Production of fuel-efficient vehicles.

In October 1982, the Government of India and Suzuki Motor Company (now Suzuki Motor Corporation of Japan) entered into a joint venture agreement. The company went into production in a short period of 13 months and the first car was rolled out from Maruti Udyog Limited, Gurgaon in December, 1983.

On September 17, 2007 the company name was changed to Maruti Suzuki India Limited (MSIL). "Maruti" is one of the strongest corporate brand names in the country, in context with awareness, trust, and customer care. It is the name that a generation of Indians has grown up with, and is well known for company's products, services, and its sales and service network across the country.

"Suzuki" in the corporate name imparts an international dimension. Besides being the parent company, SMC is a leading player in the global automobile market. Over 30 years it is the leader in Japan's mini-car market, and recently positioned itself as a complete carmaker with the success of its international strategic models like Swift, SX4, and Grand Vitara.

This international face-lift and dimension in the company's name will help Maruti as it looks, to expand its role in the international markets. The company is to launch a model for export to Europe in the next couple of years, while building on its recent success in Asian and African markets. Maruti is also developing capabilities to assume the role of being Suzuki's R&D hub for Asia outside Japan.

"India" in the corporate name, recognises the growing importance of the country across the world.

In the fiscal year 2006-07, MSIL sales were 674,924 cars including 39,295 exports. MSIL has expanded its manufacturing facility by adding another facility in Manesar near Gurgaon. This plant is currently operating with a production capacity of 100,000 cars which will be increased to 400,000 cars by 2010.

The assembly line of the new plant manufactures Swift, SX4 and the new Swift Sedan give multiple products in a single production line and thus increase the cost competency in the market. For the first time Suzuki started manufacturing diesel engines under a license agreement with Fiat. With the increased production capacity MSIL renewed its focus in global markets by way of exports.

In recent years, Maruti has taken major steps in developing itself as Suzuki's R&D Hub for Asia. More than 50 engineers have been trained at Suzuki and have been able to refresh and upgrade Maruti models. Thus, Maruti engineers have worked with Suzuki engineers in Japan in designing Suzuki's world car, Swift, and make it suitable for Indian conditions.

Suzuki has a distributor concept in international markets. Most of the export sales of Maruti come through distributor network of SMC. In very few nations, Maruti has its own network/dealership and that too will vanish in future. Zen-the world car was exported to European countries.

Overseas Distributors :

To support SMC overseas distributors with entry-level products and to develop markets where there is no presence of SMC, there is a role to be played by MSIL. The objectives are:

- To double the percentage share of global merchandise trade within the next 5 years.
- To act as an effective instrument of economic growth by giving a thrust to employment generation.

With a common platform for a range of various products like Swift, SX4, and Swift Sedan, the competence increases in terms of pricing, quality, and so on. This gives a competitive edge for selling products in developing countries.

Maruti, as a forward-looking organisation, has always encouraged exports to remain competitive in global markets. Exposure to international markets helps to bring in improvement in the quality of the product and cost. Therefore, in 1986, despite a 3-year waiting period in the domestic market, MSIL started exporting cars, only to ensure that we remain competitive in terms of cost and quality. Since then, MSIL has sold more than 450,000 cars to more than 100 countries of the world. Some of our cars have become bestsellers; such as old Zen, which was projected as the World Car, was well received in Europe. Similarly, Alto received most encouraging reviews in Netherlands, Greece, Germany, and Switzerland. Alto's superb fuel economy entitled its customers to a 1,000 euro refund from the Government of Netherlands.

But, with the new emission norms MSIL had to suspend its exports to European nations, on temporary basis. For these markets new models are being developed.

At present, MSIL exports entry-level models to many Latin American and African nations. With focus on non-European nations, MSIL has managed to bring incremental sales, and its exports to these countries have grown by 47%, 65%, and 40% in the past three years.

International spread - Europe - 280,000 units (34 nations)
- **Latin America** - 41,400 units (13 nations)
- **Asia** - 74,000 units (25 nations)
- **Africa** - 52,300 units (24 nations)
- **Oceania** - 6,300 (4 nations).

Export performance of MSIL - Region	Volume	% Share
EU	280,454	62
Non-EU	174,038	38
Total	454,492	100

Over 454,000 units exported to more than 100 countries in 5 continents.

Main Models of MSIL - Base Model	Volume (Cumulative)	% Share
M800	164,612	36
Alto	130,800	29
Zen	123,589	27
Others	35,491	8
Total	454,492	

It is expected that India's car export will touch 1 million by the year 2010. The main drivers for this higher growth in car export are as follows:

(i) **Quality Manpower & Skills :** India has better manpower available for shop floors and has quality engineers. This has made possible improving car production at lower costs.

(ii) **Component Advantage :** There is better cost advantage for auto-component manufacturers in India, which gives cost-competitive advantage for Indian manufacturers globally.

(iii) **Location Advantage :** India is closer to Pacific Rim, Europe, and East coast of the U.S. when compared to other Asian manufacturers. This imparts an advantage in terms of reduced transportation cost and reduced delivery timing. This is also one of the main reasons for Japanese and Korean manufacturers to shift their export base to India.

(iv) **Currency Advantage :** India gives an opportunity for exporting to any of the nations of EU or the U.S., depending on the currency strength, because India has double-currency advantage due to two-way movement of rupee against U.S. dollar and euro.

(v) **Ability to Cope with Norms :** India has the ability to cope with the changing stringent norms of safety and environment etc. Indian manufacturers have redefined their engines, with safety features to meet the latest norms of Europe; or are developing models with compatible features.

MSIL has been a part of all the above-mentioned growth drivers and has increased its focus to non-EU markets also, primarily comprising Latin American, African, and Oceanic markets.

Table C.1 : Shows the cumulative sales till March 31, 2007 to top countries.

Sr. No.	Country	Volume/Quantity
1.	Netherlands	67,757
2.	Italy	41,516
3.	United Kingdom	34,307
4.	Algeria	29,487
5.	Chile	25,901
6.	Germany	25,461
7.	Sri Lanka	23,352
8.	Hungary	22,924
9.	Nepal	16,539
10.	Denmark	12,921
	Total	300,165

Table C.2 : Shows the export performance in the past three years.

Region	2004-05		2005-06		2006-07	
	Units	Growth	Units	Growth	Units	Growth
EU	32,740	– 7%	11,085	–66%	138	–99%
Non-EU	16,159	1%	23,696	47%	39,157	65%
Total	48,899	–4%	34,781	–29%	39,295	13%

Strategy for global market, primarily non-EU market :

(a) Shift the focus from market share to opportunity share.

(b) Concentrate on emerging pure entry-level segment.

(c) Team of MSIL works closely with distributors in various nations.

(d) Expand the entry-level market in developing nations by emulating the experience of domestic market.

(e) Marketing efforts include advertisements, events, and sales promotions, and these efforts would vary from country to country.

MSIL's Management :

The top-level team including the then Managing Director visited about 15 countries. The distributors were invited to visit the Indian market and understand the domestic strategies. This action was with the belief that it would build confidence level. And, in the past one year almost 150 delegates from 24 countries have visited MSIL.

MSIL's four main pillars of the strategy are :

- Adequate stocks.
- Manpower
- Network.
- Retail finance.

Every country to which the MSIL exports to has the distributors of SMC.

Swift was the product that involved MSIL engineers working on the project at SMC Headquarters in Hamamatsu, Japan for over two years. They were a part of the core team and proved their competency globally for developing a product that won scores of accolades across the world.

In the fiscal year i.e. April 2007-January 2008, the exports volume for MSIL was about at 43,000 units with a growth of 51%. BY 2010-2011 MSIL is focussed to reach 250,000 annual car exports.

(Referred from International Business by
– J.D.Daniels)

CASE STUDY – 9: Enron International in India

In 1990, *Enron*, a Houston-based independent power company established a subsidiary, Enron International and gave it the mission of building and running power generation projects in the developing world. Enron's chairman appointed one of his proteges Rebecca Mark, the only 36 years old as CEO of the new unit. By 1997, the outspoken and photogenic Mark, who was fast gaining a reputation as one of the most dynamic business women in USA had built Enron International into a global operation with sales of $ 3.1 billion and annual profits of $ 220 million and a backlog of international energy projects worth over $ 20 billion. By the end of 1997, Enron International had plans to invest $ 20 billion in India. Getting to this point, however, had severely tested Mark's diplomatic skills and political acumen.

Enron's interest in India dates back to 1991, when the Prime Minister Mr. Narasimha Rao visited USA to seek help for India's economic development. Mr. Rao asked Enron if it was interested in independent power projects in the country. This request signaled out a shift of policy in India. Since Independence, political opinion in India was opposing foreign direct investment on anything other than highly favourable terms to the host country. By 1990, winds of ideological change were blowing and the national government decided to go for free market approach that included substantial deregulation and loosening of rules on foreign direct investment. In October 1991, the government liberalized India's domestic power producing sector, allowing private developers both Indian and foreigners to build and operate independent power projects with no restrictions on foreign equity ownership.

India's need for power was obvious. The demand for electricity often exceeded available power supply by more than 20 percent. The installed capacity in the early 1990's, which amounted to around 80,000-mega watts, was working only at 60 percent efficiency. Forecasts suggested that an extra 1,40,000 mega watts of capacity would be needed by 2005, but public money for such huge investment was not available. In mid 90's about 70 percent of India's electricity supply was being produced by state-owned electricity generation and distribution boards which collectively were running up losses of over $ 2 billion per year. They could not afford to fund the required expansion in capacity.

Mark accepted Rao's offer but it was realized that India's energy problems involved more than a simply lack of generating capacity. The country also lacked in a adequate supplies of fuel. To help to solve these problems, Mark articulated strategic vision that was audacious in scope. The vision called for Enron to invest up to $20 billion to become the largest distributor and consumer of liquefied national gas (LNG) in India by 2010. Under the plan, Enron would set up two LNG terminals and re-gassification units in India, one at Dabhol in Maharashtra

State and the other at Ennore in Tamil Nadu State. The company would construct two gas based power-generating plants near the terminals. Enron would also build a network of pipelines to pipe the gas to its LNG terminals from oil and gas fields near Bombay and then onward to its own and other power plants around the country. The Mumbai field was not having large enough to supply India's projected LNG needs. The company planned to import LNG from Qatar at the cost of $4 billion, which was funded by state-owned Qatar Gas & Pipeline Co.; Enron International's parent company and Royal Dutch/Shell. Enron International had promised investors in the Qatar facility 15 percent annual growth in shareholders income. Achieving this goal was highly dependent on the success of Mark's India Strategy. Without India, Enron might lack sufficient customers to absorb the LNG output from its Qatar facility.

By mid 1992, Mark was very busy with first stage of her plan and she was in deep negotiations with Indian Central and Government of Maharashtra where Dabhol power plant was to be constructed. The Dabhol project was bold step. Enron was to develop 2015-mega watts power plant that would be fixed by LNG. The total cost of the project was over $2 billion making Dabhol project the largest foreign investment in India and the biggest independent power project in the world.

Mark was aware of the political conditions in India. While the Central Government at Delhi might in principle approve the project, still Enron will have to win approval of the Maharashtra State Government and cultivate the approval of key players in India's extensive civil service. To get Dabhol project approved, the company had to get 170 different state and central permits, sort through so complicated legal questions and deal with complex web of State and Central taxes.

By early 1995, Enron had received full approval for the project and was proceeding with the initial construction. Initially, congress party was in power in Maharashtra State and Mr. Sharad Pawar was a big supporter of Enron Power Project at Dabhol. During 1994 and early 1995, series of ethnic riots swept through Mumbai. Anti Muslim hysteria had been whipped up by Shiv Sena and in February 1995, Shiv Sena formed an alliance with BJP and won the state elections. During elections campaign, Shiv Sena seized on Dabhol Project and used it to attack the Congress Party and its leader Mr. Sharad Pawar, claiming that Pawar had been bribed by Enron to support Dabhol Project. The BJP also supported Shiv Sena and added in election campaign the Gandhi doctrine of 'swadeshi' (self-reliance) and contrasted their defense of Indian rights and self-reliance against the corrupt practices of Enron, Mr. Pawar and the Congress Party.

Fuel was added to this fire when Enron official, in testimony before a committee of the US Congress that was dealing with foreign aid allocations, revealed that Enron had spent $20 million to educate Indians about the benefits of its various power projects in the country. The Enron officials tried to make innocent suggestion that the US Government might want to use its foreign aid help with such educational campaigns. But Indian Press in concert with Shiv Sena seized this revelation to claim that this $ 20 million had been in the form of bribes. As a result, Shiv Sena, BJP came in power with Shri. Manohar Joshi as the New Chief Minister.

The new state government set up a committee under the leadership of Shri. Gopinath Munde to review the Dabhol project in respect of the charges of corruption and abuse that had been leveled at Enron during election campaign. However, Rebecca Mark felt, she was on solid ground. Enron had not done anything wrong. Contracts had been properly signed and construction work on the project was underway. India needed power and agreements protected Enron from any unilateral breach of contract. If the state cancelled the project, it would be hit with a $ 200 million cancellation fee.

In mid 1995, the committee finished its report, which was not published although, excepts in which Enron was accused of deception and cost padding were leaked to the press. Enron vigorously denied these charges.

The implication was that there was a risk premium built into Enron contract with the state government. The report also criticized the previous administration for not putting the Dabhol project out to competitive bids. Enron officers argued that the Prime Minister Shri Narasimha Rao invited Enron. And it was Enron who suggested Dabhol project and Enron was the only foreign power producer willing to shoulder the risk associated with such a huge investment in India and lack of competitive bidding was the opportunity cost of getting company to come and create an industry.

The committee was not able to find out any evidence of corruption by either Enron or Indian political officials still having made such a big issue of the project the Sena-BJP coalition was not ready to backdown. On August 3, 1995, the state government issued a work stoppage order on the deal after Enron had already spent $ 100 million. Two days later, Enron served the State Government with legal notice that it would pursue arbitration in London. The state government was facing damages of $300 million with the possibility of another $ 500 million on the top of it. On August 12, Little & Co. that acted as the lawyers for the Maharashtra State Government for the last 20 years resigned and stated that the state's position was indefensible. Top civil servants in the state also repeatedly told Mr. Munde and Mr. Joshi that the government's position was untenable.

Simultaneously, Enron mounted a public relations Campaign of its own and ran full page advertisement in Indian newspapers publishing the benefits to India of its Dabhol project. It also requested Bill Clinton the President of USA to call the Indian Prime Minister to get the project started again. By September, the public opinion polls showed that 80 percent of the people in the state of Maharashtra and 60 percent of those in India wanted the project restarted.

Enron was interested in restarting the project and state government was facing the potential of heavy damages and was rapidly losing support for its position. At the same time the state government needed some evidence that its efforts had not seen for naught, it needed to save its face.

Rebecca Mark decided to bargain and a resettlement was worked out. Enron agreed to cut the price it charged for power generated by the Dabhol project by 22.6 percent. In return, Enron walked away with a deal for a 2450-mega watt plant, 450 megawatts bigger than the initial plant. According to Enron, the larger plant would realize much greater scale economies and allow Enron to maintain its projected rate of return on investment while simultaneously cutting prices.

On the basis of her experience in India, Mark states that the key to Enron's success was its intentions to help India to solve a problem and to stay engaged in the country for the long term. She and her colleagues have spent six years coming to India, talking to the same people for the same project. Mark believes that any one who worked with them doubts their intentions, goodwill and long term commitment to India. Enron's appeal to the people of India ultimately served the company well.

In February 1997, Enron reaffirmed its commitment to India when it submitted a proposal to build five to seven more power plants in India for a total cost of $ 10 billion. The first phase to generate 740-mega watts of power was completed in December 1998, three months ahead of schedule.

For India's part, Enron's experience with the Dabhol project was a public relations set back. Although the outcome reaffirmed the country's commitment to encouraging foreign direct investment, the perception has been created that the shifting political landscape, bureaucratic rules and the cross currents between national and state governments make India, a difficult place to invest in. As noted by US Ambassador to India William Clarke, the Dabhol incidence sends the right signals but unfortunately it sent off the wrong signals for a while. Just like a retraction in a newspaper, it will take long time for people to notice.

CASE STUDY – 10: Bhopal Gas Tragedy.

On December 3, 1984, about 2000 people were killed and 2,00,222 were injured when a thick cloud of poisonous Methyl Isocyanate gas was accidentally released from the Union Carbide plant in Bhopal, India.

The accident occurred when 120 to 240 gallons of water was introduced into a tank containing 90,000 pounds of Methyl Isocyanate. The tank also contained 3,000 pounds of chloroform used as a solvent in the manufacture of Methyl Isocyanate. The two chemicals should have been separated before storage, but this had not been done for some time in the operating process at Bhopal.

Following the accident, Union Carbide officials in USA strongly denied that their firm was responsible for the tragedy on the following grounds.

1. The American firm owned 50.9 percent of the Indian subsidiary but the parent corporation had been able to exercise little control. All managerial and technical persons were citizens of India at the insistence of the Indian Government. No Americans were permanently employed at the plant.

2. Safety warnings from visiting American Inspectors about the manufacture of process of Sevin had been ignored.

3. Five automatic safety devices that had been originally installed as a part of Sevin manufacturing process had been either removed or replaced by manual safety methods by the time the accident occurred-allegedly, to increase employment or for repair or as a part of cost reduction program. Automatic temperature and pressure warning signals had been removed soon after construction. The repairs on the automatic scrubber unit had extended over six months. The refrigeration unit to cool the tank had been inoperable for over an year. These were the evidences of sabotage.

4. The Bhopal plant had been built to increase employment in India. Union Carbide would have preferred to make Sevin in USA and ship it to India for distribution and sale, due to substantial economies of scale in the manufacturing process.

Waaren Anderson Chairman of Union Carbide stated that while he believed that the American company was not liable for the tragedy due to the reasons stated above, it was still morally responsible and he suggested that the firm should pay prompt financial compensation to those killed and injured in the accident.

The culpability in the choice of designs was obvious, as Prafull Bidwai and Rama Seshan have observed. Germany had prescribed an alternative safe process to manufacture the same product. This was known to Indian authorities who allowed the plant to be established. But as parent Union Carbide was not given permission to install plants in other countries.

Mr. Mukund, the Indian Works Manager denied Anderson's charges of negligence. Several accidents had occurred prior to this accident. Other reports suggest that the factory inspector never stepped into the factory on his monthly trip, though there was one major objection raised both by him and the municipality, which was overruled by the state and central governments. It was well known that political parties and influential persons got favours from the Union Carbide in several forms like employment, contracts and lavish entertainment.

The state's culpability lay in permitting the slum dwellers to stay close to the factory, apart from permitting it to operate within city limits. The state government argued that the Union Carbide never warned them about the nature of the chemicals.

The action in the case could be either criminal or civil or both. Justice Keenan of USA remitted the case back to the Indian Courts with the condition that Union Carbide, USA could not escape the provision of discovery meaning an investigation in the internal documents of the company. Meanwhile, the suffering of Bhopal victims continued unabated, all the while Union Carbide officials were saying that this was all exaggerated.

The Supreme Court wished to put an end to the misery and awarded a damage of US $ 470 million, which the company paid. They were absolved of all criminal charges. Subsequently, the revocation of criminal proceedings was withdrawn. A new twist was given to the case by the Supreme Court in 1996 when it held that no one from the company could be considered for punishment under the charge of manslaughter as they found no reason to believe that this was willful negligence. This judgement has been questioned as being too naive. It was clear that the company officials were playing with fire. The maximum punishment for normal negligence under the IPC would be two years imprisonment. The precise extent of damage is not known though the Union Carbide doctors claim it is not as much as the Indian doctors estimate. The quantum for each death victim cannot be more than Rs. 1 lakh at the most. Union Carbide would have had to pay at least hundred times more if the accident had happened in the USA.

UNIVERSITY QUESTION PAPER

APRIL 2015

Time : 2 ½ Hours   Maximum Marks : 50

Instruction :
- (i) All questions are compulsory with internal choice within the questions.
- (ii) All questions carry equal marks.

1. What do you understand International Business Environment ? Explain the importance of the study of International Business.

    OR

    Discuss the trends and development in global trading environment.

2. Describe factors influencing interest rate movements and impact of movements in interest rate on trade and investment.

    OR

    Discuss the pattern and structure of foreign investment.

3. Explain in detail WTO with objectives and functions.

    OR

    What is Agreement on Textile and Clothing ? Explain it along with various provisions.

4. Explain the issues related to foreign investment involving technology transfer, pricing and regulations.

    OR

    Examine the concept of international collaborative arrangement and strategic alliance.

5. Explain - Structure and Functioning of European Commission (EC).

    OR

    Explain in detail North American Free Trade Agreement (NAFTA).